MW00610322

In memory of
our dear wife and mother

מינדל בת ר׳ ישראל ע״ה
Marilyn Fishoff
נלב״ע כ״ד תשרי תשמ״ט

whose *midos tovos*, numerous acts of *chesed*
and exemplary manner *bein adam lechaveiro*
personified Reb Chaim's teachings.

Yechiel Ben-Zion Fishoff and Family

לזכר נשמת

ר׳ שלמה ב״ר ישראל ז״ל

האשה דברה מרים בת ר׳ מנחם מנדל ז״ל

אהבתם ומסירתם למשפחתם

ומעשי הצדקה והחסד

יהיו לנו לאור עולם

Mr. & Mrs. Max Tennenbaum
Mr. & Mrs. Yossie Mermelstein

לזכר נשמת

ר׳ מאיר מנחם ב״ר משה יוסף ז״ל

אהבתו ומסירתו למשפחתו

ומעשיו הצדקה והחסד

יהיו לנו לאור עולם

Mr. & Mrs. Moshe Kaiser
Mr. & Mrs. Michael Kaiser

למזכרת נצח

להעוסק בצרכי צבור באמונה רב פעלים ודבר טוב לעמו

ר' אלימלך גבריאל ב"ר גרשון
טרעס זצ"ל

נשיא אגודת ישראל בארצה"ב שהצליח להציל רבים
משחת בימי השואה האיום והנורא, והיה כאחיעזר
ואחיסמך בנטיעת מוסדות התורה והיהדות באמעריקע.

יהי זכרו ברוך

הלך לעולמו ב' תמוז תשכ"ז

תנצב"ה

לזכר עולם בהיכל ה'

הרה"ג ר' אברהם גרשון בן ר' אלימלך גבריאל
טרעס זצ"ל

אשר היה עמלו בתורה וחסד יחדיו, עשה נחת רוח
ליוצרו, ורבים השיב מעון.

נפטר לעולמו ביום כ"א אייר תשד"מ

יהי זכרו ברוך, ותהיה נשמתו צרורה בצרור החיים

דורש דמים אותם זכר

לזכר ולעילוי נשמות

הקדשים

ר' יצחק דוד ב"ר צבי ביסטריצר

וריעתו חי' עטיע בת ר' מרדכי

ר' אברהם ב"ר ישראל יששכר הילמן

וריעתו חי' בת ר' יעקב יוסף

נרצחו בידי ארורים באושוויץ ביום

ה' סיון תש"ד

ה' ינקום דמם

תנצב"ה

לזכרון עולם

לעילוי נשמת אבינו מורנו עטרת ראשנו

ר׳ יהודה מאיר ב״ר דוד הלוי ז״ל הורוויץ

נפטר ט׳ אדר תשמ״ה

תהא נשמתו צרורה בצרור החיים.

שלמה דוד ופיגי הורוויץ ומש׳

מנדי וחני הורוויץ ומש׳

נתן וטובה הורוויץ ומש׳

צורתה

ArtScroll Judaica Classics®

Reb Chaim's

Translated by
Rabbi Eliyahu Meir Klugman
and Rabbi A. Scheinman

Edited by
Rabbi Dr. Samson R. Weiss
with Rabbi Bezalel Rappaport

שיחות מוסר

DISCOURSES

The shmuessen of the Mirrer Rosh Yeshiva
Rabbi Chaim Shmulevitz זצ״ל

Published by
Mesorah Publications, ltd
in conjunction with the
Alumni Association of Yeshivas Mir Yerushalayim

FIRST EDITION
First Impression . . . May, 1989

Published and Distributed by
MESORAH PUBLICATIONS, Ltd.
Brooklyn, New York 11232
in conjunction with
YESHIVAS MIR YERUSHALAYIM

Distributed in Israel by
MESORAH MAFITZIM / J. GROSSMAN
Rechov Harav Uziel 117
Jerusalem, Israel

Distributed in Europe by
J. LEHMANN HEBREW BOOKSELLERS
20 Cambridge Terrace
Gateshead, Tyne and Wear
England NE8 1RP

ARTSCROLL JUDAICA CLASSICS ®
SICHOS MUSSAR
© Copyright 1989, by MESORAH PUBLICATIONS, Ltd.
4401 Second Avenue / Brooklyn, N.Y. 11232 / (718) 921-9000

No part of this book may be reproduced
in any form without **written** permission from the copyright holder,
except by a reviewer who wishes to quote brief passages in connection with a review
written for inclusion in magazines or newspapers.

THE RIGHTS OF THE COPYRIGHT HOLDER WILL BE STRICTLY ENFORCED.

ISBN:
0-89906-943-6 (hard cover)
0-89906-944-4 (paperback)

Typography by CompuScribe at ArtScroll Studios, Ltd.
4401 Second Avenue / Brooklyn, N.Y. 11232 / (718) 921-9000

Printed in the United States of America by Noble Book Press Corp.
Bound by Sefercraft, Quality Bookbinders, Ltd. Brooklyn, N.Y.

This sefer is dedicated
in honour of our parents

Wolf and Rose Feintuch שיחיו

and

Sarah Friedlander שתחי׳

May השם grant them health, happiness and long life
and may they merit to see much נחת
from their children and grandchildren.

And is further dedicated
in memory of our father

מנחם נחום בן אהרן סאבו ז״ל

שהלך לעולמו ביום י״ג חשון תשט״ז

He was taken from our midst at an early age
but his kindness and good deeds
have remained forever.

Ben and Penina Feintuch
Nachum, Ilana, Elisa and Dovid
Toronto, Canada

Publishers' Preface

Few contemporary works achieve the status of "classic" as soon as they are published. *Sichos Mussar*, in the original Hebrew, is such a work. Its popularity was due to both the man and the subject matter, and it is a popularity that continues to spread with every passing year.

Rabbi Chaim Shmulevitz, Rosh Yeshivah of the Mirrer Yeshivah of Jerusalem, had achieved fame as a Talmudic genius of the first order long before he delivered his first *mussar* discourse. When it became necessary for him to assume the traditional role of the *mashgiach*, and deliver regular discourses on ethics and Torah thought, he was equally illustrious. He had an uncanny ability to look at the Torah and find things that others had never noticed, but that seemed true and obvious once he had revealed them. His legendary breadth of knowledge and ability to find connections among farflung sources captivated new audiences for ancient thoughts.

Reb Chaim's *Shmuessen* became synonymous in the Torah world with innovation, insight, compassion, depth, and demands for self-improvement. Eventually, students of the Yeshivah began transcribing the discourses and circulating them among their peers. From this developed the Hebrew version of *Sichos Mussar*, which included three years of the very popular talks.

In homes, yeshivas, seminaries — even among the clandestine *baalei teshuvah* of Moscow and Leningrad — *Reb Chaim's Shmuessen* became inspirational textbooks that changed lives, shaped outlooks.

Several years ago, two of Reb Chaim's students undertook to make the discourses available in English. They wanted more than a translation. They wanted to consolidate ideas that, in the original transcribed version, had been spread over several discourses, and to include ideas and explanations that Reb Chaim had introduced on other occasions. The sons of the Rosh Yeshivah, distinguished scholars in their own right, cooperated and guided the project, reviewing and refining from beginning to end. Finally, the renowned scholar and thinker Rabbi Dr. Samson R. Weiss graciously consented to edit the manuscript, bringing to his work a lifetime of learning and a close friendship with the Rosh Yeshivah. Also assisting in the editing was Rabbi Betzalel Rappaport. We thank Rabbi Avrohom Yoseif Rosenberg who checked the Hebrew citations for accuracy and vowelized them.

The translators, Rabbi A. Scheinman and Rabbi Eliyahu Meir Klugman, have rendered a priceless service to the entire nation, and — not only with the discourses, but with their biographical essay and appreciation — have done justice to the legacy of one of the great teachers and leaders of our time.

As always, we are grateful to our colleague, Reb Shea Brander, who once again has presented a Torah work in a manner worthy of its content. Our appreciation goes as well to Mrs. Faigie Weinbaum, who proofread; to Mrs. Esther Feierstein, who typed the bulk of the manuscript; and to Mrs. Menucha Silver, Zissi Glatzer, and Bassie Goldstein, who assisted in the typing.

Mesorah Publications is proud to present this work to the Jewish public. It is a privilege. We are confident that the greatness of Reb Chaim will quickly become apparent to an enthusiastic new generation of students.

Table of Contents

Translators' Preface

We did not succeed.

§ § §

As the *Sichos* of our *Rosh Yeshivah* and *rebbe* are submitted for publication, we are inundated by the memories of a decade ago and more. Hagaon Harav Reb Chaim Shmulevitz was the *rosh yeshivah par excellence*. His mastery of *Bavli* and *Yerushalmi* was breathtaking. He was encyclopedic in his knowledge of *rishonim* and *acharonim*, *poskim* and *teshuvos*. When he delivered his intricately constructed *shiur*, it was as if the furthest reaches of the vast sea of the Torah were converging to prove his points and shed new light on obscure questions.

When, relatively late in his career, he assumed some of the duties of *mashgiach*, as well, a new era began — not only for him and for the Mirrer Yeshivah of Jerusalem, but for the entire Torah world. The brilliance, the scope, the breadth, the depth — everyone knew that about R' Chaim. But his insight into human nature and his way of finding insights in the narratives of *Tanach* and teachings of the Sages that spoke so directly to his listeners — these were astounding. More importantly, they had a lasting impact.

In his *mussar shmuessen*, R' Chaim did not indulge in metaphysical speculation. Nor did he use dramatic devices to evoke an emotional response from his listeners, only to leave them feeling empty when the spell ended. Rather, his *mussar* was characterized by an understanding of *Chazal* in depth, and of life and human nature in depth. By sheer power of his thought and emotion, R' Chaim would break through to the inner meaning of *Chazal*. Like a mighty river sweeping up everything in its path, he swept us up in the flow of his rich thoughts and deep feelings. For close to an hour, we would think and feel through R' Chaim's mind and heart. True, later we would return to our small selves, but the experience had been real and much of it remained with us always. Years later we would be confronted with a dilemma or a difficult choice, and R' Chaim's words and thoughts would come tumbling unbidden out of our mouths — and, more important, into our minds and hearts.

II.

What was R' Chaim's unique dimension of *mussar*? Perhaps the description of his unique approach to *Chazal* is contained in a word that is alas untranslatable. The word is *derher* — דערהער — a Yiddish expression which denotes a quality of listening. It means to listen not to the outside tones of a sound, but rather to hear the rich inner vibrations; to take in the full complement of harmonies that a chord has produced; to discern what was *meant* rather than merely to hear what was uttered.

R' Chaim had remarkably keen ears that could unerringly *derher* the meaning of a *Chazal*, the feelings of a fellow human, the significance of a historical event. He himself used this term to describe Yisro.

He would say: "Shallow people translate the verse וַיִּשְׁמַע יִתְרוֹ as *Yisro heard*. Did not everyone hear? Did not the news of Israel's miraculous redemption from Egypt and the splitting of the Sea traverse the entire world? Was there even a child unfamiliar with these unparalleled events?

"No, Yisro was not alone in hearing, but he was uniquely able to *derher*! Only he comprehended the significance of each event, and that is what brought him to *Klal Yisrael*. 'וַיִּשְׁמַע יִתְרוֹ, Yisro *derhered*.' "

This was R' Chaim's approach to *mussar* and this is what he expected of us. He would often repeat a *shmuess* almost word for word and yet say it with the vitality and freshness of someone living through it for the first time. Referring to this practice he would often emphasize, "Those who think that I repeat myself did not even understand it the first time around!" What did he mean? Repetition is a burden to the person who looks to *mussar* to provide interesting ideas or abstract intellectual stimulation. But for one whose heart is attuned to the eternal truths hidden in *Chazal*, repetition serves to drive home these truths, each time giving the listener a deeper and richer awareness of the lesson of *Chazal*. There is no limit to how far one can *derher* a *vort* if it is an expression of a Divine truth. To the person who perceives the teachings of our Sages as an extension of G-d's will, its layers of meaning are infinite.

So keen was R' Chaim's sense of *derher* that hitherto echoes were brought to our attention by his perception. His personal reactions to the reading of the Book of Ruth on *Shavuos* morning — the climax of a night of Torah and *tefillah* — was a moving example of his uncanny ability to put himself into an ancient narrative as if he had heard it for the first time. The *Seder* at night would start with a *shiur* or *shmuess* from R' Chaim. The crescendo of Torah study that followed was overwhelming. The walls of the yeshivah reverberated with the energy and thunder of hundreds of *talmidim*. At an hour or so before sunrise there would be a hurried *rekidah*, and then the *davening* would start. People's hearts — still pounding from the night's learning — were readying themselves to stand at Sinai, as it were, to receive the Torah anew. Everyone was moved by the *davening* and by R' Yechiel's [the noted *baal kriah* of the Mir] emotion-soaked *Akdamos* and Torah reading, but there was one element of the morning's prayers that only R' Chaim's heart was big enough to encompass.

At the reading of Ruth he would sob!

Everyone is impressed by the beautiful story of Ruth becoming a convert and eventually the ancestress of David HaMelech. But R' Chaim's heart trembled at the realization of the terrible price Ruth paid for the honor that would be generations in coming. She was a *princess*, a woman born and bred in aristocracy and wealth, who had grown up in esteem and dignity, and now she was reduced to being a beggar scrambling for sheaves of wheat with the riffraff of Bethlehem. Has anyone paid a greater price for her belief in the eternal truth of Torah? R' Chaim wept at the thought of her shame and humiliation, her hurt and anguish, as even her rightful redeemer rejected her. While others, perhaps, were preoccupied with the ecstasy of their own acceptance of the Torah that *Shavuos* morning, R' Chaim suffered with Ruth's torturous initiation into the Jewish people. And as we went on to read of Hashem's repayment of Ruth's travails, when she became the mother of royalty, R' Chaim would once again weep — this time tears of joy.

III.

In Netanya — where many yeshivah students would spend a few days of vacation — evening was a time for an easy stroll, a relaxed conversation, perhaps a game of chess. R' Chaim, however, was caught up in his own thoughts. He would stand transfixed by the waves pounding the shore. "Don't you hear?" he queried. "What?" we asked. "I hear the "קוֹל ה׳ עַל הַמָּיִם"" — the voice of Hashem roaring on the waters!" We listened, and through him we, too, heard.

For the person who has R' Chaim's keen sense of listening, no sound is ever drowned out. After the Six Day War, many speakers pointed out the tremendous miracles, others deplored the feeling of power and invincibility that swept through the land. Yet R' Chaim's most vivid recollection was entirely different. He would recount the by-now-famous story of the *agunah*.

The *agunah* was a woman whose husband had abandoned her twenty years earlier. She was a bitter and tormented person, who lived next door to the yeshivah. When the war broke out, she, like hundreds of others, crowded into the yeshivah dining room, which served as a bomb shelter for the neighborhood. The shells were whistling overhead, striking dangerously close to the yeshivah. Finally there was a direct hit; an explosion shook the building, people thought it was the end, and they instinctively cried out, שְׁמַע יִשְׂרָאֵל, *Hear O Israel* ...

At that moment, the *agunah's* voice was heard above all the others. She cried, "My husband left me abandoned for twenty years. I have suffered so much — but I forgive him! You, too, *Ribbono Shel Olam*, forgive the Jewish people for all we have done wrong!"

R' Chaim used to pause during his *shmuess* and cry when he described the plight of the pitiful *agunah*. Then he would say, "Her prayer saved us!"

An outsider would have been surprised. Were there no more momentous events of that war for R' Chaim to ponder? Wasn't history being made in front of our eyes? The reason for the outsider's surprise is that other people could only hear the cacophony of war sounds. To R' Chaim no cry went unheard. Even in the din of the battle his senses were keen enough to pick out the cry of an individual and her suffering.

R' Chaim heard everyone and spoke to everyone, and perhaps that is why each person could *derher* something of himself in the *shmuess*. The young *bachur*, the older Kollel fellow, the business or working man and, for many years, Jews in Russia would hear or see R' Chaim's *shmuess*, and they would feel that he was talking to them.

IV.

What was it that R' Chaim most pointedly *derherd*? Of all the areas of בֵּין אָדָם לַחֲבֵרוֹ, *relations between man and his fellow man*, that he spoke of so often, what was the most poignant?

If it is possible to isolate a particular dimension, one would have to choose "the humiliation of rejection." The worst pain and hurt that a person could feel is the terrible knowledge that he is not wanted by his fellow man. He would stress this while telling the story of the *agunah*. Her plight lay not in her meager earnings as a laundress, nor in the responsibility of raising her children alone, without even the hope of ever again having a partner. Rather it was the awesome awareness that she had been rejected — totally — by the very person who had chosen her for his life's partner. It was a knowledge that she would be condemned to live with until her dying day. It was this evaluation of her plight that made her forgiveness an act of such magnitude.

This understanding of "rejection" caused R' Chaim to feel for a certain boy in the yeshivah. He was not especially bright nor was he endowed with any of the abilities that would make him sought after as a *chavrusa* (study partner). After searching in vain for a *chavrusa*, he came to R' Chaim to pour out his heart. R' Chaim told him that if he didn't find a *chavrusa* within three days, then he himself would learn with him. And he did!

R' Chaim was not moved only by the *bachur's* need for a *chavrusa*. It was highly doubtful that he, with his very ordinary ability, would gain much from learning with one of the great geniuses of the age. Rather, R' Chaim understood that someone who could not find a *chavrusa* considered himself a failure — a person who had been rejected by the yeshivah body as a whole! Learning with R' Chaim would restore his self-confidence and dignity. R' Chaim had a new *chavrusa*.

Using this approach, R' Chaim showed us the meaning of a strange chapter in *Tanach*. The *parashah* dealt with Shmuel HaNavi's severe rebuke when he informed Shaul that he had forfeited the monarchy. Shaul then beseeched Shmuel to return with him to "honor him in front of the elders." R' Chaim would thunder, "Was Shaul living in a fool's paradise? Was that the time for him to seek a bit of false honor?"

He replied, "Shaul had just been humiliated in an unprecedented way. He had been the hope of Israel, the chosen and anointed one. He was now totally rejected, a bitter disappointment, a discarded relic in the course of history. G-d had become "disgusted" with him. If he were left in this state of rejection he would collapse under the strain and all hopes of repentance would be gone. No, he was not trying to preen himself with false glory. Rather, he was pleading with Shmuel, "Give me a minimum of dignity so that I may continue and perhaps salvage something of my life!"

And finally, his sensitivity to human nature enabled him to understand the roots of Amalek. Everyone speaks of Amalek's heresy, his intentional incitement of G-d, and his relentless wars with Israel. R' Chaim probed further. "Where does such a monstrous nation stem from?" he asked. He showed us the *Chazal* that Amalek's mother — Timna — approached Avraham Avinu with the request that he accept her as a proselyte. Avraham rejected her — quite conceivably due to her base character. She then married Elifaz (Eisav's son) and bore him Amalek. Said R' Chaim, "Why did she become the mother of Amalek. Because Avraham Avinu had slammed the door in her face. It was surely with good cause but look," he said, "look at the outcome of such an act of total rejection. She begged acceptance and Avraham Avinu rejected her.

"True, Amalek symbolizes heresy and brazenness, hatred and venom; but what causes such incorrigible evil to sprout? Rejection! Behind Amalek's profane mouth, his cruel face, and his murderous eyes lay the hopeless pain of a person rejected for eternity!"

This was the depth of R' Chaim's feelings and *derher*!

V.

We did not succeed, but R' Chaim did.

Many years ago, a tumultuous episode erupted in the yeshivah. A *bachur* had become enamored of pseudo-intellectual *haskallah* literature. His ideals and values were no longer those of the yeshivah and there was a clamor to remove him. The yeshivah was in an uproar. R' Chaim delivered one of his memorable *shmuessen*, touching upon his own so-called naiveté in assuming that the problem of the pre-War yeshivah world was eradicated, and speaking about the *bachur's* misguided search for ideals. He repeated his insights into Amalek and then he pounded on his *shtender*, roaring, "So long as no one else is affected by him, the *bachur* will stay in yeshivah. No one, no one was ever rejected by me, and no one ever will be!" The tumult died down and the *bachur* stayed on.

This story is probably remembered by many students of that era, but the writers was privileged to see a sequel to it.

The *bachur* stayed on, and in due course left the yeshivah. I had long forgotten about him. One day I got on a bus, sat down and next to me was sitting that same *bachur*. He was obviously an upright member of the Torah community. "What are you doing now?" I inquired. He replied that he was drifting from one low-paying job to another. "But hadn't you gone to law school?" I asked, puzzled. "Yes, I graduated and even worked with a law firm," he replied. "But many cases involved husband-wife litigation for custody of the children. Many times I found myself demanding custody on behalf of a client, when I thought that it would be better for the child to be with the other parent. I couldn't bear the thought of what I was doing to the children, so I resigned."

Is this not what R' Chaim so consistently instilled in us, to think about the impact of our actions on others, to feel their pain and to keep it alive in ourselves? Is this not some measure of R' Chaim's power, that even someone who had been at the periphery of the yeshivah was willing to give up a lucrative career so as not to hurt and cause pain to others?

R' Chaim succeeded.

VI.

But we did not succeed. In this work, we tried to capture something of his power, something of his thunder, something of his *derher*, something of his compassion, something of his sensitivity. We could not.

R' Chaim delivered each *shmuess* with *mesiras nefesh*. He once collapsed at a *shmuess* and upon being revived insisted on finishing. Every *talmid* who heard him was affected by him. Jews in Russia would sit and pore over his *shmuessen*, feeling that he meant them and their problems. And many of them will still tell you that in the darkness of Soviet Russia it was "Sichot Rav Shmulevitz," as they call it, that lit their way in showing them how to become observant Jews and serious *bnei-Torah*. As one of them, still a refusenik today, told me. "It was 'Sichot Rav Shmulevitz' which was *the rebbe* in *hashkafah* for the *baal teshuvah* movement in the Soviet Union."

May it be in his *z'chus* that many will study his *shmuessen* and not relegate them to the status of *vertlach*. Let each reader's heart open a bit and let him learn to feel another person's pain and sorrow, hurts and hopes — and to share another's joy. Even more, to dispel another's pain and to bring him joy.

A.S., E.M.K.

Biography

Rabbi Chaim Leib Shmulevitz זצ״ל —
Genius of Mind and Heart — A Biographical Sketch by
Rabbi Eliyahu Meir Klugman.

Reb Chaim was born in Kovno, Lithuania, on *Motzaei Rosh
Hashanah* 5663 (1902) to Reb Refoel Alter Shmulevitz and his wife,
Ettel, the daughter of Reb Yoseif Yoizel Horowitz, *Der Alter fun
Novaradok*. The *sandek* at his *bris* was Reb Yitzchok Blazer (the
famed Peterburger Rav), a Torah and *mussar* luminary, one of Reb
Yisroel Salanter's greatest disciples.

Reb Chaim's respect for his father was legendary and he quoted
him often in both Torah lectures and *mussar* discourses (on ethical
themes). He considered his father's handwritten *chiddushim* (Torah
novellae) his most valued treasure. During the Six Day War, when the
yeshivah was within range of Jordanian artillery, Reb Chaim sent
some of the manuscripts to America with his uncle, Rabbi Avraham
Yaffen, with specific instructions that he carry them by hand and not
put them in his luggage, because *"Dos iz mein gantzer leben* — This
is my whole life."

In 5680 (1920) when Reb Chaim was 17, both his parents passed
away within a very short time, orphaning him, a brother and two
sisters. As the oldest, Reb Chaim felt the responsibility of supporting
his brother and sisters, so during the day he went to the marketplace
to make a few "groshen."

"That was during the day," his brother Reb Shlomo recalls, "But
the entire night, I would see him writing his *chiddushei Torah* —
which must have occupied his mind during his day in the market!"

He was able to study Torah and think in Torah under all
circumstances wherever he was. At a meal, a *simchah*, taking a walk,
or on the bus, one could always see him with his brow furrowed in

---

Abridged from *The Torah World*, copyright 1982 ArtScroll Judaiscope Series concentration and his closed fist moving back and forth, punctuating his Torah thoughts.

He committed to paper his every *shiur, shmuess, chabura, va'ad* and public address, leaving behind thousands of handwritten pages, including *chiddushim* on every tractate of the Talmud.

When but eighteen, Reb Chaim was invited by the world famous *Gaon* Rabbi Shimon Shkop to give the third level *shiur* in the *yeshivah ketana* (preparatory academy) in Grodno. Many of his students of those years later became great Torah leaders — Rabbi Shmuel Rozovsky (Rosh Yeshivah in Ponoviez), Rabbi Yisrael Gustman (Rosh Yeshivah Netzach Yisrael) and Rabbi Dovid Lipschutz (Suvalker Rov), to mention but a few.

⋙ Mir

At the age of 22, he headed a group of students who transferred from Grodno to Mir, and for the next 54 years, Reb Chaim Stutchiner (as he was called) taught, guided, and inspired thousands of *talmidim* by word and by deed, individually and collectively, with his way of life and his approach in learning.

His *hasmadah* (diligence) and the intensity of his efforts in Torah study became legend in his lifetime.

> *A friend once asked to study with him before Shacharis. "Fine," said Reb Chaim. "How about starting at one in the morning?"*
>
> *"I can't tell you when he slept," said that friend — now a Rosh Yeshivah — "but I do know that when I went to sleep at eleven p.m., he was still up, learning. And he would awaken me at one a.m. for our pre-Shacharis seder (session)."*

❀ ❀ ❀

> *During his years in Mir, while still single, he ate the Friday night meal at the home of the Mashgiach Reb Yeruchem Levovitz ל"צז. After the meal, Reb Yeruchem gave a mussar discourse in his home to scores of students, but the Mashgiach would tell Reb Chaim not to stay: "Your mind is always occupied with your learning; during the shmuess it will be no different. Go to the yeshivah and study in peace."*

His thirst for Torah knowledge was always unquenchable. Even in his youth Reb Chaim's fame as a *masmid* with phenomenal memory in all areas of Torah had spread throughout Europe.

> *Once, on a visit to Vilna, he stopped in at the home of Rabbi Chaim Ozer Grodzensky, the acknowledged leader of Torah Jewry. When Reb Chaim entered the room where Reb Chaim Ozer was meeting with some rabbinic leaders, Reb Chaim Ozer stood up. Upon being asked why he had honored such a young man, Reb Chaim Ozer answered, "When the Torah Library of the Mirrer Yeshivah enters the room, I rise in respect."*

In 1929, he became the son-in-law of the Mirrer *Rosh Yeshivah*, Rabbi Eliezer Yehudah Finkel, and a scant few years later, at the relatively young age of 31, Reb Chaim was appointed a *Rosh Yeshivah*, delivering regular lectures. The hallmark of his lectures was depth combined with a fabulous breadth. On the subject at hand, he would bring to bear countless references from all over *Bavli* and *Yerushalmi*, *Rishonim* and *Acharonim*. It was not uncommon for him to cite 20 or 30 different sources from far-flung corners of the Talmud and its commentaries during a single lecture.

◆§ The Years of Exile

With the outbreak of World War II in 1939, the yeshivah was forced into exile, beginning one of its most glorious chapters. Years later, he would say that under these most trying circumstances, forced to flee from one place to another, the yeshivah prospered as never before. The ensuing seven years of *galus* — of exile in the most real sense — serve as a shining example of the heights a united community can scale, of the dimensions of greatness and strength of character a yeshivah can attain when its only nourishment is Torah, its only home *Bitachon BeHashem*.

On the second day of Cheshvan 5700 (1939), the yeshivah *bachurim* and faculty fled from Mir to Vilna, where they stayed for about two months, after which they moved to Kaydan, where they managed to set up the yeshivah once more. Seven months later they were ordered out of Kaydan by the Lithuanian Communist authorities, whereupon the yeshivah divided into four groups, each numbering between 80 and 100 students. So as not to attract attention, each group studied in a different town in the surrounding countryside and Reb Chaim would shuttle from one to another to say the weekly *shiur*, preparing on the bumpy ride between towns.

The *hashgachah pratis* (Divine Providence) of the next few years was patently evident. Miraculously, the yeshivah obtained transit visas for the entire group, and after much travail managed to reach Japan via the Trans-Siberian Railroad. Those involved saw Divine manipulation of events every step of the way, and the verse *"Lev malachim ve'sarim be'yad Hashem* — The hearts of kings and officials are in the hands of God" was for them a living reality.

Reb Chaim often mentioned in his *shmuessen* that one of the most important factors in its miraculous salvation was the yeshivah's staying together at all times. In this connection he often spoke of the power of the united community.

> When the Jews reached Mount Sinai, the Torah says, "Israel set camp adjacent to the Mountain." Rashi comments that the Torah employed the singular, speaking of the entire nation as one individual — "As one person with one heart." The *Or HaChaim Hakadosh* explains that this unity was a prerequisite to receiving the Torah. "Imagine," said Reb Chaim, "600,000 men, plus women and children, whose release from Egyptian bondage was only to facilitate their receiving the Torah, thereby becoming God's Chosen People. They traveled to Sinai for this reason and this reason alone. But that did not suffice. These multitudes could not have received the Torah as individuals. It was only as a nation, as a cohesive unit with one body and one heart, as it were, that they could receive the Torah and fulfill their destiny."
>
> He would elaborate further on this theme: "Those who separated themselves from the yeshivah — numbering 30 or so — and tried to make their own way out of the European inferno, did not succeed. Only the yeshivah as a unit managed with Divine guidance to escape unscathed."

The yeshivah stayed in Kobe, Japan, for about six months, and then relocated to Shanghai for the next five years. Living conditions were extremely difficult, but the yeshivah prospered. Reb Finkel had gone to *Eretz Yisrael* to obtain visas for the yeshivah and was forced to remain there. Thus, the entire responsibility of directing the yeshivah was borne by Reb Chaim and the *Mashgiach*, Rabbi Yecheskel Levenstein זצ"קל.

~§ Shanghai

The refugee population of Shanghai included contingents of students from other yeshivos, including Kamenitz, Kletzk, Lubavitch, and Lublin, among others. Each had its own place of learning, but Reb Chaim was responsible for the financial needs of all. Exchanging foreign currency in Shanghai was fraught with danger and Reb Chaim lived with a perpetual fear of being apprehended by the authorities, but this in no way deterred him from seeing to the needs of all the yeshivos, while learning and teaching with unmatched zeal.

During the years in Shanghai, Reb Chaim was like a father to all the students, many of whom had been orphaned as a result of the war. He himself would bring food and medicine to the ill. And he cared for them spiritually and emotionally, teaching them, learning with them, and raising their spirits in any possible way.

In Shanghai, the yeshivah was confined to the ghetto, together with most other Jewish refugees. As dean of the yeshivah, Reb Chaim had the privilege of living outside the ghetto. Since he studied with a *chavrusa* whenever possible, the *chavrusa* slipped out of the ghetto every night without permission to learn with him. In time, he was caught and the two of them were thrown into jail for a day or so. During his entire stay in jail, Reb Chaim was seen standing at the window engrossed in his Torah thoughts.

A short while after arriving in Shanghai, Reb Chaim received American visas for himself and his family. He refused them, saying that he would leave only when *all* the students had received their visas. This meant ultimately staying in Shanghai for five-and-a-half years.

After the war, the yeshivah had obtained visas for all the students and was ready to leave — except for two boys who had become mentally unbalanced as a result of the trauma of war and exile. The American government wasn't interested in admitting sick people to the U.S. The enormous demand for the very scarce visas made falsifying information for obtaining a visa highly dangerous, more so than in normal times. Reb Chaim took the two boys to the consulate and somehow induced them to sit still and not say a word. He did all the talking and managed to convince the consul that they were sane and eligible for visas. This he did at the very real risk of being caught, but as was his life long practice, there was little he would not do to help someone else.

> *Even when he was involved in the administrative work of the yeshivah, his mind would be occupied with learning. "Nisht azoy iz pshat in dem Rashba (This is not the explanation of the Rashba)," he'd say to himself, although involved in some task that apparently had absolutely no connection with the Rashba — but anything and everything he did reminded him of this Rashba, that Tosfos, or some other part of Torah.*

◄§ Jerusalem

In 1947 the yeshivah moved again — as always, as a single unit — this time, to the United States, where Reb Chaim spent some six months before rejoining his father-in-law Reb Eliezer Yehudah Finkel in the Mirrer Yeshivah in Jerusalem. Someone studying in Mir-Jerusalem at the time told this writer:

> *When Reb Lazer Yudel came to Jerusalem a number of years earlier, he had started the yeshivah with ten carefully chosen talmidim — ten of the finest young men in local yeshivos — among them Rabbi Yudel Shapiro (now Rosh Kollel Chazon Ish), Rabbi Chaim Brim, and Rabbi Chaim Graineman — today each an outstanding Torah personality. When Reb Chaim joined the yeshivah, the yeshivah was still quite small and all of the students went to visit him. As was the custom, the best of them related some of their recent chiddushim (Torah novellae), and interpretations on Shas and Rishonim. Reb Chaim sat through their presentations without a word. They had felt that they had suitably impressed the new Rosh Yeshivah from America.*
>
> *Only then did Reb Chaim speak, telling each in turn that whatever he had said could be found in one Acharon (later commentator) or another — and he told them where: "This you'll find in the Teshuvos Reb*

Akiva Eiger, that in the Noda Biyehudah, the next in the Yeshuos Yaakov."

"We left in a daze, awe struck that one man could have mastered so much of such variety, with total recall."

Reb Chaim remained in Mir-Jerusalem until his passing some 32 years later, disseminating Torah and *mussar* to thousands of disciples with *shiurim* and *shmuessen* (lectures on Talmud and on ethical themes), *vaadim* and *chaburos* (smaller groups convened on these respective topics), teaching *Toras Hashem*.

His influence was felt far beyond the confines of the Mirrer Yeshivah. Groups of *talmidim* from yeshivos all over the country would come at any time and request a *chaburah* on this or that *sugya* (topic), in any volume in *Shas*. "Come back in 20 minutes," he would say, and they would be treated to a *chaburah* — deeply brilliant and wide ranging, as if he had just been delving into the very topic they had requested him to expound upon.

His awesome clarity in every part of Torah was such that *Zeraim* and *Taharos* (sections dealing with agricultural laws and ritual purity) — which are not studied with the same frequency as the other *Sedarim* (sections), since no Talmud *Bavli* is extant to them, except for two *masechtos* — were as familiar to him as any popular *mesechta*. A colleague once remarked, "What really can one say about a man who knows every *Rash* in *Taharos* by heart!"

> When quoting a source during a shiur or shmuess he would open the Gemara, leaf through the pages and read. Those standing behind him would often notice that the sefer was not even turned to the appropriate page. He knew the text entirely by heart, but in his humility he made it appear as if he were reading.

❧ ❧ ❧

> A visitor to the Mir in Poland remembered spending a Shabbos at Reb Chaim's house: "Reb Chaim made Kiddush, quickly finished and joined a chavrusa waiting in the next room with a Tur Even Hoezer. Reb Chaim would recite the Tur, Bais Yosef and Bach from memory while the chavrusa read from the corresponding page in Tur."

It was in 1964, after the passing of the *mashgiach*, his brother-in-law Reb Chaim Zev Finkel ז״ל, that Reb Chaim began to give *shmuessen* in the yeshivah. Their fame spread and people from all parts of Israel would flock to Mir to hear his Sunday night *shmuess*. His eloquence, his ability to drive home a point simply and lucidly, his wide-ranging knowledge and his emphasis on matters pertaining to man and fellow were among the reasons that they attracted standing-room-only crowds.

> *Reb Chaim had a habit of standing by the bimah, waiting several minutes before speaking. Reb Shlomo Wolbe explained: "He did not need the time to prepare his words. He needed it to prepare himself for the shmuess. Until he was certain that his thoughts were mi'libo — from his heart — he would not say them."*

It was in his *shmuessen* that Reb Chaim offered his listeners a glimpse into his great heart, for his genius of mind was matched by his genius of heart and by his sterling character. As he was a giant in Torah, so he was a giant in *midos*.

His all-encompassing concern for his fellow Jew and his constant preoccupation with the well-being of others were manifestations of the love that poured forth from his great heart, a heart like that of a prince in Israel: "His heart is the heart of all Israel" (*Rambam Hilchos Melachim*).

> Reb Chaim often said, "A leader of *Klal Yisrael* must feel the joy and suffering of his fellow Jew as if they were his own." He quoted the comment of *Chazal* that Aharon merited wearing the *Urim V'Tumim* (special breast plate) over his heart, as a result of his profound joy at learning of the selection of his younger brother Moshe to be the redeemer of Israel. Reb Chaim explained: "A heart that had the capacity to truly rejoice in the good fortune of another — that heart was the appropriate place for the *Urim V'Tumim*. Through the *Urim V'Tumim*, God revealed to Aharon the solutions to the most difficult problems in a manner all but incomprehensible and unfathomable — except to him whose heart could so totally identify with the problem of his supplicant as to feel that problem as his own."

He, too, rejoiced in the good fortune of others as if his own, and he literally became ill upon hearing of their misfortunes, as was evidenced, for example, during the week-long Entebbe incident when he became physically sick with concern.

> *This writer was standing near the Rosh Yeshivah when the yeshivah was praying for the recovery of the late Gerer Rebbe, צז"ל. His body was shaking with sobs as he entreated the Almighty to spare the life of this great leader.*

❦ ❦ ❦

> *His family often hid the daily Agudah newspaper Hamodia to spare him the anguish of seeing requests for public prayer for the recovery of this or that ill person.*

❦ ❦ ❦

> *On a shivah visit to a friend who had lost his wife, Reb Chaim sat down and wept bitterly with anguish over his friend's loss. After twenty minutes, he arose, said, "Hamakom Yenachem (May God console you) ...," and left, offering the greatest comfort to the bereaved by bearing with him the agony of his loss.*

❦ ❦ ❦

> *In this vein, we can understand his deep emotions while visiting the Yad Avshalom. Reb Chaim told his students that he often would say a tefillah. He was once asked, "Wasn't Avshalom a rasha — a wicked man? Why pray at his monument?"*
>
> *He replied, "Contemplate Avshalom — he tried to kill his father; and yet when he died, his father David was broken hearted and prayed for him. This helps me understand what is meant by a 'father's mercy,' and I'm ready to beseech God: 'As a father has mercy on a son, so should God have mercy on us!'"*
>
> *Everyone's feelings are aroused by standing at the Kosel. Who but Reb Chaim could respond to Yad Avshalom?*

◄§ The Last Days

On Hoshana Rabbah 5739, Reb Chaim is lying on his bed, his body racked with pain and ravaged by disease. A young man enters the room and asks him to pray for the recovery of a sick person.

After the young man leaves, the Rosh Hayeshivah says to his son, "Please dress me, I'm going to the Kosel."

"But Father," his son protests, "you can hardly turn over in bed. How can you possibly go to the Kosel?"

"Dress me please," his father insists. "I'm going to the Kosel."

Reluctantly the son helps his father dress and with the aid of another carries him to the car which takes him to the Kosel. At the Kosel, the father, with barely enough strength to stand, gets out of the car and entreats the Almighty for the well-being of another. Then he returns to his sickbed.

A few days after *Succos,* Reb Chaim was rushed to the hospital and, for the next two months, his life hung by a thread. Even during the weeks of semi-consciousness his lips moved, and from time to time he could be heard whispering *divrei Torah.* Torah Jewry the world over stormed the gates of heaven pleading for his recovery.

On Monday night, the third of *Teves,* after the last of the *Chanukah* lights had cast its glow, this great light had shined its last. The great light that for 60 of its 76 years had illuminated the byways of Torah with loving kindness joined his colleagues in the *Mesivta D'Rakia* (Heavenly Academy).

What, really, can one say about a man who learned through the entire Torah, both written and oral, countless times (*Bavli, Yerushalmi, Midrash, Rishonim,* and *Acharonim*), and knew it so thoroughly and completely in its width, breadth and depth? What more *is* there to say about one who had the entire Torah at his fingertips and, not satisfied with his own accomplishments, spent all his days teaching this Torah by word and by deed to thousands of disciples, young and old, brilliant and ordinary?

The Torah tells us: "And Avraham came to eulogize Sarah and to weep for her." Reb Chaim asked, "Why doesn't the Torah elaborate further on this point and tell us what Abraham said?" He suggested that the answer is to be found in Rashi's comment to verse 2: "*The years of the life of Sarah.*" Rashi comments, "They were all equal in virtue."

Reb Chaim explained, "Avraham could not truly eulogize Sarah, because, as the *Chazal* tell us, she was greater than he in prophecy, limiting Avraham's capacity to fully understand Sarah's greatness. Thus he could not describe the true dimensions of her personality. He could, however, offer one all-encompassing praise — 'All her years were equally superb.' There were no lapses in her excellence. She was perfectly consistent and consistently perfect."

If we cannot evaluate Reb Chaim, we can at least apply to him Avraham's comment: *All his days were equally virtuous*, equally filled with Torah and goodness.

Reb Chaim often told us that the essence of life is giving. "What is the purpose of life if not to give of one's self to others?" With this he explained the *Gemara* (*Nedarim* 64b) that states that there are four types of persons who, although physically living, are considered dead — a beggar, a leper, a blind man, and a childless person. Reb Chaim explained that their common denominator is their dependence on others and their inability to give of themselves to their fellow: The beggar needs the support of others; according to Jewish law, the leper must live outside the community and thus cannot help others; a blind man needs constant assistance; and a person without children has no one to whom he can bequeath his legacy. In one way or another, they are all limited in their ability to give of themselves in all respects and so essentially they are not living.

Similar is the saying of our sages: A righteous man is considered living even after his death because the living world still feels the influence of his words and deeds. He is giving, so he is alive.

The great light that ceased to be on that third night of *Teves* was really not extinguished. It is only the candle that is missing. The flame, however, continues to burn brightly. Reb Chaim is still giving. The light of his Torah, his *mussar*, his *chessed*, the light of the example he set with his very being will continue to shine brightly, until the days of *Mashiach*.

Reb Chaim's
DISCOURSES

לִקְרַאת יוֹם הַדִּין

Awaiting the Day of Judgment

I.

R osh HaShanah, the Day of Judgment, is drawing near. While each of us surely feels and perceives the awesomeness of this day, yet, in a sense, we feel that as people who are by and large engaged in Divine service, and are close to Hashem, we have, somehow, less to worry about.

The truth, however, is the opposite. The closer one is to Hashem the more accountable he is for his deeds. This is the meaning of the psalmist: צִדְקָתְךָ כְּהַרְרֵי אֵל מִשְׁפָּטֶיךָ תְּהוֹם רַבָּה, *Your benevolence is like the mighty mountains, Your judgments are like the vast deep waters* (*Tehillim* 36:7). Thus we find these two seemingly diametrically opposed attributes of God — מִשְׁפָּטֶיךָ, *Your judgments*, and צִדְקָתְךָ, *Your benevolence* — expressed simultaneously. Those upon whom God bestows his benevolence are also subject to the most exacting judgments. When we come to this realization we can understand that it is even more incumbent upon us to reexamine our deeds and look for ways of preparing ourselves for the profound judgment which takes place on Rosh HaShanah.

The first step which one must take in order to face Divine judgment is deduced by *Chazal* from the very same verse which describes the awesomeness of that judgment.

צִדְקָתְךָ כְּהַרְרֵי אֵל, מִשְׁפָּטֶיךָ תְּהוֹם רַבָּה, אָדָם וּבְהֵמָה תוֹשִׁיעַ ה'. אָדָם וּבְהֵמָה תוֹשִׁיעַ ה' – אֵלּוּ בְּנֵי אָדָם שֶׁהֵן עֲרוּמִין בְּדַעַת וּמְשִׂימִים עַצְמָם כִּבְהֵמָה (חולין ה' ע"ב, עיין רש"י).

Your righteousness is like the mighty mountains, Your judgments are like the vast deep waters. Man and beast You save. Man and beast — this alludes to people who are wise in understanding and conduct themselves humbly like cattle (Chulin 5b and Rashi).

Although it is true that God does not excuse the recipients of His graciousness fom excruciating judgment, yet those humble people who *are like cattle* are spared the penetrating Divine judgment.

This is the essence of the prophet Zefaniah's declaration אֲשֶׁר ... מִשְׁפָּטוֹ פָּעָלוּ, בַּקְּשׁוּ צֶדֶק בַּקְּשׁוּ עֲנָוָה אוּלַי תִּסָּתְרוּ בְּיוֹם אַף ה'. ...*That which His justice has accomplished, seek righteousness, seek humility, perhaps you will be able to conceal yourselves on the day of God's fury (Zefaniah 2:3).* When Hashem acts in judgment, מִשְׁפָּטוֹ פָּעָלוּ, there is no escape, but if one *seeks humility* then perhaps one will be spared Divine retribution.

Chazal draw a remarkable parallel from the above principle to explain an interesting phenomenon in the laws pertaining to leprosy afflicting a house.

אָמַר ר' אֶלְעָזָר: לְעוֹלָם הֱוֵי קַבָּל וְקַיָּם. א"ר זֵירָא, אַף אֲנַן נַמִי תְּנִינָא, בַּיִת אָפֵל אֵין פּוֹתְחִין לוֹ חַלוֹנוֹת לִרְאוֹת נִגְעוֹ (סנהדרין צ"ב ע"א).

R' Elazar said: A person should always be humble and he will survive. R' Zeira stated: We too have learned that one does not open the windows of a dark house in order to examine its leprosy (Sanhedrin 92a).

Even though a house may be in fact afflicted with leprosy, yet halachically it is not טָמֵא, *ritually impure.* Since it is dark, not displaying itself nor publicizing itself, as it were, the priest does not illuminate it in order to reveal its afflictions. So too the harsh lights of rebuke and judgment will not be trained upon a humble man, though he may be tainted.

Besides the aspects inherent in and integral to human nature which prevent a person from being genuinely humble, there is the added difficulty, that גַּאֲוָה, *self-esteem,* is a necessary element in the worship of God! Thus Scriptures describes approvingly the character of Yehoshaphat as וַיִּגְבַּהּ לִבּוֹ בְּדַרְכֵי ה׳, *He held his heart high in the ways of Hashem* (II Divrei HaYamim 17:6).

Ramban demonstrates the practical application of this principle during the construction of the Tabernacle. Those who volunteered to build the Tabernacle had no previous experience nor training in their respective vocations, rather they found it within their nature to do so. They were those whom נְשָׂאוֹ לִבּוֹ, whose *hearts were stirred up* (*Shemos* 35:21); those with גַּבְהוּת הַלֵּב. It was with this strength and determination that they succeeded in constructing a magnificent Tabernacle without any previous building experience.

If self-esteem is a necessary aspect of Divine service it becomes yet more difficult to inculcate humility in ourselves in anticipation of the day of judgment. On the one hand we must fill ourselves with pride and stoutheartedness to such a degree that no feat is deemed impossible to accomplish, therefore actually finding these abilities within us. On the other hand we must be humble and unassuming similar to a בַּיִת אָפֵל, an unilluminated house whose blemishes are not scrutinized.

II.

An additional method of tempering the harshness of Divine judgment is being דָּן לְכַף זְכוּת, *judging one's fellow human being in a favorable light. Chazal* tell us, הַדָּן חֲבֵרוֹ לְכַף זְכוּת דָּנִין אוֹתוֹ לִזְכוּת, *He who judges his fellow man favorably is himself judged favorably* (*Shabbos* 127b).

At first glance the equating of human judgment with Divine judgment would seem incongruous. Human beings can never be sure of the motives of a fellow human being and therefore must judge them favorably, giving them the benefit of the doubt. How can we say the same about Divine justice? Are there any doubts before Hashem that it would be possible to attribute the possibility of דָּן לְכַף זְכוּת to Him?

The answer is that *Chazal* are not referring to a situation where we are judging if a person's actions are right or wrong. Rather, *Chazal* are referring to actions which are ostensibly right but the motives of which are unclear. The requirement to be דָּן לְכַף זְכוּת means to appraise favorably an action done with mixed motives by emphasizing its positive aspects. This is the meaning of Shlomo HaMelech's assertion, כִּי אָדָם אֵין צַדִּיק בָּאָרֶץ אֲשֶׁר יַעֲשֶׂה טּוֹב וְלֹא יֶחֱטָא, *There is no person on earth who is completely righteous who does only good and commits no wrong* (Koheles 7:20).

There are people who indeed do not sin, but no human being is free of having at least some impure motive for even the best of deeds which he performs (see *Alshich* there). It is regarding the evaluation of one's motive that דָּן לְכַף זְכוּת is reciprocated by the Divine דָּן לְכַף זְכוּת. If a person judges his fellow man's actions from the perspective of their finer and nobler motives, then Hashem will judge his actions by the same standards.

This element of Divine דָּן לְכַף זְכוּת is expressed in the following manner.

אֵלּוּ הֵן פְּרַקְלִיטִין שֶׁל אָדָם: תְּשׁוּבָה וּמַעֲשִׂים טוֹבִים. וַאֲפִילוּ תֵּשַׁע מֵאוֹת וְתִשְׁעִים וְתִשְׁעָה מְלַמְּדִים עָלָיו חוֹבָה וְאֶחָד מְלַמֵּד עָלָיו זְכוּת נִצּוֹל, שֶׁנֶּאֱמַר, אִם יֵשׁ עָלָיו מַלְאָךְ מֵלִיץ אֶחָד מִנִּי אָלֶף לְהַגִּיד לְאָדָם יָשְׁרוֹ. וַיְחֻנֶּנּוּ וַיֹּאמֶר פְּדָעֵהוּ מֵרֶדֶת שַׁחַת מָצָאתִי כֹפֶר (איוב לג:כג-כד). ר' אֶלְעָזָר בְּנוֹ שֶׁל ר' יוֹסֵי הַגְּלִילִי אוֹמֵר: אֲפִילוּ תֵּשַׁע מֵאוֹת וְתִשְׁעִים וְתִשְׁעָה בְּאוֹתוֹ מַלְאָךְ לְחוֹבָה וְאֶחָד לִזְכוּת נִצּוֹל, שֶׁנֶּאֱמַר מֵלִיץ אֶחָד מִנִּי אָלֶף (שבת ל"ב ע"א). *These are a person's defenders: repentance and good deeds. Even if nine hundred and ninety-nine argue for his guilt while one argues in his favor, he is saved, as it says, "If there is one angel, one defender among a thousand to show man what is right for him, then He is gracious to him saying, 'Deliver him from going down to the pit' " (Iyov 33:23-24). R' Eliezer son of R' Yosi Haglili said: Even if nine hundred and ninety-nine parts of that angel are unfavorable and one part is favorable, he is saved, as it says, "a defender one part of a thousand" (Shabbos 32a).*

Thus, we see that one deed, though it may contain many unworthy aspects, even if it has only one worthy dimension, that dimension can override other less worthy facets.

By judging our fellow man from the best possible angle we are assuring ourselves of also being judged favorably.

III.

Another important virtue which must be augmented before the Day of Judgment is the virtue of רַחֲמִים, *mercy*. We, ourselves, place the emphasis of our prayers during the holy days on רַחֲמִים, appealing for Divine mercy.

R' Yochanan said, "There are ten synonyms for prayer. Yet Moshe chose to employ the term תַּחֲנוּנִים to describe his own supplications" (*Devarim Rabbah* 2:1). *Matnos Kehunah* explains that the implication of this is that Moshe's prayer was neither a complaint nor a claim for that which is due, but rather a request for undeserved mercy.

I remember my father זצ"ל would pour his heart out on Rosh HaShanah when saying, "May You see before You the sacrifice of Yitzchak by Avraham on the Altar. Just as he sublimated his mercy in order to fulfill Your will, so too may Your mercy overcome Your anger." The emphasis was on the revelation and enactment of God's mercy.

But God bestows mercy only upon those who are merciful towards others. As *Chazal* have pointed out, כָּל הַמְרַחֵם עַל הַבְּרִיוֹת מְרַחֲמִים עָלָיו מִן הַשָּׁמַיִם, *He who shows compassion towards God's creatures is in turn granted Hashem's mercy* (*Shabbos* 151b).

Rabbeinu HaKadosh, the spiritual giant and the scholar who compiled the *Mishnah*, suffered terribly for thirteen years due to the lack of compassion that he expressed towards an animal. The *Gemara* recounts:

דְּהַהוּא עֶגְלָא דַּהֲווּ קָא מַמְטוּ לֵי' לִשְׁחִיטָה. אֲזַל תַּלְיָא לְרֵישֵׁיהּ בִּכְנָפֵיהּ דְּרַבִּי וְקָא בָּכֵי. אֲמַר לֵי' זִיל לְכָךְ נוֹצַרְתְּ. אָמְרֵי, הוֹאִיל וְלֹא קָא מְרַחֵם לֵיתוּ עֲלֵיהּ יִסּוּרִין וְעַל יְדֵי מַעֲשֶׂה הָלְכוּ. יוֹמָא חַד הֲוָה קָא כַּנְשָׁא אַמְתֵהּ דְּרַבִּי בֵּיתָא הֲוָה שַׁדְיָא בְּנֵי כַרְכּוּשְׁתָּא וְקָא כַּנְשָׁא לְהוּ. אֲמַר לָהּ שַׁבְקִינְהוּ. כְּתִיב, וְרַחֲמָיו עַל כָּל מַעֲשָׂיו. אָמְרֵי הוֹאִיל וּמְרַחֵם נְרַחֵם עֲלֵיהּ (בבא מציעא פ"ה ע"א).
There was a calf being taken to the slaughterhouse, when it broke away, and hid its head under Rebbi's cloak and cried [in terror]. "Go," [said Rebbi], "it is for this purpose that you were created." They declared [in Heaven], "Since he has no pity he shall suffer." Through a [different] event his suffering was relieved: One day Rebbi's maid was sweeping the house. A litter

of kittens were laying about and she was sweeping them up. He said, "Leave them alone for it says, 'And He is merciful upon all of his creatures.' " [In Heaven it was] proclaimed, "Since he is compassionate we will be merciful towards him" (Bava Metzia 85a).

If we show mercy and compassion towards others, then Heaven will show compassion towards us. We will then be able to pray, רַחֲמֵנוּ כְּרַחֵם אָב עַל בָּנִים, *Hashem, be as compassionate towards us as a father is towards his children,* for a father's feelings for his children are boundless. Avshalom rebelled against his father, even going as far as attempting to murder him. Yet, David mourned his loss greatly, crying in anguish, מִי יִתֵּן מוּתִי אֲנִי תַחְתֶּיךָ אַבְשָׁלוֹם, *Would that I have died in your stead, Avshalom.* Avshalom committed the greatest imaginable crime against his father, yet David forgave him for one reason only: He was his son. This is the essence of our prayers on Rosh HaShanah. Though we have rebelled against You, Hashem, we beg You, please be merciful towards us for we are Your children and a father forgives his children no matter how badly they may have sinned, no matter how much they may have rebelled.

בֵּין אָדָם לַחֲבֵרוֹ

Between Man and His Fellow Man

I.

אֶת זוֹ דָרַשׁ רַבִּי אֶלְעָזָר בֶּן עֲזַרְיָה: מִכֹּל חַטֹּאתֵיכֶם לִפְנֵי ה'
תִּטְהָרוּ. עֲבֵרוֹת שֶׁבֵּין אָדָם לַמָּקוֹם יוהכ"פ מְכַפֵּר. עֲבֵרוֹת שֶׁבֵּין
אָדָם לַחֲבֵרוֹ אֵין יוֹם הַכִּפּוּרִים מְכַפֵּר עַד שֶׁיְרַצֶּה אֶת חֲבֵרוֹ (יומא
פ"ה ע"ב).

*R' Elazar ben Azariah expounded as follows: [The verse
reads,] "Of all your sins before HASHEM will you be
cleansed." Yom Kippur atones for sins between man
and HASHEM. However, Yom Kippur does not atone for
sins between man and his fellow until he has attained
the forgiveness of his fellow man (Yoma 85b).*

O n Yom Kippur we stand in judgment before Hashem and ask
forgiveness for our sins. There is one group of sins,
however, that permeates almost all of man's activities for which no
forgiveness is being offered. This is the area of בֵּין אָדָם לַחֲבֵרוֹ,
personal relationships, for which judgment is passed but for
which there is no atonement until and unless the wronged party is
placated.

It would follow then that a major area in which to concentrate the efforts of תְּשׁוּבָה, *repentance*, on Yom Kippur must be that of בֵּין אָדָם לַחֲבֵרוֹ.

This aspect of Yom Kippur is also emphasized in a verse of the morning *haftarah*.

> הֵן לְרִיב וּמַצָּה תָּצוּמוּ וּלְהַכּוֹת בְּאֶגְרֹף רֶשַׁע . . . הֲלוֹא זֶה צוֹם
> אֶבְחָרֵהוּ: פַּתֵּחַ חַרְצֻבּוֹת רֶשַׁע הַתֵּר אֲגֻדּוֹת מוֹטָה וְשַׁלַּח רְצוּצִים
> חָפְשִׁים (ישעיה נח:ד,ו).
>
> Behold, you fast for strife and contention and to smite
> with the fist of wickedness ... Is not rather this the fast
> that I have chosen — to loosen the chains of wicked-
> ness, to undo the bands of the yoke, and to let the
> oppressed go free (Yeshayahu 58:4,6)?

The severity of judgment in these matters is evident from the punishment meted out to Avdan for embarrassing R' Yishmael the son of R' Yose. After detailing the discussion between them and Avdan's belittling remark, the *Gemara* relates:

> תָּאנָא בְּאוֹתָהּ שָׁעָה נִצְטָרַע אַבְדָּן וְטָבְעוּ שְׁנֵי בָנָיו וּמֵאֲנוּ שְׁתֵּי
> כַלּוֹתָיו. אָמַר רַב נַחְמָן בַּר יִצְחָק בְּרִיךְ רַחֲמָנָא דְּכַסְפֵּיהּ לְאַבְדָּן
> בְּהַאי עָלְמָא (יבמות ק״ה ע״ב).
>
> Avdan became a leper, his two sons drowned, and his
> two daughter-in-laws annulled their marriages (Yeva-
> mos 105b).

Yet, "Blessed be the Merciful One," said R' Nachman, "for punishing Avdan in *this* world" (*Yevamos* 105b). As terrible as Avdan's punishment was, R' Nachman considered it mild compared to what it could have been, and therefore pronounced a blessing that Avdan had been fortunate in receiving his punishment in this world and not in the World-to-Come. Few sins that are בֵּין אָדָם לַמָּקוֹם, *between man and Hashem*, carry anything approaching such an all-encompassing penalty.

However, it is not only the severity of the punishment that makes the judgment for hurtful personal relationships so awesome; it is also the culpability for well-intentioned actions and the range of deeds for which one is held to account, innocuous though the transgressions may seem. Thus if one harms one's fellow man even with the best of intentions, in order to be of service in some way, the punishment is no less severe.

Channah, the mother of the prophet Shmuel, was constantly taunted by Peninah about her barrenness. The Sages testify that פְּנִינָה לְשֵׁם שָׁמַיִם נִתְכַּוְּנָה, *Peninah's intention was for the sake of Heaven* (*Bava Basra* 16a), hoping to inspire Channah into praying for children, which in fact she did. Yet because of the mental anguish she caused, Peninah suffered the loss of all her children (*Pesikta Rabbasi* 44)!

Moreover, not only is one punished for hurting a human being, however well intentioned, but even just being the cause of another's pain is sufficient reason for punishment. This principle is borne out by the following incident:

רַב רְחוּמֵי . . . הֲוָה רָגִיל דַּהֲוֵי אָתֵי לְבֵיתֵי כָּל מַעֲלֵי יוֹמָא דְכִפּוּרֵי. יוֹמָא חַד מָשְׁכְתֵי שְׁמַעֲתָא. הֲוָא מְסַכְּיָא דְּבִיתְהוּ, הַשְׁתָּא אָתֵי, הַשְׁתָּא אָתֵי. לֹא אָתָא, חֲלַשׁ דַּעְתַּהּ אָחֵית דִּמְעֲתָא מֵעֵינָהּ. הֲוָה יָתֵיב בְּאִיגְרָא, אִיפְּחִית אִיגְרָא מִתּוּתֵי וְנָח נַפְשֵׁי (כתובות ס"ב:ע"ב).

R' Rachumi would usually return home every Erev Yom Kippur. Once, he became engrossed in his studies [on Erev Yom Kippur and forgot to return]. His wife was watching anxiously for him [saying to herself,] "Now he is coming, now he is coming." Seeing that he didn't come, she became upset, shedding a tear. Her husband was sitting on a roof; the roof caved in and he died (Kesubos 62b).

The death of R' Rachumi cannot be described as a punishment; no one was more affected by his death than his wife, on whose account he was punished. If she had been hurt by his tardiness, surely his permanent absence would be unbearable.

To understand the reason of R' Rachumi's death we must view the punishment meted out for interpersonal offenses in a different manner. It is not retribution in the sense of reward and punishment, rather it is part and parcel of the reality of our existence. As surely as one must be hurt by a collision with another object, so too must one be harmed when one has hurt another person's feelings. When one puts his hand into fire it will be burned, countless good reasons for doing so notwithstanding!

This insight places interpersonal relationships in a different light altogether. We cannot excuse our actions by rationalizing our intentions, for whenever we cause anguish there will be retribution. It is a cause-and-effect relationship, in which excuses and rationalizations are irrelevant.

Moreover, it is not only for positive actions that a person is held accountable, but even if one is only a passive instrument for someone else's pain he is held responsible. Thus, the *Gemara* tells us about R' Kahana whose face was disfigured in a way that he always appeared to be laughing. Once R' Yochanan, when delivering a lecture, glanced at R' Kahana and thought him to be laughing at the discourse. R' Yochanan was embarrassed and R' Kahana subsequently died. Indeed, R' Kahana had been passive, but nevertheless R' Yochanan had been hurt, and that was enough to cause R' Kahana's death.

II.

Harsh and severe as this aspect of human relationships may seem, its counterpart in the positive sense is the unlimited reward for helping one's fellow. Just as a person is held to account for unwittingly hurting someone or for even just serving as an instrument for another's embarrassment, so too, and even more so, is a person rewarded for aiding his fellow man — unintentional and passive though it may have been.

Thus we find numerous instances where an inanimate object became sacred merely because it had served as the place of spiritual elevation for man. Thus:

קָדֵשׁ? שֶׁנִּתְקַדְּשׁוּ יִשְׂרָאֵל עָלָיו (שבת פ״ט ע״א).

[Why was it called] the Wilderness of Kadesh? For Israel had sanctified [Kadosh] themselves there (Shabbos 89a).

Was there a conscious act on the part of the Wilderness to assist Israel in sanctifying themselves? Certainly not.

So, too, Mount Moriah became sanctified for all generations because it served as an instrument of elevation for Avraham and Yitzchak. R' Elazar would kiss the very stone on which R' Akiva s at when he would expound to his students, comparing the stone to Mount Moriah. These inanimate objects were rewarded, as it were, for the passive assistance they rendered to the growth of human beings. If this is the case with inanimate objects it certainly holds true for human beings.

The most outstanding facet of human relationships, however, is when the reward earned for one's own achievements is overshadowed by the reward for the role one played in aiding one's brother to accomplish the *very same* deed.

מִי גָרַם לִרְאוּבֵן שֶׁהוֹדָה? יְהוּדָה. וְעַל־יְדֵי כֵן זָכָה יְהוּדָה שֶׁיָּבֹאוּ עַצְמוֹתָיו לִמְנוּחָתָן וְיֵשֵׁב בִּישִׁיבָה שֶׁל מַעֲלָה וְזָכָה לַאֲסוֹקֵי שְׁמַעְתְּתָא אֱלִבָּא דְהִלְכְתָא (ע״פ סוטה ז׳ ע״ב).

Who caused Reuven to admit [his guilt]? Yehudah. Therefore, Yehudah merited that his bones would come to their rest, that he would sit in the Heavenly Academy, and he merited that he would arrive at a decision in accordance with Halachah (paraphrase of Sotah 7b).

We must bear in mind that Yehudah himself confessed his relations with Tamar under the most embarrassing circumstances (*Bereishis* 38:26). Yet, this did not suffice to merit these Heavenly rewards. It was only because he was instrumental in bringing about Reuven's confession that he was forgiven for his sins and rewarded with peace for his soul.

It is clear, then, that as important as it is to rectify one's own shortcomings, it pales in comparison to helping another person with his needs.

Let us utilize the time left till Yom Kippur to rectify the wrongs we have done to our fellow man, let us strengthen the good we bestow upon others and thereby we will be elevated and sanctified on this most holy of days.

מֵאִיגְּרָא רָמָא לְבֵירָא עֲמִקְתָּא

Zenith to Nadir:
Coping with Adversity

וַיֹּאמֶר קַיִן אֶל הֶבֶל אָחִיו וַיְהִי בִּהְיוֹתָם בַּשָּׂדֶה (בראשית ד:ח).
And Cain said to his brother Hevel and it came to pass when they were in the field (Bereishis 4:8).

עֲנֵי קַיִן וַאֲמַר לְהֶבֶל לֵית דִּין וְלֵית דַּיָן וְלֵית עָלַם אַחֳרָן וְלֵית לְמִתַּן אֲגַר טַב לְצַדִּיקַיָּא וְלֵית לְמִיפְרָעָא מִן רַשִּׁיעַיָּא (תרגום יונתן בן עוזיאל שם).
Cain spoke up and said to Hevel, "There is no judgment, no judge, nor any other world [besides this one]. There is no one to reward the righteous nor to punish the wicked" (Targum Yonasan Ben Uziel ibid.).

סָרוּ מַהֵר מִן הַדֶּרֶךְ אֲשֶׁר צִוִּיתִם עָשׂוּ לָהֶם עֵגֶל מַסֵּכָה (שמות לב:ח).
They have quickly strayed from the path that I have commanded them, they have fashioned for themselves a molten calf (Shemos 32:8).

This description of Israel's abrupt decline is shocking, not so much as regards the sin of the golden calf in itself but rather concerning their rapid descent into the abyss of idolatry, a sin that a Jew would not readily commit.

While one may commit other sins in the heat of the moment, one does not worship idols except as the culmination of a lengthy process of decline. *Chazal* have described this process as, כָּךְ אוּמְנוּתוֹ שֶׁל יֵצֶר הָרַע הַיּוֹם אוֹמֵר לוֹ עֲשֵׂה כַּךְ וּלְמָחָר אוֹמֵר לוֹ עֲשֵׂה כַּךְ עַד שֶׁאוֹמֵר לוֹ עֲבוֹד עֲבוֹדָה זָרָה (שבת ק״ה ע״ב), *this is the skillfull process [of ensnarement] by the evil inclination: Today he tells him, "Do thus," and tomorrow he tells him, "Do that," until he tells him, "Go worship idols"* (*Shabbos* 105b).

Yet here, Israel's prelude to the sin was the height of spirituality: standing at the foot of Mount Sinai, witnessing the most awesome of revelations and receiving the Torah. How did the evil inclination succeed in hurling Israel so suddenly from the peaks of spiritual experience to the depths of idol worship?

To answer this question we must examine a few examples of people who made similarly radical changes in their spiritual standing and the underlying cause.

The first one to deteriorate so rapidly was Cain. Cain was a true servant of God, the first to grasp on his own the essence of קָרְבָּנוֹת, *sacrifices* (see *Ramban*). In addition he communicated with Hashem like a prophet. Yet, when he arose to slay his brother, he blasphemed saying, "There is no judgment, no judge, nor any other world [besides this one]. There is no one to reward the righteous nor to punish the wicked" (according to *Targum Yonasan Ben Uziel Bereishis* 4:8).

The answer to this riddle lies in the verse, וַיִּחַר לְקַיִן מְאֹד וַיִּפְּלוּ פָּנָיו, *and Cain was very angry and his face fell* (*Bereishis* 4:5). Here we find Cain in a state of duress, hurt and shocked by Hashem's rejection of his offering. In such a mental state his susceptibility to heresy was at its strongest and in one instant the evil inclination pushed him to the depths of blasphemy.

This, too, was the case of the מְגַדֵּף, *blasphemer*, in the Wilderness (*Vayikra* 24:10-14). Here was a man living in an epoch of Israel's supreme closeness to Hashem, yet he was able to blaspheme and profane the Divine Name. The cause for this astonishing outpouring was a crushing emotional blow similar to the one by Cain. *Chazal* (cited by *Rashi* ibid.) tell us that his profaning of Hashem's Name occurred as a result of his losing a lawsuit. It had been decided that due to his antecedents he was to have no share in the land of Israel and he was to remain without tribal affiliation. It was in this distraught and disturbed state that the blasphemer lost all control of himself, and profaned God's Name.

The most poignant of examples is perhaps the story of Orpah, the sister-in-law of Ruth. Both Ruth and Orpah approached their mother-in-law Naomi and expressed the desire to convert to Judaism. וַתֹּאמַרְנָה לָהּ כִּי אִתָּךְ נָשׁוּב לְעַמֵּךְ, *And they said to her, "With you we will return to your people"* (Ruth 1:10).

They both spoke in one vein expressing one wish. Orpah had come to the same recognition of Judaism as Ruth, willing to embrace it, and to sever all her ties with family, home and nation. However when Orpah finally desisted and returned home, she did not remain the same woman of stature as before. So far and so quickly did she degenerate that *Chazal* (*Ruth Rabbah* 2:20) tell us that on the very night that she returned, she became a harlot, not even balking at the most bestial of behavior. In one day she fell from a profound recognition of the Creator and His laws to a moral low not even in line with the lowliest of people!

It was this same effect that allowed for the sudden and swift degeneration of Israel to the point of worshiping a golden calf. For until that very moment Moshe had been the teacher and leader of Israel. He had led them out of Egypt and taught them the Torah and its laws. Now the Satan confronted them with a vivid scene of their leader's death. Frightened and shocked, enveloped in darkness and confusion, they were no longer able to brake their fall. The Satan needed no series of steps to entice them to idolatry. As soon as the idea of the calf presented itself, Israel grasped at it, as a drowning man grasps at a straw.

This breakdown is not only the explanation of the sin of the golden calf but is the essence of the Jewish tragedy inherent in the destruction of the Temple as well. *Chazal* relate:

רַבִּי הֲוָה נָקִיט סֵפֶר קִינוֹת וְקָא קָרֵי בְּגַוֵּיהּ כִּי מָטָא לְהַאי פְּסוּקָא
"הִשְׁלִיךְ מִשָּׁמַיִם אֶרֶץ" נָפַל מִן יָדֵיהּ אָמַר מֵאִגְרָא רָם לְבֵירָא
עֲמִיקְתָּא (חגיגה ה׳ ע״ב).

Rebbi was holding the Book of Lamentations and read from it. When he reached the verse "He has thrown [Israel] from the Heavens to earth," it fell from his hand. He exclaimed, "Indeed [they have fallen] from a high roof to a deep pit" (Chagigah 5b).

The meaning of this comparison is puzzling. What did Rebbi see in the fall of the book that enlightened his understanding of the verse? The answer is that he realized that the place of the book in his hand or on the floor was irrelevant to its condition. It was the fall itself which damaged the book. So, too, the tragedy of Israel is not so much in its present lowly condition but rather the downfall and shock of the abrupt decline that has battered Israel terribly. This is the true understanding of the verse *He has thrown [Israel] from the Heavens to earth.* It is not the change of position from Heaven to earth which has so profoundly affected Israel, as much as the fall itself.

A person must be constantly on guard when he feels himself undergoing a period of spiritual descent, not to lose himself entirely. The plunge in itself is usually far more damaging than the level to which one has descended. If a person does take hold of himself, not losing his self-control under any circumstances, he will succeed in regaining his former stature, perhaps even being uplifted by his trying experience.

The paradigm of this strength and self-control is Shlomo HaMelech who fell from a position of ruling over the entire world to becoming a wandering pauper. *Chazal* describe his position at that time as מָלַךְ עַל מַקְלוֹ, *reigning over his cane (Sanhedrin* 20b). This describes his tremendous downfall, being left with naught but a cane. Yet on the other hand, we are told that he did not simply possess a stick but that he *ruled over it.* He used his tremendous wisdom to find a device to cushion his fall, in order that he not become lost entirely. Therefore he did not lose his regal bearing even under such degrading circumstances. And that is why in the end, he regained all he had lost and once again ruled over Israel.

With this understanding of the importance of keeping one's bearing even under the most trying of circumstances, we can comprehend a request of Shaul HaMelech. Shaul had been berated by Shmuel for not listening to Hashem's command. He was then informed that Hashem had become disgusted with him and would terminate his reign. Shaul then requests of Shmuel, כַּבְּדֵנִי נָא נֶגֶד זִקְנֵי עַמִּי וְנֶגֶד יִשְׂרָאֵל, *Show me honor before the elders of my people and before Israel (I Shmuel* 15:30).

Of what use is this meaningless honor? Had he not been informed that he had lost all his regal stature? This, from Shaul, the paradigm of humility, of whom Shmuel testified, אִם קָטֹן אַתָּה בְּעֵינֶיךָ, *You are very small in your eyes (I Shmuel* 15:17). The answer is that Shaul understood the urgent need to retain some remnant of his former regality in order to slow his descent. His plea to Shmuel was not to abolish the decree, but to slow its effect so that he not become easy prey for his evil inclination. He begged that Shmuel cushion his fall so that he would not become shattered from the impact of the fall.

מֵי נֹחַ

The Deluge

כִּי מֵי נֹחַ זֹאת לִי (ישעיה נ"ד:ט).

For this is to me as Noach's flood (Yeshayahu 54:9).

Chazal interpret this verse as implying that the flood was caused by Noach's shortcomings. The shortcoming alluded to is that Noach did not pray for the world to be spared the ravages of the flood and was therefore responsible for its destruction. Why, indeed, didn't Noach beseech God not to obliterate all of mankind? Noach slaved and labored day and night with superhuman effort and endurance to tend to and to preserve the animals in the ark in order to ensure the continuity of the world [see *Tanchuma Noach* 9]. Could it be that he did not care about the rest of humanity?

One could possibly answer that Noach's decision not to pray stemmed not from a lack of concern for humanity but rather from the knowledge that his prayers would not be answered. This reply could be supported by *Rashi* (*Bereishis* 18:32) quoting our Sages who state that Avraham did not pray that Sodom and Gemorrah be spared in the merit of eight people, for the occurrence of the flood showed that the merit of eight people, i.e., Noach, his three sons and their wives, did not suffice to save the world from destruction. The question then really is: Since Noach knew that his prayers would not be answered, why was he held responsible for not praying? Why demand of him an exercise in futility?

To answer this we must examine another perplexing statement of *Chazal*, that three people were involved in formulating the Egyptian decree against the Jewish people. Bilaam conceived the plan, Iyov kept silent and Yisro protested and subsequently fled.

בִּלְעָם שֶׁיָּעַץ נֶהֱרַג, אִיּוֹב שֶׁשָּׁתַק נִדּוֹן בְּיִסּוּרִים, יִתְרוֹ שֶׁבָּרַח זָכוּ
מִבְּנֵי בָנָיו שֶׁיֵּשְׁבוּ בְּלִשְׁכַּת הַגָּזִית (סוטה י"א ע"א).
Bilaam who devised it was slain [in battle], Iyov who silently acquiesced was afflicted with sufferings and Yisro who fled merited having his children sit in the Chamber of the Hewn Stones [the Sanhedrin] (Sotah 11a).

Why did Iyov deserve to be so terribly afflicted on account of his silence? Yisro, who did protest, was singularly unsuccessful and worse, yet he had to flee. Iyov would have accomplished nothing by speaking out, so why was he punished for not doing something whose effectiveness would be nil in any case?

The understanding of this is that the purpose of the suffering that Iyov underwent was not solely to punish him, but rather to teach and point out to him his failings and wrongdoings. [Punishment in general is to be understood in this manner.] True, had he protested the decree against Israel, his advice would not have been taken and his protests would have been of no avail. But neither, for that matter, are a suffering person's moans of any help, yet he continues to groan and cry out in pain. If Iyov kept silent, it was an indication that Israel's suffering didn't really bother him. *As es tut vay shreit men* — "When in agony, one cries out." If he would truly have felt Israel's pain and affliction, he would have cried out in protest, much as he did for his own suffering. His silence then betrayed his lack of care and empathy, and this was the lesson that was taught to him through his own pain and suffering.

This too, was the case with Noach. Had Noach been concerned with the destruction of the world and its plight, he would have prayed regardless of whether he thought his prayers would succeed or not. The fact that he did not pray for his generation revealed a lack of concern for its destruction. This is why it was named Noach's flood, decrying this very lack of concern.

If we are correct in assuming that one must pray as an expression of concern even when he is sure that his prayers will not be answered, the question arises as to why Avraham did not pray that Sodom be saved in the merit of less than ten righteous men. True, he knew that the merit of eight people did not suffice to save a city, but why did he not pray in any case?

The answer is that Avraham did express his worry for Sodom by his incessant prayers that Sodom be saved on account of fifty, forty, etc., righteous men. He only desisted when he reached the point where he realized that it was futile, something he learned from Noach's experience.

Until one has reached the limits of 'excessive prayer,' one is obligated to pray and continue praying, as Avraham did. To do otherwise betrays a lack of care and concern for one's fellow.

This then is the difference between Noach and Avraham. Noach did not feel the pain of his generation. Avraham, on the other hand, lived the anguish of the destruction of Sodom, and therefore he continued praying until he knew that any additional *tefillah* was excessive.

גָּדוֹל הַשָּׁלוֹם

Harmony

I.

הִנֵּה נָא יָדַעְתִּי כִּי אִשָּׁה יְפַת מַרְאֶה אָתְּ (בראשית יב:יא)

Now I know that you are a beautiful woman (Bereishis 12:11).

Harmony, or peace, as שָׁלוֹם is commonly translated, is one of the greatest gifts bestowed upon the Jewish people. This blessing is so great that as far as Israel is concerned it is perceived as a unique sign of their relationship with God, a consequence of נְשִׂיאַת פָּנִים, lit., *uplifting of the Divine countenance.* יִשָּׂא ה' פָּנָיו אֵלֶיךָ וְיָשֵׂם לְךָ שָׁלוֹם, *May Hashem turn His countenance to you and establish peace for you (Bamidbar 6:26).*

We are often oblivious, however, to some of the finer nuances of שָׁלוֹם. Because we relate to the concept of שָׁלוֹם in its grandest forms we don't appreciate how precious it is in its smallest application and most minute details. Let us examine the Torah's outlook of its finer and most subtle nuances.

Avraham's relationship with Sarah was one of the most noble and most elevated of relationships between man and wife. He had been married to her for decades, yet because of the modesty and saintliness prevailing, he was unaware of the true extent of her beauty (see *Rashi, Bereishis* 12:11).

One would imagine that nothing further could be, or need be, added to this wonderful marriage. Yet, the angels made a point of inquiring about Sarah לְחַבְּבָהּ עַל בַּעְלָהּ, *so as to endear her to her husband* (*Bava Metzia* 87a). By pointing out her exceptional modesty to Avraham, she would become even dearer to him. So valuable is any additional שָׁלוֹם added to a marriage!

When Sarah said, "וַאדֹנִי זָקֵן, *My master is old*," Hashem quoted her as saying, "וַאֲנִי זָקַנְתִּי, *I have aged*," all for the sake of שָׁלוֹם, so that Avraham should not be offended by her words. This despite the fact that Avraham was indeed old (he was 99) and would certainly have realized that she had no ill intentions when she had said it. Yet, to avoid that tiniest possibility of friction, to refrain from diminishing somewhat the שְׁלוֹם בַּיִת, Hashem altered her words.

We gain a similar perspective on the value of שָׁלוֹם, be it even a subtle point, if we analyze the relationship of Yaakov and Leah, and the eventual ramifications of that relationship.

The Torah tells us, וַיֶּאֱהַב גַּם אֶת רָחֵל מִלֵּאָה, *[Yaakov] loved Rachel more than Leah* (*Bereishis* 29:30); the implication is that Yaakov indeed loved Leah, but less so than Rachel. On the other hand, the Torah states, וַיַּרְא ה' כִּי שְׂנוּאָה לֵאָה, *Hashem perceived that Leah was disliked*. How do we reconcile this contradiction?

Or HaChaim explains that the overt relationship between Yaakov and Leah was certainly one of love and amity. Yet, Hashem, Who peers into the hearts of men, detected a slight antipathy for Leah. One could even say that Yaakov himself was not even conscious of it. This is implied in the expression, וַיַּרְא ה', *and Hashem saw*; it was only Hashem who realized that Yaakov's love for Leah was slightly lacking.

Based on *Or HaChaim's* insight into the subtlety of the lack of total love felt by Yaakov for Leah, let us proceed further. The birth of their third son marked the completion of that relationship between Yaakov and Leah. He was called לֵוִי for עַתָּה הַפַּעַם יִלָּוֶה אִישִׁי אֵלַי, *now my husband will accompany me* (*Bereishis* 29:34). This son whose very birth and existence cemented and finalized the love and harmony between Yaakov and Leah was consecrated amongst his fellow Jews. He did not work in Egypt nor did he worship the golden calf. And when the firstborn lost their position of priesthood, it was the Levites who received that calling. The firstborn were originally chosen to be the priestly caste, for the Almighty had saved them from death in Egypt by a spectacular and miraculous act of Providence. בְּיוֹם הַכֹּתִי כָל בְּכוֹר בְּאֶרֶץ מִצְרַיִם הִקְדַּשְׁתִּי אֹתָם לִי, *On the day that I smote all the Egyptian first-born I consecrated them to me* (*Bamidbar* 8:17).

Why were the Levites chosen? Because their existence marks the addition of yet more שְׁלוֹם בַּיִת in the household of Yaakov.

In a similar vein we find that Rachel gave the name יוֹסֵף to her firstborn son saying, אָסַף אֱלֹקִים אֶת חֶרְפָּתִי, *for Hashem has gathered in my shame* (*Bereishis* 30:23). *Rashi* explains:

> So long as a woman is childless, she has no one to blame for accidents that occur. When a child is born, she can now attribute them to her child. Thus, "Who broke the dish?" "Your child." "Who ate these dates?" "Your child."

This point is astonishing! Could it be possible that Rachel would feel this way towards Yaakov who literally gave his life for her and toiled fourteen years so that he could marry her? Would this Yaakov be angry at her for such an insignificant thing as a dish breaking? And when does she feel it important to mention this fact? On the day when her first child is born, after having been childless for so many years. It was a day on which she received a fresh lease on life, after being without children and having declared, מֵתָה אָנֹכִי, *I consider myself dead*. [*Chazal* deduced from here that a childless person is considered dead.] And on this great day of her life Rachel has no more important detail to commemorate than the fact that if something would break in the house Yaakov would not be angry with her.

It is apparent from the aforementioned that even if we don't appreciate the importance of every additional nuance of שְׁלוֹם בַּיִת, our patriarchs and matriarchs did. The elimination of any possible source of even the most minor irritation is so important that Rachel in her moment of extreme joy chose her child's name in celebration of this point. The difficulty in understanding this is due to our lack of a true appreciation of the importance of the slightest nuance of שְׁלוֹם בַּיִת.

II.

Reflecting on what generates שָׁלוֹם between husband and wife, and between man and his fellow man, leads one to the conclusion that it is כְּבוֹד הַבְּרִיּוֹת, respect and appreciation for one's fellow and spouse.

When Avraham saw the angels who came to visit him after his circumcision, he evaluated their importance in the following manner.

אָמַר [אַבְרָהָם], אִם אֲנִי רוֹאֶה שְׁכִינָה מַמְתֶּנֶת עֲלֵיהֶם אֲנִי יוֹדֵעַ שֶׁהֵן בְּנֵי אָדָם גְּדוֹלִים, וְאִם אֲנִי רוֹאֶה אוֹתָן חוֹלְקִין כָּבוֹד אֵלּוּ לְאֵלּוּ אֲנִי יוֹדֵעַ שֶׁהֵן בְּנֵי אָדָם מְהֻגָּנִים. וְכֵיוָן שֶׁרָאָה אוֹתָם חוֹלְקִין כָּבוֹד אֵלּוּ לְאֵלּוּ יָדַע שֶׁהֵן בְּנֵי אָדָם מְהֻגָּנִים (בראשית רבה מח:ט).

[Avraham] said: "If I see the Divine Presence waiting for them, then I will know that they are men of great stature. If I see them honoring one another I will know that they are upright people." When he saw them honoring one another, he knew that they were upright people (Bereishis Rabbah 48:9).

From this Midrash we see that כְּבוֹד הַבְּרִיּוֹת is not simply another *mitzvah* but rather an additional dimension of greatness. A person can be important enough for the Divine Presence to wait for him, and yet not be an אָדָם הָגוּן, *respectable person*, for he lacks respect for his fellow man. Only when Avraham perceived that the visitors were considered great people deserving to be awaited by the Divine Presence and in addition showed proper respect for each other, then and only then did he run towards them.

Conversely, we find a great act of humiliation sparked an explosion of שִׂנְאַת חִנָּם, *unwarranted hatred*, from which the Jewish people suffer to this very day. When Bar Kamtza was humiliated at his enemy's party, he set in motion a chain of events that led to the destruction of the Temple and the onset of the Diaspora. *Chazal* determined that the Second Temple was destroyed due to שִׂנְאַת חִנָּם as expressed by an act of extreme humiliation. Insult and derision provoke שִׂנְאַת חִנָּם whereas כְּבוֹד הַבְּרִיּוֹת, *respect for one's fellow*, brings about love and harmony.

אַחֲרִית דָּבָר מֵרֵאשִׁיתוֹ

The Conclusion Stems from the Origin

יֵקַח נָא מְעַט מַיִם וְרַחֲצוּ רַגְלֵיכֶם וכו׳ (בראשית יח:ד).

אָמַר רַבִּי חָמָא בַּר רַבִּי חֲנִינָא וְכֵן תָּנָא דְבֵי ר׳ יִשְׁמָעֵאל, בִּשְׂכַר שְׁלֹשָׁה זָכוּ לִשְׁלֹשָׁה. בִּשְׂכַר "חֶמְאָה וְחָלָב" זָכוּ לְמָן, בִּשְׂכַר "וְהוּא עוֹמֵד עֲלֵיהֶם" זָכוּ לְעַמוּד הֶעָנָן, בִּשְׂכַר "יֵקַח נָא מְעַט מַיִם" זָכוּ לִבְאֵרָה שֶׁל מִרְיָם (בבא מציעא פ״ו ע״ב).

Let some water be taken and bathe your feet etc. (Bereishis 18:4).

R' Chama the son of R' Chaninah said and the Academy of R' Yishmael also taught: As a reward for the three [deeds of Avraham], Israel obtained three things. As a reward for the "milk and butter" [which Avraham served to his visitors] they received manna, as a reward for "and he stood upon them" they received the pillar of the cloud, as a reward for "let some water be taken" they were granted the well of Miriam (Bava Metzia 86b).

The *Maharsha* asks: The *Gemara* in *Tannis* (9a) attributes these three gifts to the merits of Moshe, Aharon and Miriam respectively. How, then, does the above *Gemara* deny them the merit of these three gifts and attribute them to Avraham?

The answer is that the gifts bestowed upon Israel were the result of a process, not of a single event. Just as a seed that grows into a tree needs soil, water and sun to develop, so too did the 'seed' of Avraham's deed require fertile ground on which to develop. Moshe, Aharon· and Miriam were not the initial cause for the manna, cloud and drinking well. Rather they watered and brought to fruition the seed planted by Avraham's hospitality.

This process is alluded to in the verse בְּאֵר חֲפָרוּהָ שָׂרִים כָּרוּהָ נְדִיבֵי הָעָם בִּמְחֹקֵק בְּמִשְׁעֲנֹתָם, *The well, dug by princes, carved out by the nobility with the sceptre, their staffs (Bamidbar 21:18).*

Targum Yonasan interprets the verse as follows: בֵּירָא דְחָפְרוּ יָתָהּ אֲבָהָת עַלְמָא אַבְרָהָם יִצְחָק וְיַעֲקֹב רַבְרְבָנַיָא דְמִלְקַדְמִין חָפְרוּ יָתָהּ רֵישֵׁי עַמָּא מֹשֶׁה וְאַהֲרֹן, *The well that was dug up by the fathers of the world, Avraham, Yitzchak and Yaakov, was dug up [again] by the leaders of the nation, Moshe and Aharon* (ibid.) Thus the well itself was dug by the deeds of the patriarchs; it was developed and deepened by the next generation of leaders, Moshe and Aharon.

Similarly, we find the *mitzvah* of *tzitzis* attributed to the merit of both Shem (see *Rashi, Bereishis* 9:23) and Avraham (*Chullin* 89a). Again, we must differentiate between Shem, who planted the 'seed' by covering his father's shame, and Avraham, who developed and nurtured its fruition.

Just as a good deed has stages of beginning and stages of development, similarly, wicked acts are to be seen as the result of a process. They begin with an almost imperceptible aberration and grow into full-bodied wickedness, פֶּן יֵשׁ בָּכֶם שֹׁרֶשׁ פֹּרֶה רֹאשׁ וְלַעֲנָה, *lest there be among you a root which grows gall and wormwood (Devarim 29:17).*

Ramban explains:

> פֶּן יֵשׁ בָּכֶם שֹׁרֶשׁ רָע שֶׁיִּפְרֶה וְיִשְׁגֶּה וּבַיָּמִים הַבָּאִים יוֹצִיא פְּרָחִים רָעִים וְיַצְמִיחַ מְרוֹרוֹת. וְזֶה עַל אֲשֶׁר אֵינֶנּוּ פֹּה הַיּוֹם כִּי הָאָב שֹׁרֶשׁ וְהַבֵּן נֵצֶר מִשָּׁרָשָׁיו יִפְרֶה, וְהִזְכִּיר הַשֹּׁרֶשׁ לוֹמַר כִּי הוּא יָכוֹל לְהָבִיא בָּאָלָה הַדּוֹרוֹת הַבָּאִים (רמב"ן שם).
>
> *Perhaps there is among you an evil root that will blossom and grow and in the coming days will produce poisonous buds and grow bitter herbs. This refers back to "him that is not here with us today," for the father is*

*the root and the son is the twig growing from this root.
[The Torah] mentioned 'root' in order to relate that he
can bring the coming generations into this curse
(Ramban ibid.).*

Chazal explain the institution of עֶגְלָה עֲרוּפָה, *a calf brought in
atonement for a slain wayfarer*, in a similar manner. It is described as
atonement for both the living and the dead.

כַּפֵּר לְעַמְּךָ יִשְׂרָאֵל אֲשֶׁר פָּדִיתָ – אֵלּוּ הַמֵּתִים. מְלַמֵּד שֶׁהַמֵּתִים
צְרִיכִים כַּפָּרָה. נִמְצִינוּ לְמֵדִים שֶׁשּׁוֹפֵךְ דָּם חוֹטֵא עַד יוֹצְאֵי מִצְרַיִם
(ספרי דברים כא:ח).

*Forgive Your people whom You have redeemed — this
refers to the deceased [i.e., those redeemed from Egypt].
This teaches us that the dead too need forgiveness.
Thus we see that he who sheds blood has sinned,
tracing back [the sin] until those who left Egypt (Sifri
Devarim 21:8).*

The explanation is as follows. If someone sheds blood it is proof
positive that the 'seed' for that deed was planted by an ancestor of his
in Egypt. It lay dormant for generation after generation until it
sprouted and bore fruit in the form of a murderer. It is for this
'implanted seed' that the forebearer must be atoned even though he
certainly did not take part in the murder itself.

When Yaakov was on his deathbed he castigated his sons Shimon
and Levi and asked that his name not be mentioned as their ancestor
in connection with the sins of Korach and Zimri, the descendants of
Shimon and Levi, respectively. בְּסֹדָם אַל תָּבֹא נַפְשִׁי בִּקְהָלָם אַל תֵּחַד כְּבֹדִי,
*In their counsel let my soul not enter, in their assembly let my honor
not be defiled (Bereishis 49:6).*

Indeed, when the Torah enumerates the forebears of Zimri and
Korach it does not mention Yaakov.

The difficulty is obvious. It is common knowledge that Shimon
and Levi were the children of Yaakov and hence, their progeny are
descended from Yaakov as well. What then is gained by the omission
of Yaakov's name?

The answer is that the Torah is not merely listing the forebears of
these sinners for purposes of identification. Rather, this genealogical
enumeration is to indicate that the root of their misdeeds was already
present in their ancestors. By eliminating Yaakov's name, the Torah

made it clear that the misdeed was entirely Korach's; no element of it stems from Yaakov.

If we understand the act of sinning as a process, instead of a sudden event, starting with an imperceptible root, which grows and expands until fully manifested, then we can resolve the seemingly conflicting accounts concerning the causes that led the *Mishnah* scholar Acher [Elisha ben Avuyah] to become a heretic.

The *Gemara* describes Acher as becoming a heretic after having cast off the yoke of Torah and desecrating the Sabbath. *Tosafos* quotes the *Yerushalmi* in order to explain the reason for Acher's decline:

לָמָּה אֵרַע לוֹ כָּךְ . . . אָמַר לוֹ רַבִּי עֲקִיבָא רַבָּךְ לֹא כַךְ דָּרַשׁ, אֶלָּא טוֹב אַחֲרִית דָּבָר שֶׁהוּא טוֹב מֵרֵאשִׁיתוֹ. וּבִי הָיָה הַמַּעֲשֶׂה. אֲבוּיָה אָבִי הָיָה מִגְּדוֹלֵי יְרוּשָׁלַיִם וּבְיוֹם שֶׁבָּא לְמְהוּלִי קָרָא לְכָל גְּדוֹלֵי יְרוּשָׁלַיִם וְהוֹשִׁיבָן בְּבַיִת אֶחָד, וּלְרַבִּי אֱלִיעֶזֶר וּלְרַבִּי יְהוֹשֻׁעַ בְּמָקוֹם אַחֵר. מִן דְּאָכְלִין וְשָׁתִין . . . יָשְׁבוּ וְנִתְעַסְּקוּ בְּדִבְרֵי תּוֹרָה. יָרְדָה אֵשׁ מִן הַשָּׁמַיִם וְהִקִּיפָה אוֹתָן וכו' אָמַר, הוֹאִיל וְכַךְ כֹּחָהּ שֶׁל תּוֹרָה אִם יִתְקַיֵּם הַבֵּן הַזֶּה, לְתוֹרָה אֲנִי מַפְרִישׁוֹ. וּלְפִי שֶׁלֹּא הָיְתָה כַּוָּנָתוֹ לַשָּׁמַיִם לֹא נִתְקַיְמוּ בּוֹ (תוספות חגיגה ט''ו ע''א).

Why did this happen [to Acher]? He replied, "Has not your teacher R' Akiva expounded, 'That ending is good which is the result of a good beginning?' I experienced this. For my father Avuyah was one of the great men of Jerusalem. On the day of my circumcision he invited all the great men of Jerusalem and put them into one room and R' Eliezer and R' Yehoshua in a different room. As they were sitting and eating and drinking . . . They were engaged in the study of Torah and a heavenly fire descended and surrounded them. Avuyah [proclaimed], 'If this is the power of Torah, then I will dedicate my son to its study.' Because his motive was impure, therefore it was not fulfilled" (*Tosafos Chagigah 15a*).

The *Gemara*, however, gives us two different reasons for his becoming a heretic. In one place the *Gemara* states, *he never stopped humming Greek tunes. It was said about Acher, that when he would stand up from his seat in the beis midrash, heretical books would fall from his lap* (*Chagigah 15a*). The *Gemara* in *Kedushin* (39b) gives us still another reason for his decline: *He saw the tongue of Chutzpis the*

Translator being dragged about by a pig. He exclaimed, "Can a mouth that uttered Torah lick the dust?" Whereupon he became a heretic (*Kiddushin* 39b).

To fit together the bits and pieces comprising Acher's downslide, let us turn again to R' Akiva's quote: טוֹב אַחֲרִית דָּבָר שֶׁהוּא טוֹב מֵרֵאשִׁיתוֹ, *That ending is good which is the result of a good beginning.* R' Akiva understood that although Acher's heresy was the result of his own misdeeds, still, had the root been perfect, then the plant could never have turned bitter. So, R' Akiva probed Avuyah's deeds for the root of Acher's heresy. He realized that instead of his father desiring that his son learn Torah because it is the Divine word and the essence of life, he was impressed rather by its outward grandeur and honor. Thus, the seed was sown which would later become Acher.

Acher's own heresy was also the culmination of a process, rather than an abrupt break with faith. He started with Greek songs which then led him to Greek philosophy. Immersing himself in philosophy, he was confronted by the disbeliefs and questions contained therein. Certainly, he grappled with the problems and attempted to reconcile them, but the disbelief remained embedded in his heart. When he was confronted by the shock of seeing R' Chutzpis' tongue being dragged through the streets, his doubts and questions which had lain dormant were reawakened and caused his final break with belief in God.

Many people, simple as well as learned, have experienced events and tragedies as bad if not worse. Yet, they retained their faith and, instead, rose in their spiritual stature by witnessing God's judgment. But Acher was different. The seed for heresy had been planted in him and was waiting to bear fruit. No sooner did the opportunity present itself, that it burst into full bloom.

It is therefore incumbent upon us not to limit our חֶשְׁבּוֹן הַנֶּפֶשׁ, *introspection,* to that which we are, but to that which is latent in us. One tainted seed can subsequently develop into evil incarnate. On the other hand, a tiny seed of a good deed can develop ultimately into manna, water and Clouds of Glory for the entire nation of Israel.

הִסְתַּגְּלוּת
The Ability to Adapt

Human beings are endowed with the gift of adaptability. No matter how harsh one's living conditions, no matter how difficult the environment, a human being is able to adapt and survive. We have seen in our lifetime people who have undergone the unspeakable horrors of the Nazi hell and survived. However, since their conditions gradually worsened and their suffering increased, step by step, they found the ability to adapt to their surroundings, eventually surviving the war and rebuilding their lives.

It is the understanding of this process which will clarify for us the difference between Avraham's reaction to Hashem's command to bring Yitzchak as a sacrifice, as opposed to that of Sarah's. Avraham repressed his instincts of mercy and went eagerly to fulfill Hashem's command. Sarah, on the other hand, when she heard what had transpired, could not bear the news and died instantly. How is it that these two great people reacted so differently to the same events? This question takes on added strength if we bear in mind that in regard to prophecy, Sarah's greatness surpassed that of Avraham's (see *Rashi* on *Bereishis* 21:12).

The answer is that Avraham was made aware in a gradual manner that Yitzchak was to be brought as a sacrifice, thus allowing his feelings and emotions to adapt themselves to the challenge awaiting him. Hashem told him first: קַח נָא אֶת בִּנְךָ, *Please take your son*, then:

אֶת יְחִידְךָ, *your only son*, אֲשֶׁר אָהַבְתָּ, *whom you love*. And only then did He inform him: אֶת יִצְחָק, that He was referring to Yitzchak. Why the procrastination? *Rashi* explains: וְלָמָּה לֹא גִלָּה לוֹ מִתְּחִלָּה? שֶׁלֹּא לְעַרְבְּבוֹ פִּתְאוֹם, וְתָזוּחַ דַעְתּוֹ עָלָיו וְיִטָּרֵף, *Why did he not reveal [that Yitzchak would be the sacrifice] at the outset? So as not to confuse him and disorient him, causing him to lose his mind.*

Thus, even Avraham, had he been confronted suddenly with the awareness that it was Yitzchak who was to be sacrificed, would not have survived. It was the gradual realization of this fact which enabled him to assimilate this knowledge gradually and consequently perform Hashem's command with equanimity. Such was not the case with Sarah who was suddenly overwhelmed by the knowledge of what had transpired, and consequently died from the sudden shock.

We find a similar case of an instantaneous shock overwhelming a person, in *Gemara Kesubos* 62b. R' Chananyah ben Chachinai had been away from home for a period of thirteen years, and arrived home suddenly. His wife was immersed in housework and before she saw him visually, her "heart felt his presence" (see *Rashi* ibid.). She could not stand the shock and died.

Had she seen him visually, she would not have died. The gap in time between the actual sighting of her husband and the awareness thereof would have cushioned the shock and tempered its effect. What actually transpired was the sudden overwhelming of her mind and heart with his presence, and this was beyond her capacity.

Conversely, in another instance, we find that the suddenness of someone's perception of a situation was beneficial. The *Gemara* (*Sotah* 13a) tells of Esav contesting the title to Yaakov's burial plot, the Cave of Machpelah. When Yaakov died and was brought to Canaan for burial, Esav came and protested that the plot of land belonged to him. A debate ensued and it was decided that Naphtali would return to Egypt to retrieve the deed certifying Yaakov's purchase of the plot. A deaf grandson, Chushim the son of Dan, who was present at this scene, inquired as to the cause of the delay. When they told him, he exclaimed, "What? And until the deed is brought, grandfather is to lie in degradation?" Whereupon he killed Esav.

Why was it that Chushim, a grandson, was more concerned about Yaakov's honor than Yaakov's own children? The answer is hinted at in the *Gemara* by its reference to Chushim's deafness. All the brothers had been slowly drawn into the argument with Esav, gradually dulling their sensitivity to their father's shame. Chushim, being deaf, was completely unaware of the litigation. When he was abruptly informed of the situation, he could not contain his wrath, and killed Esav instantly.

However, as vital as adaptation is for a person's survival, it is also detrimental to his spiritual growth. A person may become stimulated to some spiritual endeavor, but the passage of time usually dulls the original inspiration and renders one insensitive to its demands. It is therefore of utmost importance to constantly renew and revitalize those stimuli that serve to elevate a person.

Thus the prophet Yechezkel describes the gateways to the Third Temple and their usage,

הַבָּא דֶרֶךְ שַׁעַר צָפוֹן לְהִשְׁתַּחֲוֹת יֵצֵא דֶרֶךְ שַׁעַר נֶגֶב, וְהַבָּא דֶרֶךְ שַׁעַר נֶגֶב יֵצֵא דֶרֶךְ שַׁעַר צָפוֹנָה, לֹא יָשׁוּב דֶרֶךְ הַשַּׁעַר אֲשֶׁר בָּא בוֹ כִּי נִכְחוֹ יֵצֵא (יחזקאל מו:ט).

He who enters through the northern gate in order to prostrate himself shall leave via the south gate, and he who enters through the south gate shall leave by the north gate. He shall not return by the gate that he entered therein but rather through the opposite one shall he exit (Yechezkel 46:9).

The Chasid Yaavetz (*Avos* 1:4) explains that the rationale for this was so that one does not become too familiar with the Temple. Even though the *mitzvah* of עֲלִיָה לְרֶגֶל was performed thrice annually, still the need to avoid רְגִילוּת, *over-familiarity*, is indicated by the stricture. Even three times a year can lead to עֲלִיָה לְרֶגֶל becoming rote.

It was this feeling of familiarity which allowed Israel to make a golden calf in spite of their awareness of the Divine Presence in their midst. This indeed was what prompted Moshe to move his tent outside the *Shechinah* compound so that his feelings of awe towards the Divine Presence would not become dulled by routine and familiarity.

This is a lesson meant to apply to all spiritual stimulation. A person must constantly be on guard not to allow routine and habit to dampen the flame kindled by that inspiration.

We find another method used to retain one's original inspiration, and to guard it from the ravages of time.

The *Gemara* (*Sanhedrin* 19b) tells us of Palti ben Layish who was forced to marry Michal, the daughter of Shaul HaMelech, whom he considered as previously betrothed to David. He lived many years being "married" to her without ever approaching her. *Chazal* ask, "What did he do to [control himself]?" He drove a sword between the two beds, and proclaimed, "He who engages [in sin] should be pierced by this sword."

The question is obvious. What power does a lifeless sword have against the passions and desires of a man? What was there to stop him from simply removing the sword and sinning undisturbed? The answer is that it was not the sword that prevented Palti from transgressing, but rather his resolution at the moment when he was forced to "marry" his "wife." *Chazal* did not ask how he controlled himself, but rather, how was it that he could retain the power of his original resolution. The answer lies in the sword that he implanted between the two beds. The sword served to remind him of his powerful awareness at the time of marriage that she was forbidden. This reminder kept fresh the firmness of his resolve and kept him from sin.

❧ ❧ ❧

There is another way to explain the difference between Avraham and Sarah's reaction to the sacrifice of Yitzchak.

The *Gemara* [*Sanhedrin* 107a] states that a person ought to avoid נִסְיוֹנוֹת, *tests of one's moral commitment*, just as David HaMelech was unable to withstand the נִסָּיוֹן of Batsheva, a spiritual test that he himself had requested. The explanation of this principle is that when Hashem tests a human being he correspondingly endows that person with the ability and strength needed to withstand his test. Not so when one is not given the test or trial by Hashem, but rather brings it on himself as did David HaMelech in the case of Batsheva. In such a case it is not certain at all that a human being will have the ability to pass the test.

The same principle may be applied here. Avraham was tested by God to see if he would sacrifice Yitzchak. He was therefore endowed with the superhuman strength needed to withstand the accompanying emotions. Sarah, on the other hand, was not given this test, and therefore was not endowed with these capabilities and hence could not withstand the accompanying emotions, even though she was superior to Avraham in the area of prophecy.

כִּי נָפַלְתִּי קָמְתִּי

My Fall Is the Cause of My Rise

אַל תִּשְׂמְחִי אֹיַבְתִּי לִי, כִּי נָפַלְתִּי קָמְתִּי, כִּי אֵשֵׁב בַּחֹשֶׁךְ ה׳ אוֹר לִי
(מיכה ז:ח).

*Rejoice not over me, my enemy, for though I have
fallen, I have [also] arisen, though I sit in darkness,
Hashem is a light for me (Michah 7:8).*

אִלּוּלֵי שֶׁנָּפַלְתִּי לֹא קַמְתִּי, וְאִלּוּלֵי שֶׁיָּשַׁבְתִּי בַּחֹשֶׁךְ, לֹא הָיָה ה׳
אוֹר לִי (מדרש שוחר טוב, תהלים).

*Had I not fallen, I would not have arisen, had I not sat
in darkness, Hashem would not have been a light for
me (Midrash Shocher Tov, Tehillim 5).*

Paradoxical as it may seem, Israel's lapses and dark nights serve as
both preparation to and prerequisite of its ascension to greatness.
This is true not only of Israel as a nation, but also each individual in
his own battle with his *yetzer hara* (*evil inclination*) experiences
periods of darkness. And it is these periods of darkness which enable
one to clearly perceive the truth, discerning the light by its contrast to
the darkness.

Chazal describe most vividly two people who fell to depths of
depravity, such as could only be described as בְּגִידָה, *treason*. In the
depths of the abyss they were able to perceive the light that had

escaped them earlier and it was this perception which enabled them to repent.

וַיָּרַח אֶת רֵיחַ בְּגָדָיו וַיְבָרֲכֵהוּ (בראשית כז:כז).

[כְּגוֹן יוֹסֵף מְשִׁיתָא וְיָקוּם אִישׁ צְרוֹרוֹת.] בְּשָׁעָה שֶׁבִּקְּשׁוּ שׂוֹנְאִים לְהִכָּנֵס לְהַר הַבַּיִת אָמְרוּ: יִכָּנֵס מֵהֶם וּבָהֶם תְּחִלָּה. אָמְרִין לֵיהּ עוֹל וּמַה דְּאַתְּ מַפִּיק דִּידָךְ. נִכְנַס וְהוֹצִיא מְנוֹרָה שֶׁל זָהָב. אָמְרוּ לוֹ אֵין דַּרְכּוֹ שֶׁל הֶדְיוֹט לְהִשְׁתַּמֵּשׁ בְּזוֹ, אֶלָּא עוֹל עוֹד זְמַן תִּנְיָנוּת וּמַה דְּאַתְּ מַפִּיק דִּידָךְ, וְלֹא קִבֵּל עָלָיו וכו'. אָמַר לֹא דַּי שֶׁהִכְעַסְתִּי לֵאלוֹקַי פַּעַם אַחַת, אֶלָּא שֶׁאַכְעִיסֶנּוּ פַּעַם שְׁנִיָּה. מֶה עָשׂוּ לוֹ? נָתְנוּ אוֹתוֹ בַּחֲמוֹר שֶׁל חָרָשִׁים וְהָיוּ מְנַסְּרִים בּוֹ. הָיָה מְצַוֵּחַ וְאוֹמֵר, וַי, אוֹי אוֹי שֶׁהִכְעַסְתִּי לְבוֹרְאִי (בראשית רבה סה:כב).

And he smelled the scent of his garments (בְּגָדָיו) *and he blessed it* (Bereishis 27:27).

[The word 'בְּגָדָיו' *as* 'בּוֹגְדָיו' *(traitors) refers to Yosef of Shisa and Yakum of Tzroros.] When the enemies [of the Jewish people] desired to enter the Temple Mount, they declared, "Let a Jew enter first." They told him [Yosef], "Enter, and whatever you bring out is yours." He entered and brought out a golden candelabra. They told him, "It is not fitting for a commoner to use this, but enter again and whatever you bring out is yours." He, however refused, saying, "Enough that I have angered my Creator once, shall I anger him a second time?" What did they do to him? They put him into a carpenter's vise and dragged him over it. He cried again and again, "Woe unto me that I have angered my Creator"* (Bereishis Rabbah 65:22).

The depths of depravity to which Yosef had sunk are indescribable. He dared enter the place that even Israel's enemies feared to enter. He emerged carrying the *menorah*, without the most elementary understanding that "it is not befitting a commoner to make use of it" — an understanding that even the Romans had. It was only when this grievous error was pointed out to him that he became aware how low he had sunk. It was this profound awareness of the darkness surrounding him that caused Hashem to enlighten him, and prompted him to defy the Romans, proclaiming, "Enough that I have angered my Creator once." He resisted the Roman torture, screaming not in pain but in repentance, "Woe unto me that I have angered my Creator." It is clear that had he not sunk so low, he would never have risen to such heights. Had he not been in the blackest darkness, he would never have been able to act in so courageous a manner. It was as a result of his initial feelings that he rose to the heights of martyrdom; a martyrdom comparable to that of R' Akiva and his colleagues.

Chazal give another example of a 'traitor' who repented, and there too, we catch a glimpse of that light whose source is darkness:

יָקוּם אִישׁ צְרוֹרוֹת הָיָה בֶּן אֲחוֹתוֹ שֶׁל ר' יוֹסֵי בֶּן יוֹעֶזֶר אִישׁ צְרֵידָה וַהֲוָה רָכִיב סוּסְיָא בְּשַׁבְּתָא. אָזַל קוּמֵי שְׁרִיתָא לְמִצְטַבְלָא אָמַר לֵיהּ חָמֵי סוּסִי דְּאַרְכְּבִי מָרִי וְחָמֵי סוּסֵךְ דְּאַרְכְּבָךְ מָרָךְ. אָמַר לֵיהּ, אִם כַּךְ לְמַכְעִיסִים קַל נָחְמֶר לְעוֹשֵׂי רְצוֹנוֹ. אָמַר לֵיהּ עָשָׂה אָדָם רְצוֹנוֹ יוֹתֵר מִמֶּךָּ? אָמַר לוֹ וְאִם כַּךְ לְעוֹשֵׂי רְצוֹנוֹ קַל נָחְמֶר לְמַכְעִיסָיו נִכְנַס בּוֹ הַדָּבָר כְּאֶרֶס שֶׁל עַכְנָא; הָלַךְ וְקִיֵּם בְּעַצְמוֹ אַרְבַּע מִיתוֹת בֵּית דִּין, סְקִילָה שְׂרֵפָה הֶרֶג וְחֶנֶק ... נִתְנַמְנֵם יוֹסֵי בֶּן יוֹעֶזֶר אִישׁ צְרֵידָה וְרָאָה מִטָּתוֹ פּוֹרַחַת בָּאֲוִיר. אָמַר בְּשָׁעָה קַלָּה קְדָמַנִי זֶה לְגַן עֵדֶן (בראשית רבה סה:כב).

Yakum of Tzroros was the nephew of R' Yossi ben Yoezer of Tzeredah. Once he was riding a horse on Shabbos when he came upon his uncle who was being carried on a horse on his way to the gallows. He exclaimed, "Look at the horse that my master let me ride and look at the horse that your Master has made you ride" (i.e., I am indulging in sin and am fortunate in my lot, while you are engaged in Torah and mitzvos all your life and will probably be hung). [R' Yossi] replied, "If this is the lot of those who anger Hashem, how much more the reward of those who do His will?" Countered [Yakum], "Has anyone done His will more than you?" He replied, "If this is how [Hashem] acts towards those who do His will, how much more with those who anger Him?" The impact of this reply entered into his heart like a serpent's venom. He went and subjected himself to the four methods [of execution] ... Yossi fell asleep and saw Yakum's bed flying in the air. He exclaimed, "In a brief moment he has preceded me into the Garden of Eden" (Bereishis Rabbah 65:22).

Yakum had watched his uncle being led to his execution without displaying the slightest bit of compassion and sensitivity. To the contrary, he mocked R' Yossi about his faith and beliefs and told him that his martyrdom was in vain. Instead of supporting his uncle in those trying moments, he mocked him. It was because of this callousness and stoneheartedness that when R' Yossi's words did make an impact on him, they struck him like the venom of a serpent. "Had it not been for the darkness enveloping him, he would never have perceived the light."

Having seen how it is sometimes sin itself that paradoxically serves as a springboard to achievement we can understand the uniqueness of the בַּעַל תְּשׁוּבָה, the *penitent*.

Chazal tell us, בְּמָקוֹם שֶׁבַּעֲלֵי תְשׁוּבָה עוֹמְדִין צַדִּיקִים גְּמוּרִים אֵינָם עוֹמְדִין, *In the place that penitents stand, even the completely righteous cannot stand* (Berachos 34b). In a similar vein the verse heralding the call to *teshuvah*, repentance — שׁוּבָה יִשְׂרָאֵל עַד ה' אֱלֹקֶיךָ, *Return, Israel, unto Hashem your God* — describes *teshuvah* as reaching to the throne of the Almighty (see *Yoma* 86a). The reason being כִּי כָשַׁלְתָּ בַּעֲוֹנֶךָ, *for you have stumbled by your sins* (Hoshea 14:2). It is the stumbling itself on the obstacles of sin that carries within it the potential to elevate a person to the very throne of the Almighty.

Why is it so? How does sin serve as the lever to elevate a person? The answer is that the primary impediment to self-improvement and growth is the lethargy of routine and inertia. Not only does it hamper a person's spiritual growth but it renders him totally insensitive, as well. This finds expression in Yeshayahu's rebuke:

יַעַן כִּי נִגַּשׁ הָעָם הַזֶּה, בְּפִיו וּבִשְׂפָתָיו כִּבְּדוּנִי וְלִבּוֹ רִחַק מִמֶּנִּי,
וַתְּהִי יִרְאָתָם אֹתִי מִצְוַת אֲנָשִׁים מְלֻמָּדָה (ישעיה כט:יג).
Because this nation has approached Me, honoring Me with their mouths and lips, but their heart was far from Me, and their fear of Me was only by force of habit (Yeshayahu 29:13).

Once Israel's worship of God was 'by force of habit,' their hearts were automatically 'far from Me'. All that they did became but lip service. All, even their fear of God, was an external performance divorced from and devoid of any heartfelt inspiration. The passion and fire were gone, extinguished by the 'force of habit.'

Habit and routine can turn even the fear of God into a mechanical reflex! So, too, does Moshe describe Israel's downfall as being the nadir of a process of habituality. Thus, כִּי תוֹלִיד בָּנִים וּבְנֵי בָנִים וְנוֹשַׁנְתֶּם

בָּאָרֶץ וְהִשְׁחַתֶּם וַעֲשִׂיתֶם פֶּסֶל, *When you will beget children and grandchildren, and you will remain in the land for a long time, you will become corrupt and you will make an idol* (Devarim 4:25). According to *Ramban*, it is the נוֹשַׁנְתֶּם, *becoming old, well worn*, i.e., set in one's ways, that spawns the corruption of idolatry. It is only the shock of the clear perception of one's downfall that awakens and rouses one to action. The impact of this realization when fully harnessed can elevate one to new heights, indeed עַד ה׳ אֱלֹקֶיךָ, to the very throne of the Almighty.

The preservation of the element of surprise, in order to shock people out of their lethargy, was the reason that Moshe delayed telling Israel about the double portion of manna on *Shabbos*. *Rashbam* (*Shemos* 16:22) explains that Moshe had already been told on Sunday that on Friday there would be two portions. However, he waited until Friday to tell the Children of Israel in order that they should be astonished when on Friday they would suddenly find a double portion to gather. Had he told them about it on Sunday, then the effect would have worn off by Friday. That is why he held back from publicizing his prophecy for so long, so that it would make the proper impact on Israel.

Similarly, the Midrash (*Devarim Rabbah* 1:11) states that Avraham was not told about the manna so that prior knowledge of this miracle should not dull its impact.

These are the sentiments one feels upon entering the Yeshivah after בֵּין הַזְּמַנִּים, *intersession*. The gap in learning ... the darkness enveloping the *Beis Medrash*. Let us use this 'downfall' and 'darkness' as a springboard to yet greater achievement. אִלּוּלֵי שֶׁנָּפַלְתִּי לֹא קַמְתִּי וְאִלּוּלֵי שֶׁיָּשַׁבְתִּי בַּחֹשֶׁךְ, לֹא הָיָה ה׳ אוֹר לִי, *Had I not fallen, I would not have arisen, had I not sat in darkness, Hashem would not have been a light for me* (Midrash Shocher Tov, Tehillim 5).

הָאוֹר וְהַחשֶׁךְ שֶׁבָּאָדָם

The Light and the Darkness in Man

וַיִּשַּׁק יַעֲקֹב לְרָחֵל וַיִּשָּׂא אֶת קֹלוֹ וַיֵּבְךְ (בראשית כט:יא).
And Yaakov kissed Rachel, and he raised his voice and wept (Bereishis 29:11).

Rashi explains that the reason Yaakov cried was because he had not brought any gifts for Rachel. Although he had set out on his journey laden with gifts, his nephew Elifaz, Esav's son, had waylaid him on his journey and had taken all his possessions. Esav had instructed him to kill Yaakov, but having grown up under Yitzchak's guidance, Elifaz could not bring himself to do it. He stood there caught in a dilemma between disobeying his father on the one hand and committing the heinous act of murdering his uncle on the other. It was Yaakov who solved his problem by advising Elifaz to take all he had, thereby impoverishing him. This would be considered as carrying out his father Esav's instructions, for עָנִי חָשׁוּב כְּמֵת, *a poor man is considered as dead* (see *Nedarim* 7b).

Let us take a closer look at Elifaz's inner conflict at the time that he met up with Yaakov. On the one hand, being a disciple of Yitzchak, the injunction against murder was so deeply ingrained in him that he could not bring himself to kill Yaakov. On the other hand, his father's exhortation to kill Yaakov had to be fulfilled in order to 'honor his father.' Here then, is an example of a person in whom both good and evil are exerting a powerful influence; indeed a tug-of-war between light and darkness in his soul.

This incident involving Elifaz contains an even more profound example of the intermingling of 'light and darkness.' The basis for his intended act of murder was the fulfillment of the *mitzvah* of honoring his father! The very 'light' itself had become corrupted and distorted by the darkness.

This then, is the meaning of the words of the prophet, מִי חָכָם וְיָבֵן אֵלֶּה, נָבוֹן וְיֵדָעֵם, כִּי יְשָׁרִים דַּרְכֵי ה' וְצַדִּקִים יֵלְכוּ בָם וּפשְׁעִים יִכָּשְׁלוּ בָם, *Who is wise and understands all these, understanding and knows them, for the ways of Hashem are straight — the righteous traverse them and the wicked stumble upon them* (Hoshea 14:10).

Rashi explains that the very same path of God which serves to elevate the righteous serves to make the wicked stumble. The very same *mitzvah* of honoring one's father is elevated in the hands of the righteous but becomes an instrument of murder in the hands of an Elifaz.

Chazal make a similar point with regard to the study of Torah: לְמַיְמִינִים בָּה סַמָּא דְחַיֵּי. לְמַשְׂמְאִילִים בָּה סַמָּא דְמוֹתָא, *For [those who study Torah] diligently, it becomes a source of life. For those who study it laxly, it becomes a deadly poison* (Shabbos 88b and *Rashi*).

The very Torah that is lifegiving to one person becomes a deadly poison to the one who is lazy in its study rather than merely a harmless hobby.

We now understand why it was precisely Elifaz, of all Esav's children, who was the progenitor of the wicked nation of Amalek. For the other children had only the wicked nature of Esav to propagate, which in itself could not produce the absolute evil of Amalek. It was only an Elifaz who had studied under Yitzchak and had absorbed his teachings, in addition to the evil essence of his father Esav, who would distort and corrupt the teachings of the Torah to such an extent as to transform them into the evil colossus known as Amalek. The essence of Amalek, then, is not merely evil incarnate, rather, it is the fusion of evil and goodness which forms a monstrosity which is not possible to be produced by evil alone.

When we comprehend how especially pernicious is the result of an evil feeding upon and drawing from the sources of good, we can understand the prophet Eliyahu's exhortation to Israel, עַד מָתַי אַתֶּם פֹּסְחִים עַל שְׁתֵּי הַסְּעִפִּים, אִם ה' הָאֱלֹקִים לְכוּ אַחֲרָיו, וְאִם הַבַּעַל לְכוּ אַחֲרָיו, *How much longer will you hesitate between two doorsteps? If Hashem is the true God then follow Him, and if the Baal is, then follow him* (I Melachim 18:21).

"Indeed, if you believe it is the Baal," Eliyahu told them, "then serve him alone but do not combine it with the Divine." The worship of Baal alone is not nearly as bad as combining it with the worship of God. The 'light' of Torah, when combined with Baal, does not mitigate its evil but rather feeds and fans its flames.

A thought of a similar nature is expressed by *Or HaChaim* (*Bamidbar* 19:2). In discussing some of the concepts of טוּמְאָה, *ritual impurity*, he explains that a Jew can become טָמֵא as opposed to a gentile who cannot, for that which is profane and impure seeks to cleave to that which is elevated and spiritual. Therefore, טוּמְאָה cleaves only to one who is spiritually elevated, the Jew. There exists a specially affinity on the part of evil to be attracted by and cleave to the good and the uplifted of this world.

How do we understand this duality of forces brought to bear on man? Does not מְעַט מִן הָאוֹר דּוֹחֶה הַרְבֵּה מִן הַחֹשֶׁךְ, *a bit of light dissipate a lot of darkness?*

The answer is that 'darkness' in the human being is not merely the absence of light. It is a rather a powerful force in its own right, asserting itself in a person even in the presence of a powerful source of light. This is similar to the darkness of the macro-world, as the prophet declared: יוֹצֵר אוֹר וּבוֹרֵא חֹשֶׁךְ, *Who forms light and creates darkness* (*Yeshayahu* 45:7); darkness is described as a positive entity, a 'creation.' *Ramban* also uses this concept to explain the darkness of Egypt as being not the absence of sunlight but rather an entity of darkness which descended upon Egypt and extinguished all light (see *Ramban, Shemos* 10:21).

The understanding of this dimension of 'darkness' will clarify for us a few incidents where we find individuals who, despite the fact that they had become fully aware of the ultimate truth, were able to deny it.

One incident is that of Yeravam who stood offering sacrifices to an idol (see *I Melachim* 13:46). When the prophet came to rebuke him, the altar split open and Yeravam's hand became paralyzed, in fulfillment of the prophecy. Yeravam had no alternative but to plead with the prophet that he pray for him that his hand be healed. Yet, even in his request to the prophet to pray for him, he referred to Hashem as *your God* (i.e. the prophet's God). *Chazal* explain that the implication was: *Your God, but not mine* (*I Melachim* 13:4-6, *Rashi*).

Here we have no less a person than Yeravam ben Nevat who clearly sees the instant fulfillment of the prophet's words and the immediate Divine retribution. Yet, he obstinately refuses to acknowledge Hashem as his God.

Even more astounding is the case of the idol of Michah. *Chazal* (*Sanhedrin* 103b) tell us that this idol went with Israel across the Red Sea from Egypt. Even as the Israelites witnessed קְרִיעַת יַם סוּף, *the splitting of the Red Sea*, one of the most awesome miracles of all time, they carried an idol! רָאֲתָה שִׁפְחָה עַל הַיָּם מַה שֶׁלֹּא רָאָה יְחֶזְקָאל בֶּן בּוּזִי, *The lowliest servant girl beheld of the Divine at the splitting of the Red Sea more than Yechezkel ben Buzi [the prophet] ever saw* (*Mechilta Shemos* 15:2).

She was able to point at revelation of the Divine and proclaim זֶה קֵלִי וְאַנְוֵהוּ, *This is my God and I shall beautify him* (ibid.). It was an unequaled moment in history. Yet, at the very same time the idol went with them! And when the manna descended from Heaven, yet another miracle, they took a portion of this heavenly food and offered it to the idol! (see *Mechilta Shemos* 15:2, *Yalkut Shoftim*).

The fact that God's presence was so readily apparent did not contradict their worship of an idol. The great light of the Divine presence did not dissipate the darkness of paganism. The servant girl beheld the Divine, yet remained a servant girl.

The darkness of evil is not simply a lack of clarity about God's existence. It is rather an entity of its own, creating a lust and an urge which must be consciously overcome and overpowered. This is not accomplished by the mere awareness of the Divine by the 'light' in oneself. If a person does not uproot the bad and evil within him, then light and darkness will continue to influence him equally. This confluence of forces can lead to the most paradoxical of behaviors, for the 'light' fuels the 'darkness,' creating evil of a new dimension — Amalek!

גַּם זוּ לְטוֹבָה

This too Is for the Good

I.

One of the great *Tanaim*, a teacher of R' Akiva, is referred to by *Chazal* as נַחוּם אִישׁ גַּם־זוּ (Nachum who always said 'this too'). The title 'Rebbi' had already been in use since the days of Hillel and Shamai, yet Nachum was not called Rebbi but simply Ish Gamzu. Although the *Gemara* attributes this title to a certain event and to Nachum's remarkable reaction to the test to which he was put, still it must be that his conduct was indicative of a great stature; indeed so great that the title Gamzu would be even more meaningful than the term Rebbi.

To understand the importance of the meaning of the word גַּמְזוּ let us examine the portion of וַיֵּצֵא which deals with Yaakov's travails and difficulties in exile. The entire portion of וַיֵּצֵא does not contain any פְּתוּחוֹת וּסְתוּמוֹת, blank spaces between sections which serve to denote the end of a topic and whose purpose is לְהִתְבּוֹנֵן בֵּין פָּרְשָׁה לְפָרְשָׁה, to allow contemplation between sections about what one previously learned.

Baal HaTurim and *Baalei Tosefos* both explain that the reason וַיֵּצֵא does not contain any פְּתוּחוֹת וּסְתוּמוֹת is so that it should mirror Yaakov's escape from Esav (described in וַיֵּצֵא) which was quiet and secretive. This, however, is puzzling because if as *Chazal* say פְּתוּחוֹת וּסְתוּמוֹת were inserted so as to allow Moshe time to think about each portion before going on to the next, where is the pause between the portions of וַיֵּצֵא to enable contemplation of the various events?

To understand the reason for the way in which וַיֵּצֵא is written, let us examine a Midrash which interprets the prophet's words as a criticism of our father Yaakov.

מֵעוֹלָם לֹא אָמַר יַעֲקֹב אָבִינוּ דָּבָר שֶׁל בַּטָּלָה אֶלָּא כָּאן. אָמַר
הַקָּדוֹשׁ בָּרוּךְ הוּא אֲנִי עוֹסֵק לְהַמְלִיךְ אֶת בְּנוֹ בְּמִצְרַיִם וְהוּא אוֹמֵר

לָמָּה הֲרֵעֹתֶם לִי? הד״א "לָמָּה תֹאמַר יַעֲקֹב... נִסְתְּרָה דַרְכִּי
מֵה״, (בראשית רבה צא:יג עפ״י מתנות כהונה).

*Why do you say, O Yaakov, "... my way is hidden
from God?" (Yeshayahu 40:28). Yaakov never said an
idle word save on this occasion. The Holy One, Blessed
is He, said, "I am busy crowning your son [Yosef] king
and you complain that I am treating you badly?" Thus
it says, "Why do you say, Yaakov, 'my way is hidden
from God?'" (Bereishis Rabbah 91:13, according to the
text of the Matnos Kehunah).*

Yaakov was criticized for looking at the details and particular
events, while ignoring the total picture. If one looks at particulars, one
gets a distorted view of how things really are. Yaakov suffers when
looking at Yosef's disappearance itself; but it is the beginning of
Yosef's monarchy when looked at in context of subsequent events.

This then is the reason that there are no פָּרְשׁוֹת פְּתוּחוֹת in וַיֵּצֵא,
because it is the beginning of the history of the children of Israel and
as such one should not and may not contemplate any part of Israel's
history separately. Israel's history, of which וַיֵּצֵא is the beginning, can
be understood only as a whole, not each event by itself.

This was the greatness of Nachum Ish Gamzu. His response to the
events that occurred to him was not merely a demonstration of simple
faith, but rather a perspective of events in their overall context. While
each event in its own was bad, 'this too' would add up to a
benevolent total, which in fact it did. He was able to view God's
deeds with the approach of מִשְׁפְּטֵי ה' אֱמֶת צָדְקוּ יַחְדָּו, *God's judgments
are true, they [His deeds] are righteous when taken all together*
(Tehillim 19:10).

Nacham Ish Gamzu transmitted this perspective to his illustrious
student, R' Akiva. We are told about R' Akiva:

הֲוָה קָאָזֵיל בְּאוֹרְחָא מָטָא לְהַהִיא מָתָא בָּעָא אוּשְׁפִּיזָא. לֹא יָהֲבֵי
לֵיהּ, אָמַר כָּל דְּעָבֵיד רַחֲמָנָא לְטַב. אָזַל וּבָת בְּדַבְרָא. וַהֲוָה בַּהֲדֵיהּ
תַּרְנְגוֹלָא וַחֲמָרָא וּשְׁרָגָא. אָתָא זִיקָא כַּבְיֵהּ לִשְׁרָגָא אָתָא שׁוּנְרָא
אַכְלֵיהּ לְתַרְנְגוֹלָא אָתָא אַרְיֵה אַכְלֵיהּ לַחֲמָרָא. אָמַר כָּל דְּעָבֵיד
רַחֲמָנָא לְטַב בֵּיהּ בְּלֵילְיָא אָתָא גַּיָּיסָא שַׁבְיֵיהּ לְמָתָא. אָמַר לְהוּ,
לָאו אָמְרִי לְכוּ כָּל מַה שֶׁעוֹשֶׂה הַקָּדוֹשׁ בָּרוּךְ הוּא הַכֹּל לְטוֹבָה
(ברכות ס:ע״ב).

*R' Akiva was traveling and came to a city. He asked
for a place of lodging and was refused, so he went and*

*came into a field. He had with him a rooster a donkey
and a candle. A wind extinguished the candle, a cat ate
the rooster and a lion devoured the donkey. R' Akiva
exclaimed, "Whatever the Holy One does is for the
good." That night an armed band came and captured
the town. R' Akiva declared, "Did I not tell you that all
God does is for the good?" Rashi explains: For had the
candle remained lit, the donkey brayed or the rooster
crowed, I would have been taken into captivity together
with the people of the town (Berachos 60b).*

One can imagine R' Akiva's situation that night, with no house to
shelter him, no light to guide him and no donkey to ride on. Yet he
was conscious of the fact that this was all for his benefit. R' Akiva
was fortunate in that he was allowed to perceive the overall situation
immediately after he suffered his misfortunes. As for us, even though
we may not be privileged to perceive the full scope of events, we, too,
have to learn to look at things in the context of the whole.

The Vilna Gaon writes in a letter to his family, "Bear in mind,
about that which you laugh today you will cry tomorrow, and about
that which you cry today you will laugh tomorrow." The Gaon was
in fact admonishing his family not to react to situations in the context
of their momentary effect but rather in the context of the wholeness
of a person's existence, this world and the World-to-Come.

II.

There is, however, another and deeper aspect to this perspective of
Nachum Ish Gamzu regarding Hashem's deeds. Besides taking a
person's own experiences and viewing them together in order to see
them in their proper perspective, one must also include the
macrocosmic implications in order to fully comprehend and understand Hashem's actions.

לְכוּ וּרְאוּ מִפְעֲלוֹת אֱלֹקִים. נוֹרָא עֲלִילָה עַל בְּנֵי אָדָם. אַף
הַנּוֹרָאוֹת — שֶׁאַתָּה מֵבִיא עָלֵינוּ, בַּעֲלִילָה אַתְּ מְבִיאָן. כַּךְ אָמַר
אָדָם לִפְנֵי הַקָּדוֹשׁ בָּרוּךְ הוּא: „רִבּוֹנוֹ שֶׁל עוֹלָם עַד שֶׁלֹּא בָּרֵאתָ
עוֹלָמְךָ קֹדֶם שְׁנֵי אֲלָפִים שָׁנָה הָיְתָה תוֹרָה אֶצְלְךָ טָמוֹן וכו׳ וּכְתִיב
בָּהּ זֹאת הַתּוֹרָה אָדָם כִּי יָמוּת בְּאֹהֶל וכו׳ אֶלָּא אֶלָּא בָּאתָ לִתְלוֹת בִּי
אֶת הָעֲלִילָה.

וְכֵן הוּא אוֹמֵר בְּיוֹסֵף. וַיִּרְאוּ אֶחָיו כִּי אֹתוֹ אָהַב אֲבִיהֶם וגו'.
בִּשְׁבִיל כְּתֹנֶת פַּסִּים גָּרַם לְכָל הַשְּׁבָטִים לֵירֵד לְמִצְרָיִם. וְאָמַר רַבִּי
יוּדָן הָיָה הַקָּדוֹשׁ בָּרוּךְ הוּא מְבַקֵּשׁ לְקַיֵּם גְּזֵרַת יָדֹעַ תֵּדַע כִּי גֵר
יִהְיֶה זַרְעֲךָ וגו', וְהֵבִיא עֲלִילָה לְכָל דְּבָרִים אֵלּוּ כְּדֵי שֶׁיֶּאֱהַב יַעֲקֹב
אֶת יוֹסֵף וְיִשְׂנָאוּהוּ אֶחָיו (תנחומא וישב).

Go and see the workings of God. Awesome is His
planning upon men (Tehillim 66:5) ... Even the fearful
things that You [i.e., God] bring upon us are brought
with a design. Thus Adam exclaimed: Two thousand
years before You created the world, the Torah was
hidden with You, wherein it is written, "This is the law.
A man who dies in a tent," and yet You found an
excuse to blame me for causing the curse of death in the
world by eating from the tree of knowledge.

Similarly regarding Yosef it says, "And his brothers
saw that their father loved him" — due to a multicol-
ored cloak all of Yaakov's children went down to Egypt.
R' Yuden explained, The Holy One wanted to fulfill the
decree of "You shall surely know that your children
will be strangers etc.," and therefore He planned all
these things so that Yaakov should love Yosef and his
brothers should hate him (Tanchuma Vayeishev).

Here we have the perfect example of two separate patterns
meshing together and acting in unison. On the one hand, there was
a preordained plan to bring Israel to Egypt and to redeem them. On
the other hand, Yaakov and his children had their own particular set
of circumstances which manifested itself in Yosef's being sold to
Egypt. So independent are the two 'plots' from one another that we
establish a halachah [i.e., that a person ought not show favoritism to
one of his children over the others] based on the premise that it was
the brothers' jealousy that caused the sale of Yosef. Two separate sets
of events and yet both are part of a grand overall plan.

This profound perception of events in their broader and macrocosmic scope is portrayed in Megillas Esther. Events that took place
over a period of a decade are fitted together to give a broad picture of
the events that occurred in Shushan. The sin of the Jewish people
participating in the feasts of Achashverosh, the preparation of
Mordechai and Esther as Israel's saviours, the decree against Israel
and their subsequent triumph are all details that comprise the broader

story of Purim. So remarkable is the fitting together of disparate events and their portrayal in the *Megillah* that it is the opinion of our Sages that it was written by the Divine spirit; it being questionable whether human intelligence is capable of comprehending the grand picture all by itself (*Megillah* 7a).

This then is the eternal answer to our questions concerning God's justice. Iyov asked, "Who shall tell me that I would find Him . . . and present my case before Him?" (*Iyov* 23:2). To which the Holy One replied, "Where were you when I established the earth?" (*Iyov* 38:4). At the time of creation the entire tapestry of history had already been woven as it says, "He showed Adam each generation and its leaders" (*Sanhedrin* 38b). One who attempts to understand history frame by frame is doomed to failure. It is only by placing events in their universal context that one can truly perceive God's handiwork.

כָּל הַגָּדוֹל מֵחֲבֵרוֹ

The Strength of the Evil Inclination

כָּל הַגָּדוֹל מֵחֲבֵרוֹ יִצְרוֹ גָדוֹל הֵימֶנּוּ (סוכה נב:ע״א).
*Whoever is greater than his fellow man, his evil
inclination, too, is greater (Succah 52a).*

It seems that the reason for this phenomenon is so that every person
can maintain בְּחִירָה חָפְשִׁית, *free will*. The greater a person, the
greater his ability to overcome the יֵצֶר הָרַע, *evil inclination*, thus
upsetting the balance of his free choice. It is therefore necessary that
the great man's יֵצֶר הָרַע be increased proportionally in order to allow
the same degree of free choice as exists for his fellow human being.
However, this reason does not suffice to explain the phenomenon of
כָּל הַגָּדוֹל מֵחֲבֵרוֹ יִצְרוֹ גָדוֹל הֵימֶנּוּ, *Whoever is greater than his fellow
man, his evil inclination, too, is greater*, for we find that the יֵצֶר הָרַע
of great people is *disproportionately* stronger and more aggressive
than that of people of lesser stature.

וְאֵת הַצְּפוֹנִי אַרְחִיק מֵעֲלֵיכֶם וגו', וְעָלָה בָאְשׁוֹ וְתַעַל צַחֲנָתוֹ כִּי
הִגְדִּיל לַעֲשׂוֹת וְאֵת הַצְּפוֹנִי – זֶה יֵצֶר הָרַע שֶׁצָּפוּן וְעוֹמֵד בְּלִבּוֹ
שֶׁל אָדָם וכו'. וְעָלָה בָאְשׁוֹ וְתַעַל צַחֲנָתוֹ – שֶׁמֵּנִיחַ אֻמּוֹת הָעוֹלָם

וּמִתְגָּרֶה בְּשׂוֹנְאֵיהֶם שֶׁל יִשְׂרָאֵל. כִּי הִגְדִּיל לַעֲשׂוֹת – אָמַר אַבַּיֵי
וּבְתַלְמִידֵי חֲכָמִים יוֹתֵר מִכֻּלָּם (סוכה נב:ע"א).

And I will remove the northern one from you, and his foulness shall rise, and his ill savor shall ascend, for he has perpetrated terrible deeds.

'And I will remove the northern one' — refers to the evil inclination who is concealed and lurks in a man's heart. 'And his foulness shall arise and his ill savour shall ascend' — he leaves the other nations in peace and attacks only Israel. 'For he has perpetrated terrible deeds' — said Abaya, "[evil deeds] against Torah scholars more than against anyone else" (Succah 52a).

The *Gemara* continues with a story of Abaya who expressed his admiration of a simple man who refrained from sinning in a certain situation when faced with great temptation. Abaya averred that had he been exposed to the same situation he would not have stood the test, and leaned in anguish against a doorpost. An old man came up to him and taught him, "Whoever is greater than his fellow man, his evil inclination, too, is greater."

We see clearly from this story that the יֵצֶר הָרַע which provokes the תַּלְמִיד חָכָם, *wise man*, is *disproportionately* greater than the יֵצֶר הָרַע which tempts a person of lesser stature. Had the temptation been exactly in proportion to his greatness, Abaya would not have been comforted by the old man's words because Abaya should also have been able to control himself. It must be that the יֵצֶר הָרַע intensifies his efforts to ensnare the תַּלְמִיד חָכָם above and beyond the proportionate effort expended on a lesser person and consequently the hardship and danger that the תַּלְמִיד חָכָם falls victim to is greater than the common man's trial.

This is also evident from the special punishment, which according to this *Gemara* was meted out to the יֵצֶר הָרַע for provoking תַּלְמִידֵי חֲכָמִים. Had the efforts of the יֵצֶר הָרַע to provoke תַּלְמִידֵי חֲכָמִים been merely an effort to make their temptation equal to that of lesser people then he would not be punished. It is only because the יֵצֶר הָרַע goes beyond his mandate in tempting and provoking the great people that his punishment is intensified.

But let us consider the story of Abaya. We could understand that the יֵצֶר הָרַע places greater obstacles before the תַּלְמִיד חָכָם than he does before the simpler person. But how could the very same object of temptation be more difficult for the תַּלְמִיד חָכָם to resist?

In order to answer this question we must gain a deeper understanding of the *modus operandi* of the יֵצֶר הָרָע.

> אר"ר אַבָּא הַיֵּצֶר הַזֶּה דוֹמֶה לְלִיסְטִים שָׁפוּף שֶׁהָיָה יוֹשֵׁב בְּפָרָשַׁת דְּרָכִים. לְכָל מַאן דְּעוֹבֵר הֲוָה אָמַר הַב מַה דַעֲלָךְ. עָבַר פִּקֵּחַ אֶחָד וְרָאָה שֶׁאֵין בּוֹ תּוֹחֶלֶת לִגְזוֹל לוֹ כְּלוּם הִתְחִיל מְכַתְּתוֹ (בראשית רבה כב:ו).
>
> *R' Abba said: The yetzer hara can be compared to a decrepit [man who posed as a] robber sitting at a crossroads and ordering whoever passed by to surrender his possessions, until a shrewd person walked by and saw that he was too feeble to rob anyone and beat him (Bereishis Rabbah 22:6).*

Chazal have given us here the key to understanding the tactics of the יֵצֶר הָרָע. In reality, he is weak and impotent. His strength lies only in the pretense and illusion that he creates. When one realizes that the יֵצֶר הָרָע is but a fantasy, a mirage, merely the illusion of reality, then one can avoid being entrapped by him. *Chazal* (ibid.) also describe the יֵצֶר הָרָע as a dog who pretends to be asleep to distract the baker's vigilance, enabling the dog to grab a loaf of bread. Thus, the יֵצֶר הָרָע is described as someone who is too weak to openly confront the human being, but rather must wait to catch him with his guard lowered.

This profound understanding of the essence of the יֵצֶר הָרָע was revealed to Yaakov by the Angel of Esav when the two wrestled at the Yabok river crossing. After overpowering the Angel, Yaakov asked him, "הַגִּידָה נָּא שְׁמֶךָ, *Please tell me your name.*" He replied, "לָמָּה זֶּה תִּשְׁאַל לִשְׁמִי, *Why do you ask for my name?*" (*Bereishis* 32:30). By asking for his name, Yaakov was actually asking him to explain his essence (see *Sforno*). The 'name' of an entity defines its essence. This we learn from the fact that Adam's greatness expressed itself in his ability to give names to all living creatures, thereby defining their essence. This, then, gives us an understanding of the Angel's reply, "Why do you ask for my name?" The Angel of Esav was not posing a question, but rather giving a reply. "My strength lies in the fact that people do not pause to examine me more closely to know my name, my essence, for if they would, it would dispel the illusion that I present." Thus the Angel of Esav truly answered Yaakov's question as to his 'name.'

Another possible understanding of the Angel's reply to Yaakov is that in truth he has no name, for a name denotes a tangible reality. There is none by the *yetzer hara* since the יֵצֶר הָרַע does not exist as the reality that he presents, he is in fact nameless. Hence, לָמָּה זֶּה תִּשְׁאַל לִשְׁמִי, *Why do you ask for my name for I have none.*

My father זצ"ל explained the following verse in *Koheles* in this vein:

עִיר קְטַנָּה וַאֲנָשִׁים בָּהּ מְעָט וּבָא אֵלֶיהָ מֶלֶךְ גָּדוֹל וְסָבַב אוֹתָהּ וּבָנָה עָלֶיהָ מְצוֹדִים גְּדֹלִים. וּמָצָא בָהּ אִישׁ מִסְכֵּן חָכָם, וּמִלַּט הוּא אֶת הָעִיר בְּחָכְמָתוֹ (קהלת ט:יד).

There was a small city with only a few inhabitants; and a mighty king came upon it and surrounded it, and built great siege works around it. There was [in the city] a poor but wise man who by his wisdom saved the city (Koheles 9:14).

Shlomo HaMelech does not give any clue as to how the wise man succeeded in destroying all the mighty siege works with his wisdom. My father זצ"ל explained this verse in accordance with the Midrash, that Shlomo is alluding here to the battle against the יֵצֶר הָרַע. He explained that the wise man opened the people's eyes to the fact that the great king and all the siege works were . . . merely an illusion! It is not strength that is needed to break the stranglehold of the enemy but rather the discerning eye of a wise man.

We now have the key to comprehend the most puzzling יֵצֶר הָרַע of all: the יֵצֶר הָרַע of idol worship. The *Gemara* in *Sanhedrin* (102b) tells us that Menashe — the infamous and idolatrous king — appeared to R' Ashi in a dream. R' Ashi asked him, "Since you are so wise, how could you have bowed down to an idol?" Menashe replied, "Had you been there, you would have lifted your coat [to be able to run faster] and hastened after me."

R' Ashi was not bothered by a wise man's inability to withstand temptations and desires of various kinds, for they are not contradicted by a person's wisdom. Idolatry, on the other hand, seems to be in stark contradiction to reason and logic. R' Ashi could not understand how the יֵצֶר הָרַע could fool a wise man. Menashe explained that idolatry, too, was presented by the יֵצֶר הָרַע through illusion, not in its reality. R' Ashi was free to ponder its irrationality because he had been freed of the illusion engineered by the יֵצֶר הָרַע. [For the אַנְשֵׁי כְּנֶסֶת הַגְּדוֹלָה, the Men of the Great Assembly, had destroyed the יֵצֶר הָרַע of idolatry.] Had R' Ashi been living at the time when the יֵצֶר הָרַע for idolatry was still extant, he, too, would have been swept up in the swirl of fantasy of worshiping idols.

We now have a clear picture of the methodology of the יֵצֶר הָרַע, and of the way that it is possible for the same sin to tempt different people in varying degree. If the dimensions of a sin would be clearly perceived as they really are, then man would be able to withstand the enticements of sin. However, since the provocation of the יֵצֶר הָרַע is based on illusion, one is blinded, and one's reaction is not guided by reason. This is what *Chazal* meant when they said, אֵין אָדָם חוֹטֵא אֶלָּא אִם כֵּן נִכְנָס בּוֹ רוּחַ שְׁטוּת, *A person does not sin unless a spirit of foolishness enters into him* (Sotah 3a).

It is in this way that the יֵצֶר הָרַע is able to pose stronger and more difficult challenges to greater people. The circumstances may be equal, but the illusion and 'the spirit of foolishness' induced by the יֵצֶר הָרַע vary from person to person. The illusion which is foisted upon the תַּלְמִיד חָכָם goes beyond what is needed to preserve the balance which affords one free will.

On the day that the יֵצֶר הָרַע will finally be destroyed, this difference in the way sin is presented will be clearly seen by all.

לֶעָתִיד לָבוֹא מְבִיאוֹ הַקָּדוֹשׁ בָּרוּךְ הוּא לְיֵצֶר הָרַע וְשׁוֹחֲטוֹ בִּפְנֵי הַצַּדִּיקִים וּבִפְנֵי הָרְשָׁעִים. צַדִּיקִים נִדְמֶה לָהֶם כְּהַר גָּבוֹהַּ וּרְשָׁעִים נִדְמֶה לָהֶם כְּחוּט הַשַּׂעֲרָה. הַלָּלוּ בּוֹכִין וְהַלָּלוּ בּוֹכִין. צַדִּיקִים בּוֹכִין וְאוֹמְרִים הֵיאָךְ יָכֹלְנוּ לִכְבּוֹשׁ הַר גָּבוֹהַּ כָּזֶה וּרְשָׁעִים בּוֹכִים וְאוֹמְרִים הֵיאָךְ לֹא יָכֹלְנוּ לִכְבּוֹשׁ אֶת חוּט הַשַּׂעֲרָה הַזֶּה (סוכה נב:ע"א).

In the time to come, the Holy One will bring the evil inclination and slaughter him in the presence of both the righteous and the wicked. To the righteous it [the evil inclination] will have the appearance of a towering mountain and to the wicked it will have the appearance of a hair thread. Both will weep. The righteous will weep saying, "How were we able to overcome such a towering mountain?" The wicked will also weep saying, "How could we not have conquered this hair thread?" (Succah 52a).

The selfsame יֵצֶר הָרַע appears in various forms. He is but an insignificant thread when he tempts the wicked, but like a high mountain when he does all within his means to provoke the righteous to sin.

לְפוּם צַעֲרָא אַגְרָא
In Proportion to the Pain
Is the Reward

I.

וַיֵּשֶׁב יַעֲקֹב (בראשית לז:א).

בִּקֵּשׁ יַעֲקֹב לֵישֵׁב בְּשַׁלְוָה קָפַץ עָלָיו רָגְזוֹ שֶׁל יוֹסֵף. צַדִּיקִים
מְבַקְשִׁים לֵישֵׁב בְּשַׁלְוָה. אָמַר הַקָּדוֹשׁ בָּרוּךְ הוּא לֹא דַּיָּן לַצַּדִּיקִים
מַה שֶּׁמְּתֻקָּן לָהֶם לָעוֹלָם הַבָּא אֶלָּא שֶׁמְּבַקְשִׁים לֵישֵׁב בְּשַׁלְוָה
בָּעוֹלָם הַזֶּה (רש"י שם).

And Yaakov dwelled (Bereishis 37:1).

*Yaakov wished to live in tranquility but the affair of
Yosef came upon him. The righteous wish to live
tranquilly. Said the Holy One [to them], "Are the
righteous not satisfied with what is prepared for them
in the World-to-Come, that they seek tranquility in this
world too?" (Rashi ibid.).*

Certainly, Yaakov did not desire tranquility for its own sake, to
enjoy the comforts of this world. Rather, after all his tribulations,
he yearned for the tranquility that would enable him to pursue the
study of Torah and the worship of God without hindrance or

distraction. The question is self-evident. Why was Yaakov criticized for this well-intentioned desire? Was it not for spiritual purposes?

To answer this question we must look at man's purpose in this world from a different perspective. This world was not created in order to afford people the opportunity to serve God in tranquility and repose. Rather, this world is a place where one is to serve God while overcoming obstacles and impediments in the face of adversity and enmity. Thus, טוֹב לוֹ לָאָדָם דָּבָר אֶחָד בְּצַעַר מִמֵּאָה בְּרֶנַח, *Better one [deed] accomplished in hardship than a hundred [deeds] done with ease* (*Avos d R' Nosson* 3:6).

The *Mishnah* in *Avos* underscores this concept. לְפוּם צַעֲרָא אַגְרָא, *In proportion to the pain is the reward* (*Avos* 5:26). If the reward increases in proportion to the hardship, it must be that a human being's primary task in this world is to overcome those hardships and difficulties in his service of his Creator.

While success in the face of adversity constitutes an important element of any spiritual endeavor, it is indispensable as far as the study and the acquisition of Torah is concerned. Hashem's desire is also that we should 'labor' in Torah. The way to 'labor' is taught to us by our Sages:

כַּךְ הִיא דַרְכָּהּ שֶׁל תּוֹרָה, פַּת בַּמֶּלַח תֹּאכַל וּמַיִם בַּמְּשׂוּרָה תִּשְׁתֶּה וְעַל הָאָרֶץ תִּישָׁן, וְחַיֵּי צַעַר תִּחְיֶה, וּבַתּוֹרָה אַתָּה עָמֵל (אבות פ"ו:ד).

This is the path of Torah: Bread with salt you shall eat, water with measure you shall drink, on the earth you shall sleep, and a life of privation you shall live, and in Torah you toil (*Avos* 6:4).

Until one has adopted such a way of life and can overcome difficulty and discomfort, one cannot begin to toil in Torah. The hardship and sacrifice mentioned in the *Mishnah* are sine-qua-non for the study of Torah.

But adversity is not only a means of worshiping God or toiling in Torah; it is a goal in its own right. The very act of appropriating and using something which is not a necessity in and of itself reduces one's share in the World-to-Come. For one increases his share in this world only at the expense of his share in the next.

מַעֲשֶׂה בְתַלְמִיד אֶחָד שֶׁל רַבִּי שִׁמְעוֹן בֶּן יוֹחַאי שֶׁיָּצָא חוּצָה

לָאָרֶץ וּבָא עָשִׁיר וְהָיוּ הַתַּלְמִידִים רוֹאִין אוֹתוֹ וּמְקַנְאִין בּוֹ, וְהָיוּ
מְבַקְשִׁים הֵן לָצֵאת לְחוּצָה לָאָרֶץ וְיָדַע רַבִּי שִׁמְעוֹן וְהוֹצִיאָן
לְבִקְעָה אַחַת עַל פְּנֵי מֵירוֹן וְהִתְפַּלֵּל. וְאָמַר, בִּקְעָה בִּקְעָה מִלְאִי
דִנְרֵי זָהָב הִתְחִילָה מוֹשֶׁכֶת דִּנְרֵי זָהָב לִפְנֵיהֶם. אָמַר לָהֶם, אִם זָהָב
אַתֶּם מְבַקְשִׁים הֲרֵי זָהָב, טְלוּ לָכֶם. אֶלָּא הֱיוּ יוֹדְעִין כָּל מִי שֶׁהוּא
נוֹטֵל עַכְשָׁיו, חֶלְקוֹ שֶׁל עוֹלָם הַבָּא הוּא נוֹטֵל, שֶׁאֵין מַתַּן שְׂכַר
הַתּוֹרָה אֶלָּא לָעוֹלָם הַבָּא. הֱוֵי, וַתִּשְׂחַק לְיוֹם אַחֲרוֹן (שמות רבה
פרשה נב:ג).

A disciple of R' Shimon bar Yochai once went abroad,
and returned a wealthy man. The other disciples
saw him and became envious, and also wished to
go abroad. Thereupon, R' Shimon bar Yochai brought
them to a valley in Meron and prayed, "Valley,
valley, fill up with dinars of gold." It began to fill with
gold. He then exclaimed, "If you are looking for gold,
take all of this. But remember, he who takes riches now
is taking his share of the World-to-Come, for the
sole reward of Torah is received in the World-to-
Come." This is the meaning of [the verse], 'and she
rejoiced at the time to come' (Mishlei 31:25) [Shemos
Rabbah 52:3].

From this we learn that it is incumbent upon every person to fulfill
his life's mission while taking from this world only as much as
necessary. Enjoying more comfort and luxury than is necessary is not
merely a harmless supplement to the means available to carry out
one's task. It is taken, rather, at the expense of one's reward, from
one's portion of his World-to-Come.

This self-limitation of the absolute necessities of life includes and
embraces all the ways of man's worship in his world. The same R'
Shimon bar Yochai who, in the above-mentioned story, chastised his
students for desiring wealth, and told them that it would be at the
expense of their World-to-Come, made the following statement:
אִלְמָלֵא יוֹתָם בֶּן עֻזִיָּהוּ עִמָּנוּ יָכַלְנוּ לִפְטוֹר אֶת כָּל הָעוֹלָם כֻּלּוֹ מִן הַדִּין מִיּוֹם
שֶׁנִּבְרָא הָעוֹלָם עַד סוֹפוֹ, Were Yosam ben Uziyahu to join my son and
myself, we could free the world from judgment for eternity (Succah
45b). Rabbeinu Chananel explains that Yosam's greatness lay in the
fact that he took neither honor nor luxuries from this world. It was,
therefore, that he could free the world from judgment until the end of
days.

The *Gemara* makes a similar statement regarding R' Chanina ben Dosa:

בְּכָל יוֹם וָיוֹם בַּת קוֹל יוֹצֵאת וְאוֹמֶרֶת, כָּל הָעוֹלָם כֻּלּוֹ נִזּוֹן בִּשְׁבִיל
חֲנִינָא בְּנִי, וַחֲנִינָא בְּנִי דַּיּוֹ בְּקַב חָרוּבִים מֵעֶרֶב שַׁבָּת לְעֶרֶב שַׁבָּת
(תענית כד ע"ב).

A heavenly voice proclaims each day, "The whole world is sustained because of Chanina my son, and Chanina himself subsists on a measure of carobs from Friday to Friday" (Taanis 24b).

It is quite obvious that the *Gemara* is not merely telling us two separate praises of R' Chanina, but rather that it is because of his frugality that his merit sustains the entire world.

It would be superficial, however, to understand ascetism and restraint only in the light of *spiritual* welfare. The *Mishnah* explicitly states that if one limits his physical consumption he will be "happy in this world" aside from "benefiting in the World-to-Come." A person who is consumed by passion and pursues constant gratification is never satisfied, and spends his life chasing after imaginary pleasures, never content with the share of good bestowed upon him. A person who lives his life and seeks only its necessities is spared the tortures of jealousy and lust, and lives out his days in happiness and contentment.

In light of the extreme importance of living with only necessities, it would be useful to see how it is possible to live in such a manner.

The desire for worldly goods and luxuries is felt most strongly when a person sees someone else enjoying them. In this case, another person's luxuries become his necessities. If, however, one makes a point of observing people less fortunate then oneself, one can begin to appreciate those gifts that one does possess. This is the lesson that Eliyahu the prophet taught R' Akiva:

רַבִּי עֲקִיבָא אִתְקַדְּשֵׁית לֵיהּ בְּרַתֵּיהּ דְּכַלְבָּא שָׁבוּעַ. שָׁמַע כַּלְבָּא
שָׁבוּעַ אַדְּרֵיהּ הֲנָאָה מִכָּל נִכְסֵיהּ. אָזְלָה וְאִתְנְסִיבַת לֵיהּ בְּסִיתְוָא, הֲוָה
גָּנוּ בֵּי תִּבְנָא ... אָתָא אֵלִיָּהוּ אַדְּמֵי לְהוֹן כְּאֱנָשָׁא וְקָא קָרֵי אַבָּבָא
אָמַר לְהוּ הָבוּ לִי פּוּרְתָּא דְּתִבְנָא דְּיָלְדַת אִתְּתִי וְלֵית לִי מִדַּעַם
לַאֲגוּנָהּ. אָמַר לָהּ רַבִּי עֲקִיבָא לְאִנְתְּתֵיהּ חֲזִי גַּבְרָא דַּאֲפִלּוּ תִּבְנָא
לָא אִית לֵיהּ אָמְרָה לֵיהּ זִיל הֲוֵה בֵּי רַב (נדרים נ ע"א).

R' Akiva married the daughter of Kalba Savua. Upon hearing this, Kalba Savua disinherited her. She married him during the winter and they slept on straw [not having any pillows or blankets] . . . Eliyahu came and appeared as a pauper and knocked on the door, saying, "Give me some straw, for my wife has given birth and I have nothing for her to lie on." R' Akiva turned to his wife and remarked, "Behold this person does not even have straw." She replied, "If so, go and study" (Nedarim 50a).

What Rachel, R' Akiva's wife, realized was that there were people in more dire straits than themselves, and that in contrast they had all the *necessities*, and so there was no reason for R' Akiva not to study Torah. By observing another person's need she realized how her situation was relatively satisfactory. And it was this insight or realization which gave birth to and made possible the development of a 'Rabbi Akiva'.

Chovos Halevovos gives similar advice: לִהְיוֹת עֵינוֹ תָּמִיד עַל מִי שֶׁהוּא לְמַטָּה מִמֶּנּוּ בְּרוֹב הַטּוֹבוֹת, לֹא עַל מִי שֶׁהוּא לְמַעֲלָה מִמֶּנּוּ, *Always keep in mind those people less fortunate than yourself, not those more fortunate than you* (Shaar Avodas Elokim 7).

II.

At a higher level, this contentment with necessities also includes being content with one's daily requirements and not worrying about tomorrow. Thus, the *Gemara* tell us:

מִשֶּׁחָרַב בֵּית הַמִּקְדָּשׁ פָּסְקוּ אַנְשֵׁי אֲמָנָה מִיִּשְׂרָאֵל אָמַר רַבִּי יִצְחָק אֵלוּ בְּנֵי אָדָם שֶׁהֵם מַאֲמִינִים בְּהַקָּדוֹשׁ בָּרוּךְ הוּא דְּתַנְיָא רַבִּי אֱלִיעֶזֶר הַגָּדוֹל אוֹמֵר כָּל מִי שֶׁיֵּשׁ לוֹ פַּת בְּסַלּוֹ וְאוֹמֵר מָה אֹכַל לְמָחָר? אֵינוֹ אֶלָּא מִקְטַנֵּי אֲמָנָה (סוטה מח ע"ב).

Since the day that the Temple has been destroyed, Israel has lost its men of faith . . . R' Yitzchak explained, "These are men who trust in the Holy One, as we have been taught;" R' Eliezer the Great said, "He who has bread in his basket and is worried about the next day's provisions belongs to those who have little faith" (Sotah 48b).

This is what *Chazal* meant when they said that Hagar, Avraham's wife, was lacking in faith. She worried about her supply of water to a degree that she filled up her gourd with more water than she needed for immediate use (see *Bereishis Rabbah* 53:14). She was found lacking in בִּטָחוֹן, *trust*, for this unnecessary worrying, in spite of the fact that she was in the desert with a sick child!

The ability to trust in God and not to worry about tomorrow can transform the harshest of curses into the most sublime blessing.

We learn, וְהָיוּ חַיֶּיךָ תְּלֻאִים לְךָ מִנֶּגֶד, וּפָחַדְתָּ לַיְלָה וְיוֹמָם, וְלֹא תַאֲמִין בְּחַיֶּיךָ, *and your lives will hang in suspense, and you shall be terrified day and night, and you will not believe that you are alive* (*Devarim* 28:66).

Chazal (*Menachos* 103b) explain that this verse refers to a situation where one has increasingly less and less to eat, the ultimate curse being when one must seek his bread each day. Yet, if this state of extreme insecurity and worry is the epitome of unhappiness, how do we understand the following statement of *Chazal*?

שָׁאֲלוּ תַּלְמִידָיו אֶת רַבִּי שִׁמְעוֹן בֶּן יוֹחַאי, מִפְּנֵי מַה לֹּא יָרַד לָהֶם לְיִשְׂרָאֵל מָן פַּעַם אַחַת בַּשָּׁנָה. אָמַר לָהֶם אֶמְשׁוֹל לָכֶם מָשָׁל לְמָה הַדָּבָר דּוֹמֶה, לְמֶלֶךְ בָּשָׂר וָדָם שֶׁיֵּשׁ לוֹ בֵּן אֶחָד. פָּסַק לוֹ מְזוֹנוֹתָיו פַּעַם אַחַת בַּשָּׁנָה. וְלֹא הָיָה מְקַבֵּל פְּנֵי אָבִיו אֶלָּא פַּעַם אַחַת בַּשָּׁנָה עָמַד וּפָסַק מְזוֹנוֹתָיו בְּכָל יוֹם, וְהָיָה מְקַבֵּל פְּנֵי אָבִיו כָּל יוֹם. אַף יִשְׂרָאֵל, מִי שֶׁיֵּשׁ לוֹ אַרְבָּעָה וַחֲמִשָּׁה בָנִים הָיָה דוֹאֵג וְאוֹמֵר שֶׁמָּא לֹא יֵרֵד מָן לְמָחָר, וְנִמְצְאוּ כֻלָּם מֵתִים בְּרָעָב. נִמְצְאִים כֻּלָּם מְכַוְּנִים אֶת לִבָּם לַאֲבִיהֶן שֶׁבַּשָּׁמַיִם (יומא ע"ו ע"א).

The students of R' Shimon bar Yochai asked him, "Why did the manna not fall once annually" [in sufficient quantity for the entire year]? *He replied, "I will answer you with a parable. There was once a king of flesh and blood who had one son, whom he provided with maintenance once a year. He would only visit his father once a year. Therefore he began providing him every day, so that he would see him every day. So too, Israel; one who had four or five children would worry saying perhaps there would not be manna the next day and they would starve. Thus, they all directed their attention to their Father in Heaven"* (*Yoma* 76a).

This situation, then, is not a curse but a blessing, since it made them turn to Hashem and trust in Him. Surely the generation of the desert, the recipients of the Torah, were not subject to the harshest curse of the *tochachah* (dire predictions).

The answer is that the Torah specifically does not mention any lack of food, but rather the dread thereof, as being the curse. Such a situation is unbearable for the man of little faith. For the man who has faith and trust in Hashem, however, this situation becomes the means of a daily closeness to God, the greatest of blessings. His daily bread becomes imbued with the essence of manna.

שְׁלֵמוּת הַמַּעֲשֶׂה

The Complete Mitzvah

וַיַּכֵּר יוֹסֵף אֶת־אֶחָיו (בראשית מב:ח).
And Yosef recognized his brothers (Bereishis 42:8).

בִּלְעָדָי, אֱלֹקִים יַעֲנֶה אֶת שְׁלוֹם פַּרְעֹה (בראשית מא:טז).
It is beyond me, God will answer as to Pharaoh's welfare (Bereishis 41:15).

וַיֶּאְסֹר יוֹסֵף מֶרְכַּבְתּוֹ וַיַּעַל לִקְרַאת יִשְׂרָאֵל אָבִיו גֹּשְׁנָה וַיֵּרָא אֵלָיו
וַיִּפֹּל עַל צַוָּארָיו וכו' (בראשית מו:כט).
And Yosef harnessed his chariot and ascended to meet his father, Yisrael, in Goshen. He presented himself to him and he fell on his neck ... (Bereishis 46:29).

וַיֵּרָא אֵלָיו: יוֹסֵף נִרְאָה אֶל אָבִיו (רש"י שם).
And he presented himself to him: Yosef presented himself to his father (Rashi ibid.).

Rashi's explanation itself needs clarification. What is *Rashi* adding or clarifying that is not already stated in this verse? Moreover, as *Ramban* points out, the verse itself is seemingly redundant. Certainly Yosef "presented himself" to his father; the verse continues by telling us that he fell upon his neck, etc.

To understand this verse and *Rashi's* comment, let us consider for a moment the emotions assailing Yosef as he went to meet his father. On the one hand, Yosef himself yearned to see his father, as would any son who had not seen his father for so many years. Yosef was especially bound to his father by the special love that Yaakov showered upon him, וְיִשְׂרָאֵל אָהַב אֶת יוֹסֵף מִכָּל בָּנָיו, *Israel loved Yosef over all his other children* (*Bereishis* 37:3), the love that would naturally be reflected in the attachment that Yosef had to his father. In addition Yaakov was not only his father but his teacher as well, as *Rashi* says, "All that Yaakov learned from Shem and Ever he taught to Yosef." Surely, this produced an even more profound relationship.

Yet there was a second reason for Yosef's meeting with his father. Yosef knew of his father's anguish and bereavement at having 'lost' his son for twenty-two years. To be reunited with his son after so many years of separation would cause Yaakov supreme joy and happiness; it would be a moment of unsurpassed exultation for Yaakov. Yaakov himself expressed it, when he told his children, אֵלְכָה וְאֶרְאֶנּוּ בְּטֶרֶם אָמוּת, "*I will go and see him [Yosef] before I die*" (*Bereishis* 45:28), and upon seeing Yosef he exclaimed, אָמוּתָה הַפָּעַם אַחֲרֵי רְאוֹתִי אֶת פָּנֶיךָ, "*Now I can die after having seen your face*" (*Bereishis* 46:30).

It is to these two disparate emotions that *Rashi* is alluding. Yosef's reason for seeing his father was so that "his father would see him" and rejoice. In traveling to see his father he suppressed all of his own emotional fulfillment and yearning. He journeyed to his father solely for the purpose of causing Yaakov the happiness of finding a long-lost son. It was an act done for the purest of motives — "to present himself to his father," as *Rashi* stresses.

But why? Why did Yosef find it necessary to suppress that emotion as a reason for going to meet his father, a father such as Yaakov?

The answer is that being that such an emotion would gratify and satisfy Yosef's own needs, it would in essence be 'selfish'. To meet Yaakov, for that reason as well, would mean that no longer would the *mitzvah* be done in purity, for its own sake, but a strain of self-gratification would insert itself and tarnish the deed. This is what Yosef sought to avoid by suppressing his emotions and acting solely for his father's sake.

It was this same character trait of Yosef that typified his treatment of his brothers in Egypt. The Torah tells us וַיַּכֵּר יוֹסֵף אֶת־אֶחָיו, *and Yosef recognized his brothers* (*Bereishis* 42:8).

Rashi, quoting a Midrash, explains that this 'recognition' does not refer merely to the fact that he identified them, but rather that he acted towards them as a brother, i.e., mercifully. How does this correlate with the Torah's description of Yosef's harsh treatment of his brothers?

The answer must be that although he indeed was outwardly harsh to them, nevertheless, the reason he acted this way in order to make them repent and regret their grievous error of selling him. Inwardly, his motives were solely for his brother's own good. Thus, Yosef's heart was so cleansed of selfish motives that not one iota of desire for revenge found its way into his heart. All that he did and said was for their benefit, as the verse testifies, *And Yosef recognized his brothers* (ibid.).

❦ ❦ ❦

Shimshon, who judged Israel for twenty years, acted in the same manner and was totally selfless during all his years as a judge. Bound and blinded by the Philistines he cried out זָכְרֵנִי נָא וְחַזְּקֵנִי נָא אַךְ הַפַּעַם הַזֶּה ... וְאִנָּקְמָה נְקַם אַחַת מִשְׁתֵּי עֵינַי מִפְּלִשְׁתִּים, *Remember me, I beseech You, and strengthen me just this time ... and I shall revenge one of my two eyes from the Philistines* (Shoftim 16:28).

Rashi elaborates: זְכוֹר כ' שָׁנָה שֶׁשְׁפַטְתִּי אֶת יִשְׂרָאֵל וְלֹא אָמַרְתִּי לְאֶחָד מֵהֶם הַעֲבֶר לִי מַקֵּל מִמָּקוֹם לְמָקוֹם, *Remember me that I judged Israel for twenty years and did not ask of anyone to pass me my stick.*

Had Shimshon but once requested a favor, his leadership would have been tainted with a touch of selfishness, of self-gratification. All his twenty years of impeccable leadership (see *Sotah* 10a) would not have stood in his favor to avenge himself of the Philistines if he would have tarnished it by garnering some favor from the Jewish people.

This injunction against taking for one's self any benefit applies not only in conjunction with *mitzvos* but is an ideal in its own right.

וַיְהִי יוֹסֵף יְפֵה תֹאַר וִיפֵה מַרְאֶה (בראשית לט:ו).

רש"י: כֵּיוָן שֶׁרָאָה עַצְמוֹ מוֹשֵׁל, הִתְחִיל אוֹכֵל וְשׁוֹתֶה וּמְסַלְסֵל בְּשַׂעֲרוֹ. אָמַר הַקָּדוֹשׁ בָּרוּךְ הוּא, אָבִיךָ מִתְאַבֵּל וְאַתָּה מְסַלְסֵל בְּשַׂעֲרֶךָ? אֲנִי מְגָרֶה בְךָ אֶת הַדּוֹב. מִיַּד, וַתִּשָּׂא אֵשֶׁת אֲדוֹנָיו וגו' (רש"י שם).

And Yosef was of handsome countenance and of handsome appearance (Bereishis 39:6).

> Rashi: When [Yosef] saw that he was put in charge, he began to eat, drink and to groom his hair. Said the Holy One, "Your father is in mourning for you, and you are grooming yourself? I will bring upon you the bear, [i.e., Potiphar's wife]." Thereupon, "and the wife of his master ..." (Rashi ibid.).

The act of "eating, drinking, etc." in the context of his father's bereavement was an act of unwarranted self-indulgence. For this self-indulgence he would have to undergo the difficulties of Potiphar's wife to seduce him and her subsequent libel against him and his imprisonment.

The self-indulgence from which one must refrain pertains not only to physical pleasures but to emotional and egoistic gratification, such as pride and honor as well. Thus, when Eliezer began his conversation with Lavan and Besuel, he made a point of declaring עֶבֶד אַבְרָהָם אָנֹכִי, I am Avraham's servant (Bereishis 24:34). Chazal explain that Eliezer resembled Avraham in his appearance and was mistaken by many people for Avraham. Therefore, he immediately made his identity clear. But why the urgency? His identity would very soon become clear with the next sentence.

The answer is that Eliezer was wary of enjoying an extra moment of undeserved honor. To garner undeserved and unwarranted pleasure is wrong even if it is but the nebulous pleasure of honor due to mistaken identity.

Similarly we find that the angels who destroyed Sodom were punished for falsely priding themselves for the upcoming destruction. They said כִּי מַשְׁחִתִים אֲנַחְנוּ, We will destroy, falsely claiming the power for themselves (see Bereishis Rabbah 20). Although they subsequently clarified their meaning by stating, "and God sent us to destroy it," they were punished for the fleeting moment of unwarranted glory.

Until now, we have touched on the negative aspects of selfish motives and pursuit of self-gratification. Let us examine the positive aspect of one who acts with purity of motive and does not expect any additional gratification at all.

Pharaoh had Yosef released from jail to interpret his dream. Pharaoh told him, "I have heard about you that you can listen to a dream and divine its meaning." Yosef replied immediately, בִּלְעָדָי, אֱלֹקִים יַעֲנֶה אֶת שְׁלוֹם פַּרְעֹה, It is beyond me, God will answer as to

Pharaoh's welfare (Bereishis 41:15-16). It was this answer of Yosef's which impressed Pharaoh to such an extent that he deemed Yosef worthy of ruling Egypt and immediately appointed him as king of Egypt second only to himself. What did Pharaoh see in Yosef's answer that so impressed him? He saw a man who did not take any honor and credit for himself but rather attributed it to its true source. Such a person was worthy to be appointed king of Egypt.

Indeed, this was the manner in which Yosef ruled over Egypt. *Chazal* tell us that Yosef amassed an astounding fortune from the taxes that he collected in Egypt. Yet, he gave it all to Pharaoh, not keeping any of the wealth for himself or for his family *(Midrash Al Yis'hallel)*.

This quality of selflessness is also what set Boaz apart and what made him worthy of being the progenitor of Israel's royal family. Boaz offered to let Tov, a relative of his, redeem Ruth, telling him, "If you wish to redeem her, then do so" *(Ruth* 4:4). He knew that if Tov would redeem her, then he, Boaz, would not establish the line of royalty. Yet having deemed it proper that the other relative be given the opportunity of redemption, he put personal consideration aside, acting without any self-interest whatsoever. This utter unselfishness, indeed, is the hallmark of royalty in Israel.

אוֹי לָנוּ מִיּוֹם הַתּוֹכָחָה

Woe to Us on the Day of Rebuke

I.

וַיֹּאמֶר יוֹסֵף אֶל אֶחָיו, אֲנִי יוֹסֵף . . . וְלֹא יָכְלוּ אֶחָיו לַעֲנוֹת אֹתוֹ כִּי
נִבְהֲלוּ מִפָּנָיו (בראשית מה:ג).

*And Yosef told his brothers "I am Yosef" . . . and his
brothers could not answer him for they were overwhelmed by him (Bereishis 45:3).*

אָמַר רַבִּי שִׁמְעוֹן בֶּן אֶלְעָזָר . . . אוֹי לָנוּ מִיּוֹם הַדִּין אוֹי לָנוּ מִיּוֹם
הַתּוֹכָחָה וכו׳. יוֹסֵף קָטָן שֶׁל שְׁבָטִים הָיָה, וְלֹא יָכְלוּ אֶחָיו לַעֲנוֹת
אוֹתוֹ כִּי נִבְהֲלוּ מִפָּנָיו. לִכְשֶׁיָּבֹא הַקָּדוֹשׁ בָּרוּךְ הוּא וְיוֹכִיחַ כָּל אֶחָד
וְאֶחָד לְפִי מַעֲשָׂיו, עַל אַחַת כַּמָּה וְכַמָּה (ילקוט שם).

*R' Shimon son of Elazar said: Woe to us on the Day of
Judgment, woe to us on the day of rebuke — for Yosef,
though he was the youngest of the brothers, overwhelmed them, and they could not answer him.
Certainly this will be the case on the day that the Holy
One will rebuke each person in accordance with his
deeds (Yalkut ibid.).*

The reference in the Midrash to Yosef's rebuke is puzzling. While
the verse tells of the shock of the brothers at the revelation that

this was Yosef, it does not, however, mention any rebuke at all. Yosef merely said, "I am Yosef." Where is the תּוֹכָחָה, *rebuke*, that the Midrash refers to?

This implies that תּוֹכָחָה in essence is not the verbal castigation that we have come to see it. Rather, it is making a person aware of the fact that he has erred. When a person realizes that he has lived his life with a totally mistaken perspective, then תּוֹכָחָה has accomplished its purpose.

Thus, no greater תּוֹכָחָה than Yosef's can be imagined. The very act of selling Yosef into slavery became the stepping stone to Yosef's ascension to royalty. The very actions perpetrated in order to prevent the fulfillment of his dreams became the means for their realization. Yosef's simple declaration "I am Yosef" was absolute proof that he was not a בַּעַל הַחֲלוֹמוֹת, a grandiose dreamer, as they had accused him of being, but rather a prophet of God conveying the Divine word. It was the shock of this תּוֹכָחָה in the face of their strong convictions that so overwhelmed the brothers and left them speechless.

When R' Shimon ben Elazar pondered this he exclaimed, "Woe unto us from the day of rebuke." If the youngest of the brothers can cause such shame and agony to his brothers simply by revealing the truth, how great will be our agony when we will be shown by the Holy One how our lives were so filled with mistakes.

Thus, when Yitzchak realized that, contrary to his longstanding belief, Esav was not the one to whom the blessing belonged, the verse says, וַיֶּחֱרַד יִצְחָק חֲרָדָה גְּדֹלָה עַד מְאֹד, *And Yitzchak shook with a very mighty tremble (Bereishis* 27:33). R' Chama explains עַד מְאֹד, *mighty,* to mean, "even more then he trembled on the Altar" [when his father prepared him for sacrifice] (*Yalkut* ibid.). What caused this great fear? The answer is that in one swift instant, Yitzchak came to the realization that all his life he had viewed his children from a totally mistaken perspective. He had assumed Esav to be the righteous son, worthy of his blessings, and Yaakov as the lesser son. In that moment of truth he saw the wicked Esav as he really was, poised on the threshold of *gehinnom*. He realized that, to the contrary, it was Yaakov who was worthy of his blessings. This moment of realization — the understanding that he had been wrong all his life — was indeed a moment of trembling.

But it is not only because one had a distorted perspective per se that one will be so severely embarrassed in the World-to-Come. It is also the fact that one behaved and acted based on his erroneous beliefs and viewpoint. When a person realizes that his perspective was wrong, it automatically means that the entire chain of his deeds and actions was one continuous error. Therefore, *Chazal* refer to the day of judgment as, 'the day when Hashem will rebuke each and every person on account of his deeds.' For when the very goals and ideas upon which one bases his actions evaporate, then the deeds become mere empty gesticulation. Thus, the day of rebuke is harder for the person than the day of judgment.

Moreover, often a person will perform an act with the knowledge that something is wrong but nevertheless feels the act is justified by its outcome, by the fact that it is but a means to a worthy goal. When that goal, however, is proven to be false or meaningless, then not only is the act without redeeming value but it stands out in its fullest measure of evil.

The brothers of Yosef justified their cruelty to him by the belief that he was a vainglorious dreamer, as they declared, "And let us see what will be of his dreams." When the presumption was refuted, the act of selling Yosef became a wrong and sinful act. Thus, the feelings of shame and contrition that Yosef's brothers experienced when he uttered the few words: "I am Yosef your brother."

II.

A person should not determine his course of action solely for the purpose of the accomplishment. A person is obligated to do that which is demanded of him, and it is for Hashem to bring results. It is incumbent upon man to act, not to accomplish. Any other approach is a declaration that כֹּחִי וְעֹצֶם יָדִי עָשָׂה לִי אֶת הַחַיִל הַזֶּה, *My power and the might of my hand have gotten me all this success* (*Devarim* 8:17). While this injunction literally applies to physical endeavors and accomplishment, it applies to the spiritual as well.

With this we can attain a deepened understanding of *Chazal's* portrayal of spiritual accomplishment as יָגַעְתָּ וּמָצָאתָ, *toiling and finding.* Man's role is that of 'toil,' while the results are מָצָאתָ, *found,* a gift of Hashem, as it were. This idea finds expression in the prayer of R' Nechuniah ben Hakanah, אֲנִי עָמֵל וּמְקַבֵּל שָׂכָר, *I toil and am rewarded* (*Berachos* 28b). For it is for the toil itself that man is rewarded, not for the result. To be more exact, the accomplishment and attainments are a part of the reward.

Chazal tell us: אֵיזֶהוּ גִבּוֹר? הַכּוֹבֵשׁ אֶת יִצְרוֹ, *Who is strong? He who subdues his evil inclination* (*Avos* 4:1).

On the other hand, *Chazal* say, אִלְמָלֵא הקב"ה עוֹזְרוֹ אֵינוֹ יָכוֹל לוֹ, *Were it not for the assistance of the Holy One, [man] could not conquer [his evil inclination]* (*Succah* 52b). How then can *Chazal* attribute the subordination of the evil inclination to strength?

The answer is that Hashem's assistance is commensurate to man's efforts. Man battles; God conquers. If man has succeeded in overcoming his evil inclination, it is indeed testimony to his strength.

Rosh proves that Moshe was a גִבּוֹר, *a strong person*, from the fact that he singlehandedly assembled the walls of the *Mishkan*, a feat requiring great strength (*Nedarim* 38a).

Maharsha asks: The Midrash states that it was through a miracle that the walls were assembled. If so, then how does this feat demonstrate Moshe's strength?

A similar question may be asked on the Midrash which states that because Moshe had no part in the construction of the *Mishkan* he was told that he would be the one to assemble its walls. The question arises once again: If it was through a Divine miracle that the *Mishkan* was assembled, how would Moshe have his share in its construction?

The answer is that as with all human endeavor and accomplishment the final outcome, in this case the assembly of the walls, is Hashem's doing. So long as Moshe expended all his efforts and energies towards constructing the *Mishkan*, it was rightfully considered his doing, no less so than an act which would have *seemed* to be his doing. For a גִבּוֹר is not one who has great physical strength, but rather one who has exerted himself to the utmost.

Similarly, Aharon is titled a גִבּוֹר (*Vayikrah Rabbah* 26:9), on account of his lifting tens of thousands of Levites in one day. While this was clearly a miracle, since Aharon exerted his utmost in order to accomplish this feat, it was rightfully considered *his* deed and is genuine proof of Aharon's גְבוּרָה. Since man's attainments are not his doing, but rather the result is God's doing, commensurate to man's efforts, therefore, there are no bounds to man's abilities! No wonder then that man is capable of superhuman efforts.

גָּלוּת הַשְּׁכִינָה

The Exile of the Divine Presence

I.

„וַאֲנִי בְּבֹאִי מִפַּדָּן מֵתָה עָלַי רָחֵל בְּאֶרֶץ כְּנַעַן בַּדֶּרֶךְ בְּעוֹד כִּבְרַת
אֶרֶץ לָבֹא אֶפְרָתָה וָאֶקְבְּרֶהָ שָּׁם בְּדֶרֶךְ אֶפְרָת הִוא בֵּית לָחֶם"
(בראשית מח:ז).

*"And as for me, when I came from Paddan, Rachel died
on me in the land of Canaan on the way, when there
was but a stretch of land to go to Efrat; and I buried her
there in the road to Efrat, which is Bethlehem"*
(Bereishis 48:7).

Our father Yaakov, on his deathbed, requested his son Yosef to
bury him in Hebron. In order to assuage Yosef's possible resentment
that his mother, Rachel, was not accorded a similar honor but was
buried at the roadside, Yaakov explains that it was a Divine
command. Yet, Yaakov does not tell him so immediately. As *Rashi*
explains, each part of his request contains a rebuttal of any other
motive for burying her at the roadside. Thus, "Do not think that it
was too far" — *There was but a stretch of land till Efrat.* "Do not
think that the weather did not allow" — *for it was dry,* and so on.

Why did Yaakov not tell him immediately that it was a Divine command? Would Yosef not have believed his own father on his deathbed?

The answer to this question lies in an understanding of the concept of גָּלוּת הַשְּׁכִינָה, *the exile of the Divine Presence*.

The Midrash tells of a dialogue between Hashem and David HaMelech concerning גָּלוּת הַשְּׁכִינָה.

אָמַר לוֹ הַקָּדוֹשׁ בָּרוּךְ הוּא, דָּוִד בְּנִי אֲפִלּוּ אַתְּ מְקִימֵנִי כַּמָּה
פְּעָמִים אֵינִי קָם. וְאֵימָתַי אֲנִי קָם? ... ,,עַתָּה אָקוּם,'' כָּל זְמַן שֶׁהִיא
מוּכְפֶּשֶׁת בְּעָפָר כִּבְיָכוֹל אַף אֲנִי כֵן. אֶלָּא כְּשֶׁיַּגִּיעַ אוֹתוֹ הַיּוֹם
שֶׁכָּתוּב בּוֹ ,,הִתְנַעֲרִי מֵעָפָר קוּמִי,'' בְּאוֹתָהּ שָׁעָה ,,הַס כָּל בָּשָׂר
מִפְּנֵי ה׳.'' לָמָה? כִּי ,,נֵעוֹר מִמְּעוֹן קָדְשׁוֹ.''
אָמַר רַבִּי אַחָא, כַּהֲדָא תַּרְנְגוֹלְתָּא דִמְנַעֲרָה אֲגַפָּה מִן קִיטְמָא
(בראשית רבה עה:א).

Hashem told [David:] Even if you petition Me to rise many times, I will not arise. And to awaken Me, you shall not succeed, as long as Jerusalem wallows in mud. When indeed will I arise? When the words of the prophet, 'Shake off your dust, come and sit up, O Jerusalem' (Yeshayahu 52:2), will be fulfilled. At that time all living flesh will be silent before the Almighty. Why? For He will have arisen from His holy dwelling place.

R' Acha said: This resembles a fowl shaking itself free of dust (Bereishis Rabbah 75:1).

This Midrash gives us an insight into the concept of גָּלוּת הַשְּׁכִינָה. As long as the 'fowl', a metaphor for the *Shechinah*, is covered with dust and grime, we can only have a limited perception of it. It is only after the 'fowl' has divested itself of its mantle of concealment that we can perceive its true nature to the best of our understanding.

But what 'dust and grime' are alluded to in the universal sense of the Midrash? This layer of dust refers to what we call 'nature,' the seemingly normal and self-contained chain of cause-and-effect that appears to us to be the ruling force of the universe. It is this layer of nature that obscures and conceals the Divine Presence, making it all but imperceptible. Only after this layer will be shaken off completely will the Divine Presence be truly revealed to us.

This explains why Yaakov had to refute all rational explanations for not burying Rachel with due honor. For so long as there remains a semblance of a rational explanation, implausible as it may be, to that extent one does not truly discern the Divine command. Only after Yaakov had totally refuted every conceivable explanation could the Divine command become apparent. Indeed, Rachel was to be buried at the roadside, so that almost a millennium later, when Nevuzaradan would exile her children, they would pass her gravesite and she would intercede for them on High (*Rashi* ibid.).

Moreover, even an event as overwhelming and as powerfully persuasive as the Divine Revelation at Sinai had to be preceded by the silencing of all other forces of the universe:

אָמַר רַבִּי אַבָּהוּ בְּשֵׁם ר' יוֹחָנָן: כְּשֶׁנָּתַן הַקָּדוֹשׁ בָּרוּךְ הוּא אֶת הַתּוֹרָה, צִפּוֹר לֹא צָוַח, עוֹף לֹא פָּרַח, שׁוֹר לֹא גָּעָה, אוֹפַנִּים לֹא עָפוּ, שְׂרָפִים לֹא אָמְרוּ קָדוֹשׁ, הַיָּם לֹא נִזְדַּעְזֵעַ, הַבְּרִיּוֹת לֹא דִּבְּרוּ. אֶלָּא הָעוֹלָם שׁוֹתֵק וּמַחֲרִישׁ, וְיָצָא הַקּוֹל, אָנֹכִי ה' אֱלֹקֶיךָ (שמות רבה כט).

R' Avahu said in the name of R' Yochanan: When the Holy One gave the Torah, no bird twittered, no fowl flew, no ox bellowed, no angels flew, no seraphim proclaimed "Holy," the sea did not move, the creatures did not speak. Rather the whole world was in total silence. And then the voice proclaimed, "I am Hashem your God" (Shemos Rabbah 29).

Although all phenomena of nature are testimonies to Hashem's omnipotence, yet as far as the full Revelation of the Divine is concerned they are but obstructions. True, the ox with its bellow and the bird with its twitter acclaim the wonders of Creation. The ocean roars with the "voice of Hashem upon the waters" (*Tehillim* 29:3), and the angels and the *seraphim* proclaim God's glory. However, for the full import of the proclamation "I am Hashem your God" to totally permeate the being of all those present, this entire symphony had to fall silent.

The Midrash continues:

וְאִם תָּמֵהַּ אַתָּה עַל זוֹ הֲרֵי אֵלִיָּהוּ כְּשֶׁבָּא לְכַרְמֶל כָּנַס כָּל הַכּוֹמְרִים וְאָמַר לָהֶם קִרְאוּ בְּקוֹל גָּדוֹל כִּי אֱלֹהִים הוּא מֶה עָשָׂה הַקָּדוֹשׁ בָּרוּךְ הוּא הִדְמִים כָּל הָעוֹלָם וְהִשְׁתִּיק הָעֶלְיוֹנִים וְהַתַּחְתּוֹנִים וְהָיָה הָעוֹלָם תֹּהוּ וָבֹהוּ כְּאִלּוּ לֹא הָיָה בְּרִיָּה בָּעוֹלָם שֶׁנֶּאֱמַר אֵין קוֹל וְאֵין עוֹנֶה שֶׁאִם עוֹנֶה הֵם אוֹמְרִים הַבַּעַל עֲנָנוּ. *Perhaps you will wonder at this [need to silence the universe in order to present the Revelation]. Do not wonder, because we also find that Eliyahu Hanavi at Mount Carmel told the priests of the Baal, "Call out in a great voice, and let Him answer you!" What did Hashem do? He silenced the entire universe, quieting those above and below, the world appearing as desolate as before Creation, as it says, "There was no sound" (I Melachim 18:26). For had there not been total silence, the false prophets would have insisted, "It is the Baal who has answered us."*

In order to prove beyond all doubt that it is Hashem who is Lord of the universe, every possible voice had to be stilled, even those above, and yet *Eliyahu* still had to plead:

עֲנֵנִי ה' עֲנֵנִי (מלכים א' יח:לז).
עֲנֵנִי — שֶׁתֵּרֵד אֵשׁ מִן הַשָּׁמַיִם
עֲנֵנִי — שֶׁלֹּא יֹאמְרוּ מַעֲשֵׂה כְשָׁפִים הֵם (ברכות ט:ע"ב).

Answer me, Hashem, answer me (I Melachim 18:37).
Answer me — by sending down fire
Answer me — that people will not attribute it to sorcery
(Berachos 9b).

Thus even though every force in the universe had been silenced, there still existed a possibility that people would believe that the entire episode was merely the work of sorcery. So great is man's ability to disregard Divine Revelation!

This understanding of the mechanism of rationalization inherent in man will give us an understanding of the criteria for those miracles selected to be described in *Tanach* and those relegated to תּוֹרָה שֶׁבְּעַל פֶּה, the *Oral Torah*.

Ibn Ezra calculates that, according to the Oral Tradition, Yocheved was a hundred and thirty years old when she gave birth to Moshe. If so, he asks, why is this not mentioned in the Torah? Does this miracle not surpass the miracle of Sarah's bearing a child at the age of ninety?

Ramban responds, "Only those miracles that had been announced in advance by an angel or a prophet are recorded in the written Torah." The reason for this is that those miracles that were not foretold contain the semblance of fitting into some natural context of cause-and-effect. Only when people are clearly informed beforehand of the coming miracle does the subsequent event stand out as an act of Providence. Therefore only Sarah's childbearing — having been foretold — became a part of the written Torah.

We too witnessed Divine Providence when the Mirrer Yeshiva was saved from the Holocaust by a series of extraordinary 'coincidences' that culminated in the escape to Shanghai. But because each separate incident was attributable to some 'natural' cause with a rational explanation, a clear perception of the Divine Revelation was blurred. Similarly, during the Six Day War there were countless miracles, yet so skillfully did God interweave them with the 'normal' military process that, unfortunately, they did not produce a lasting effect.

II.

Why is this so? Why does Divine Providence present itself in this manner, blending miracles in the natural process, making the "hand of Hashem" all but imperceptible? Why "envelop the fowl in dust," beclouding all clear observation of it?

The answer to this question is to be found in the necessity to enable man to enjoy freedom of choice. If man wishes he can discern the "hand of God" in the innermost recesses of the most natural event and on the other hand he can disregard it in the most blatant of circumstances.

Moreover, we too are enjoined to assist in this process. *Chinuch* (*Mitzvah* 132) explains this to be the rationale for the *mitzvah* to constantly keep a flame burning on the Altar:

> For it serves to disguise the fire from Heaven that was always on the Altar. It is known that the miracles that God in His mercy bestowed upon His people are usually hidden, appearing as natural or quasi-natural phenomena. Even as great a miracle as the Splitting of the Sea contained the natural element of "Hashem moved the seas with a strong eastern wind all night" (Chinuch 132).

Fortunate is the person who applies himself to hear the voice of God while the Divine Presence is still "enveloped in dust." For the voice of God is constantly ringing out, awaiting the attentive and receptive ear, until the day comes that: וְנִגְלָה כְּבוֹד ה׳ וְרָאוּ כָל בָּשָׂר יַחְדָּו כִּי פִּי ה׳ דִּבֵּר, *The glory of Hashem shall be revealed and all flesh together shall see that the mouth of Hashem has spoken* (*Yeshayahu* 40:5).

אֲשֶׁר הַחַיִּים

The Joy Inherent in Life Itself

No prayer or hope lies closer to the Jewish heart than the desire for life. Yet with all our yearnings and quest for life, we are often ignorant of the true meaning of life, grasping its peripheral aspects but remaining oblivious to its essence. We visualize life as but a means for joy and pleasure — as merely the medium through which to experience these fulfillments. We talk about things 'worth living for,' yet, in our superficial view of life we fail to appreciate the most profound joy of all: life itself.

Let us take a look at life from the perspective of our Sages and we shall see how it is to be evaluated and what constitutes its true essence.

הָבָה נִתְחַכְּמָה לוֹ (שמות א:י).

ג׳ הָיוּ בְאוֹתָהּ עֵצָה, בִּלְעָם יָעַץ, אִיּוֹב שָׁתַק וְיִתְרוֹ בָּרַח. בִּלְעָם שֶׁיָּעַץ נֶהֱרַג בַּחֶרֶב. אִיּוֹב שֶׁשָּׁתַק נִדּוֹן בְּיִסּוּרִים. יִתְרוֹ שֶׁבָּרַח זָכָה וּבָנָיו יָשְׁבוּ בְּלִשְׁכַּת הַגָּזִית (ילקוט שמעוני שם).

Let us outsmart them (Shemos 1:10).

Three people were involved in this plan. Bilaam advised, Iyov remained silent, and Yisro fled. Bilaam's punishment was that he was killed in battle. Iyov was punished with pain and suffering for his silence, while

> *Yisro who fled [in protest] merited having sons who sat in the lishkas hagazis [seat of the Sanhedrin]* (Yalkut Shimoni ibid.).

To our sense of justice this verdict appears incongruous. Why was Bilaam, the evil protagonist, given a swift and merciful death, while Iyov, guilty of only silence, was afflicted with every pain and torment? The very name Iyov has become the synonym for suffering!

The answer is that it is our shallow understanding of the value of life that does not allow us to understand Hashem's verdict. We have no appreciation of life's true essence. Were our eyes to be opened, we would see that Iyov's punishment was by far the easier of the two. True, he suffered greatly, but he lived. Bilaam was spared suffering, but put to death. Better a thousand times pain than the 'merciful' death of Bilaam.

This is, perhaps, best reflected in David HaMelech's cry, יַסֹּר יִסְּרַנִּי הּ׳ וְלַמָּוֶת לֹא נְתָנָנִי, *Hashem has caused me to suffer terribly, but He has not given me over to death* (Tehillim 118:18). King David is able to reflect on a life filled with pain and sorrow and put it into proper perspective regarding the gift of life itself.

In order to gauge one's own appreciation of life, one must observe in what perspective one places his own problems and troubles. Just as a person who has just received or won a great fortune does not feel a small loss, so, too, a person in full cognizance of the tremendous gift that is his, i.e., life, is oblivious to the relatively unimportant travails that he must undergo. Against the background of the fabulous gift of life, even the tribulations of Iyov are unimportant. Thus, the verse exclaims, מַה יִּתְאוֹנֵן אָדָם חָי, *Of what can a living man complain* (Eichah 3:39).

Rashi explains: How can a man complain of misfortunes befalling him, after I have bestowed life upon him?

As with other gifts that the Creator bestows upon humanity, the gift of life, too, is only granted to those who appreciate it. Even our father Yaakov — who was pursued by Esav and Lavan, who was humiliated by the affair of Dinah and who suffered twenty-two years of anguish over Yosef's disappearance — was punished for complaining about his travails. When Pharaoh asked Yaakov his age, he replied: . . . . מְעַט וְרָעִים הָיוּ יְמֵי שְׁנֵי חַיַּי, *Few and harsh have been my years* (Bereishis 47:9). *Chazal* tell us that for each word of complaint uttered, he lost a year of life, thirty-three in number. The gift of life is for those appreciating it; those slighting it, or complaining about it, lose it.

Furthermore, if we take a closer look at the conversation and count the 'thirty-three words' we realize that Pharaoh's question about his age is included in the punishment. Why? The reason must be that Pharaoh's question was not asked out of mere politeness; it was prompted by Yaakov's appearance. In the creases and folds of Yaakov's face one could read of a lifetime filled with anguish and suffering. Taken aback, he was prompted to ask, "How many years have you lived?" Not only was it expected of our father Yaakov that his words describe the true appreciation of life, but even his appearance and bearing was expected to portray the radiance of a man endowed with God's greatest gift (see *Daas Zekeinim*).

The *piyut* recited on *Shavuos* also points out this so-called shortcoming of Yaakov. The *piyut* explains, briefly, why the Torah was given only through Moshe and not through any of his illustrious predecessors. Avraham and Yitzchak had their respective faults while Yaakov's shortcoming is described as "not having been tranquil." This lack of tranquillity is meant to describe the absence of appreciation mentioned in the Midrash above.

Having shown the importance of properly evaluating the gift of life, we are left with the question, "What indeed is this joy of life?" or stronger yet, "What is the essence of life and what does it mean to be alive?" Let us touch upon two points that lie close to the core of that which is called life.

Chazal teach us that all the pleasures of this world are naught compared to a moment's delight in the World-to-Come. It has been noted that not only is a moment of the next world more pleasurable than all of this world's joys, but even a mere sniff of its fragrance is superior to anything this world can offer. Yet *Chazal* conclude:

יָפָה שָׁעָה אַחַת בִּתְשׁוּבָה וּמַעֲשִׂים טוֹבִים בָּעוֹלָם הַזֶּה מִכֹּל חַיֵּי הָעוֹלָם הַבָּא (אבות ד:ז).

Far better an hour of repentance and good deeds in this world than a lifetime in the World-to-Come (Pirkei Avos 4:22).

How are we to understand this?

The explanation is that the pleasure of the World-to-Come consists of the closeness to Hashem that one has attained in this world during his life. True, the enjoyment is infinite but its scope is limited to that which one has achieved during his lifetime. Thus it is our humble existence in this world which carries in it the potential for infinite closeness to Hashem. True, this relationship is often clouded and not easily perceived but it is there. The full realization and awareness thereof is to be had in the World-to-Come, but it is here that the potential of such achievement is unlimited.

This is the understanding of the well-known story of the Vilna Gaon's weeping on his death bed. Those with him asked him the reason for his tears. He held his *tzitzis* in his hand and replied, "I am leaving a world where for but a few pennies one can perform such wonderful *mitzvos*, while in the World-to-Come the opportunity no longer exists."

A second facet of life worth pondering is that it affords the possibility for man to relate to his fellow human being, share his joy, help shoulder his sorrow and most of all this world affords one the opportunity to give of one's self to one's fellow man.

The Midrash bears out this point. *Chazal* tell us that the wife of R' Shimon ben Chalafta had an argument with Rabbeinu HaKadosh about the propriety of accepting a heavenly gift. Rabbeinu HaKadosh assured her, "If you will be missing anything in the World-to-Come, I will replace it with my own." To which she replied, "Will you then see me in the World-to-Come? Does not each *tzaddik* dwell in his own world?" (*Shemos Rabbah* 52:3). Thus we see that as magnificent as the World-to-Come is, it is a place where in contrast to this world, man resides alone!

Do not belittle this wonderful gift of relating to another person. Adam lived in *Gan Eden*, untainted by sin and administered by angels, yet it was of him that Hashem declared, "It is not good for man to be alone!"

The *Kuntres Hasfekos* in the introduction to his *sefer* quotes the *Ri Muskato*: "Even if a person was to ascend the heavens and observe all the beauty and wonders thereof, he would not be happy unless he could share his observations with someone else." This necessity to share one's life with others is not a derivative of human limitation but rather the hallmark of its greatness.

יֵשׁ קוֹנֶה עוֹלָמוֹ בְּשָׁעָה אֶחָת

Immortalizing the Fleeting Moment

I.

וַיְדַבֵּר ה' אֶל מֹשֶׁה וְאֶל אַהֲרֹן וַיְצַוֵּם אֶל בְּנֵי יִשְׂרָאֵל וְאֶל פַּרְעֹה מֶלֶךְ מִצְרָיִם לְהוֹצִיא אֶת בְּנֵי יִשְׂרָאֵל מֵאֶרֶץ מִצְרָיִם (שמות ו:יג).
And Hashem spoke to Moshe and to Aharon and commanded them to the Children of Israel and to Pharaoh King of Egypt to redeem the Children of Israel from Egypt (Shemos 6:13).

אָמַר רַבִּי שְׁמוּאֵל בַּר יִצְחָק עַל מַה צִנָּם? עַל פָּרָשַׁת שִׁלּוּחַ עֲבָדִים צִנָּם (ירושלמי ר"ה פ' ג:ה)
R' Shmuel bar Yitzchok said: What did He command them? About the laws of setting free one's slaves (Yerushalmi Rosh HaShanah 3:5).

Why did Hashem feel it necessary to command Israel with this specific *mitzvah* at this particular time?

The *Gemara* relates that before doing *teshuvah*, R' Elazar ben Dordia consorted with every loose woman in the world. The cause of his repentance was a chance remark by a woman with whom he was engaged in sin, to the effect that he, Elazar, was incapable of repentance. Her words had such a powerful effect on him that he sat down on a mountain ... and wept until he died. A Heavenly voice proclaimed, "R' Elazar has entered *olam haba*, the World-to-Come." When Rebbi heard this, he began crying and remarked, "There are some who acquire their share of *olam haba* in but a moment!"

Why did Rebbi cry? Should his reaction not have been one of joy that R' Elazar had raised himself out of such degrading and debasing circumstances to the extent that he instantly acquired a share in the World-to-Come? The answer is that Rebbi did not weep for R' Elazar's sake, but rather for all of humanity. When he was told the story of R' Elazar, he realized that each one of us, too, experiences a moment of such import that is capable of changing one's entire life. Yet only one out of a thousand in fact utilize this moment. If every person does indeed have such a moment in his life, why do so few make use of it? This is why Rebbi cried.

When the Jewish people left Egypt the whole earth was shaken. "The princes of Edom fell into disarray, the powerful ones of Moab were overtaken by trembling and the inhabitants of Canaan melted" (*Shemos* 15:15). But what followed? Edom pulled themselves together, continuing their murderous ways. Moab calmed themselves and returned to their idolatry, while Canaan carried on with their perversions. Only one man, Yisro, succeeded in transforming this powerful impression into a change in his way of life. *And Yisro heard* — "What did he hear? He heard about the splitting of the sea, and about the war with Amalek" (*Rashi*). Many *heard*; but only he *listened*.

However, besides the change one must effect at the time of the initial impact, it is even more important to find some way of keeping alive those original feelings even many years. *Chazal* tell us that Palti ben Layish, the son-in-law-to-be of Shaul, was even saintlier than Boaz because Boaz had to restrain himself but one night, when Ruth came to the granary. Palti, on the other hand, was given Shaul's daughter as a wife after she had been betrothed to David. While Shaul thought the betrothal to be null and void, Palti knew otherwise. Though ostensibly they lived together, he refrained from any marital relations with her. When Palti was first forced to 'marry' her he had a moment of great resolve and decided that he would not live with her. How was he able to control himself for so long afterwards? *Chazal* tell us that he stuck a sword between his bed and hers and declared, "Whoever crosses this line deserves death!" But what power rests in a lifeless sword against someone caught up in the heat of passion? What prevents him from brushing aside the sword or ignoring it entirely?

The answer lies in the understanding that it is not the sword that prevents the sin. But the sword is a reminder of the previous resolve, forged in a moment of strength and holiness. The sword is but a testimonial that serves to evoke the previous powerful commitment.

This was the intention of Ezra HaSofer when he required women "to wear a *sinor* (special garment) for the sake of modesty" (*Bava Kamma* 82). *Rashi* explains that this was meant to serve as a deterrent to sin. The *sinor* did not act as a physical deterrent; rather it reawakened the feelings of modesty and reminded the wearer of the time she had committed herself to fidelity, and thus served to prevent her from sin.

This form of emotional reinforcement was revealed to us by God in the form of the rainbow. After the Flood, Hashem swore to never again destroy the world. As a token and reminder of this covenant He formed the rainbow in the sky. This was not meant as a reminder to Hashem, so to speak, but rather as a lesson to us, that no matter how strong or determined one's resolve, it is still necessary to design a reminder to evoke the original emotions when necessary.

II.

Until now we have described this concept of immortalizing those fleeting moments in a personal context and within the scope of but a single lifetime. However, we shall see that this concept embraces all of *Klal Yisrael* and spans the eternity of the Jewish people.

Israel was at the verge of its redemption. Moshe had already warned Pharaoh to free them and he would soon commence with the plan which would culminate in the deliverance of Israel. "And Hashem spoke to Moshe and to Aharon [*vayetzavem*] and commanded them to the Children of Israel." The *Yerushalmi* explains that Moshe was told to charge Israel with a specific *mitzvah:* the *mitzvah* of the mandatory freeing of slaves after a specified period (שִׁלּוּחַ עֲבָדִים). Why was it necessary to charge them at this very moment with this particular *mitzvah*, a *mitzvah* which would not even be applicable for almost half-a-century?

One must understand that it was extremely difficult to give up a slave when the owner perceived him as an intrinsic part of his estate. Although the slave suffers terribly under the yoke and bond of his enslavement, and yearns for freedom, it is difficult for the owner to identify and sympathize with him. The only way to convince an owner to free his slaves was by utilizing the emotions that the Jewish people felt on the day that they themselves gained their freedom. Thus, in the midst of their own realization of freedom they were commanded with the *mitzvah* of *shiluach avadim*.

This was meant not only to last the duration of their lifetimes but for the eternity of *Klal Yisrael*. Almost five hundred years later, the prophet Yirmiyahu rebuked them for transgressing a *mitzvah* which they had received at the time when they were set free. "Thus said Hashem, God of Israel: I have made a covenant with your forefathers on the day that I took them out of Egypt out of the house of bondage, saying: At the end of seven years, set free your brethren ... because you have not listened to Me, etc." (*Yirmiyahu* 34:13-14). It is precisely to give them a true understanding of this *mitzvah* that they received it at that particular time — hence the mention of the timing of the *mitzvah*, being an integral part of the commandment of the Jewish people. Had Hashem waited until the giving of the Torah to command them concerning this *mitzvah*, it would have been beyond their scope of understanding to grasp its essence.

The *Yerushalmi* says that R' Hilah uses this verse to prove that the central cause of Israel's suffering was because they neglected this *mitzvah*. The severity of their punishment was because the *mitzvah* had been given "on the day that I set your forefathers free." It was expected of them that they would have taken the force of their own emotions to endow this *mitzvah* with the necessary impetus to fulfill it. Having failed to do so they not only committed a sin; in addition, they had frittered away one of the most potentially inspiring moments in the history of *Klal Yisrael*. The way in which a person preserves the elevation attained at those rare moments of spiritual achievement and awareness is by constantly reminding oneself and reliving that moment by devices such as the sword of Palti ben Layish. The person who does so can acquire his share of *olam haba* in but a moment!

נְקָמָה

Vengeance

נָכוֹן כִּסְאֲךָ מֵאָז, מֵעוֹלָם אָתָּה (תהלים צג:ב).
Your throne is established from then, You are forever
(Tehillim 93:2).

אַף עַל פִּי שֶׁמֵּעוֹלָם אָתָּה לֹא נִתְיַשֵּׁב כִּסְאֲךָ וְלֹא נוֹדַעְתָּ בְּעוֹלָמְךָ
עַד שֶׁאָמְרוּ בָנֶיךָ שִׁירָה, לְכָךְ נֶאֱמַר נָכוֹן כִּסְאֲךָ מֵאָז (שמות רבה
כג:א)
*Although You are eternal, Your throne was not firmly
established, nor were You known in the world until
Your children sang [at the sea]. Thus, "Your throne is
established from then"* (Shemos Rabbah 23:1).

וַיִּקְרְבוּ יְמֵי דָוִד לָמוּת. וַיְצַו אֶת שְׁלֹמֹה בְנוֹ לֵאמֹר, אָנֹכִי הֹלֵךְ
בְּדֶרֶךְ כָּל הָאָרֶץ וגו'. וְשָׁמַרְתָּ אֶת מִשְׁמֶרֶת ה' אֱלֹקֶיךָ לָלֶכֶת
בִּדְרָכָיו לִשְׁמֹר חֻקֹּתָיו מִצְוֹתָיו וּמִשְׁפָּטָיו וגו'. וְהִנֵּה עִמְּךָ שִׁמְעִי בֶן
גֵּרָא בֶן הַיְמִינִי מִבַּחֻרִים , וְהוּא קִלְלַנִי קְלָלָה נִמְרֶצֶת בְּיוֹם לֶכְתִּי
מַחֲנָיִם. וְהוּא יָרַד לִקְרָאתִי הַיַּרְדֵּן וָאֶשָּׁבַע לוֹ בַה' לֵאמֹר אִם
אֲמִיתְךָ בֶּחָרֶב. וְעַתָּה אַל תְּנַקֵּהוּ כִּי אִישׁ חָכָם אָתָּה, וְיָדַעְתָּ אֵת
אֲשֶׁר תַּעֲשֶׂה לּוֹ וְהוֹרַדְתָּ אֶת שֵׂיבָתוֹ בְּדָם שְׁאוֹל (מלכים א
ב:א-ח).
*The days of David drew near to his death. And he
charged his son Shlomo saying, "I am going the way of
all the earth . . . keep the charge of the Lord your God to*

*walk in His ways, to keep His statutes, His command-
ments, and His judgments . . . And behold you have
with you Shimi ben Gaira of Bachurim the Benjaminite,
who cursed me with a grievous curse on the day when
I went to Machanaim. He came down to meet me at the
Jordan, where I swore to him in God's Name saying
that I would not kill him with the sword. Now, do not
leave him guiltless for you are a wise man and know
what you ought to do to him; to bring his hoary head to
a bloody death (I Melachim 2:1-8).*

This last testament of David to his son Shlomo is perplexing. Is it
appropriate for one's last will and testament to be one of a quest
for revenge? Does not even the basest of persons forgive his
adversaries on his deathbed? And how do we reconcile this final
request of David with the *Gemara* (*Bava Basra* 17a) which states that
David was free of his evil inclination? Moreover, this will of
David became a part of the Holy Scriptures, remaining a lesson to all
of us, to be studied and understood. How indeed do we understand
this?

Our amazement at David's words stems from the fact that we have
no notion of what נְקָמָה, *vengeance*, really is. We associate it with
simple and savage lashing back at adversaries — revenge. But נְקָמָה in
its real form is an act of spiritual character and essence. It is a
sentiment of the soul rather than a coarse reaction of the body. Thus
the prophet describes a vision, "I saw the Lord sitting on His throne,
and all the Hosts of Heaven stood upon Him at His right and at His
left. God asked, 'Who will lure Achav into going to battle and being
slain at the mountains of Gilead . . .' and the spirit went out and stood
before God and said, 'I will delude him' " (*I Melachim* 22:19-21).
Rashi, drawing on *Chazal*, explains that this was the spirit of Navos
who had been murdered by Achav and was now seeking revenge (see
Sanhedrin 102b and *Rashi*).

If a soul residing in a world that is only spiritual and has no
physical attributes, a soul which has no body and no evil inclination
can seek vengeance, then it must be that this trait is a product of the
spirit and not of the body. Indeed, it must be that vengeance is rooted
in an elevated and lofty world.

Chazal point out the unique status of נְקָמָה by saying, גְּדוֹלָה נְקָמָה

שֶׁנִּתְּנָה בֵּין שְׁתֵּי אוֹתִיּוֹת שֶׁנֶּאֱמַר קֵל נְקָמוֹת ה', *Great is vengeance which has been set between two names [of God], as it says, 'The Lord is the God of vengeance'* (Berachos 33a). What then is the essence of נְקָמָה? It is the manifestation and revelation of the enactment of justice in this world. Thus, true נְקָמָה can be an unparalleled כְּבוֹד שָׁמַיִם, showing that there is an ultimate judge, and that justice is eventually carried out. It must be noted, however, that although the purpose of נְקָמָה is to reveal the justice of God, the injured party is the one obligated to carry it out. Having been wronged, he is more keenly aware of the need for justice.

If this is the definition of נְקָמָה — the revelation of God's justice — then we can understand it to apply to reward as well. Thus, *Chazal* explain the repetition of the word נְקָמָה in the verse קֵל נְקָמוֹת ה', **נְקָמוֹת הוֹפִיעַ**, *Hashem is a God of vengeance, the God of vengeance had appeared*, as referring to both reward and punishment. Both are equal evidence to God's just rule over the world.

This dimension of נְקָמַת ה' is what makes קְרִיעַת יַם סוּף, *the splitting of the sea*, rank as one of the most preeminent revelations of Divine justice.

נָכוֹן כִּסְאֲךָ מֵאָז, מֵעוֹלָם אָתָּה (תהלים צג:ב).
Your throne is established from then, You are forever (Tehillim 93:2).

אַף עַל פִּי שֶׁמֵּעוֹלָם אָתָּה, לֹא נִתְיַשֵּׁב כִּסְאֲךָ וְלֹא נוֹדַעְתָּ בְּעוֹלָמֶךָ עַד שֶׁאָמְרוּ בָּנֶיךָ שִׁירָה, לְכָךְ נֶאֱמַר נָכוֹן כִּסְאֲךָ מֵאָז (שמות רבה כג:א).
Although You are eternal, yet Your throne was not firmly established nor were You known in the world before Your children sang [at the sea]. Thus, "Your throne is established from then" (Shemos Rabbah 23:1).

Hashem himself is eternal and no change occurs in Him. Rather, His manifestation in the world as ruler and judge was concealed until Israel sang at the sea, perceiving God's נְקָמָה — the just retribution exacted from the Egyptians. This perception of נְקָמָה as a means of furthering כְּבוֹד שָׁמַיִם gives us insight into the extraordinary reward bestowed upon Pinchas when he took God's revenge on Zimri, a prince of the Tribe of Shimon, for publicly committing adultery with a pagan woman. *Sforno* explains that בְּרִיתִי שָׁלוֹם, *the covenant of peace*, assured to Pinchas, means peace from the angel of death himself and this is what accounted for Pinchas' extraordinary longevity, all this in reward for being נוֹקֵם נִקְמַת ה׳ — for showing God's justice in this world.

This, then, is נְקָמָה as understood by *Chazal*. It is the revelation of God as judge and executor of justice. It is an intrinsic part of the world of the spirit making Navos and David willing messengers to carry out the requisite נְקָמָה; not as a private act of vendetta, which has no place in the Heavens, but rather to show the world that the wicked are eventually punished for their wrongdoings.

We can similarly understand the נְקָמָה which is mentioned in association with our father Yaakov's burial. *Chazal* relate that when Yaakov was brought to his grave in the Cave of Machpelah in Chevron, his wicked brother Esav interfered and refused to allow him to be buried. Chushim, the son of Dan, then decapitated Esav whereupon Yaakov opened his eyes and smiled. *Chazal* quote: יִשְׂמַח צַדִּיק כִּי חָזָה נָקָם — *the righteous man rejoices for he has witnessed revenge* (see *Sotah* 13a).

Certainly Yaakov had no satisfaction after his death in personal vengeance. Rather, it was the joy of seeing justice triumph in this world that caused him such satisfaction.

But there is one condition to be met before one can assume the role of exacter of נְקָמָה. The Torah says, וַיַּרְא פִּינְחָס בֶּן אֶלְעָזָר בֶּן אַהֲרֹן הַכֹּהֵן וַיָּקָם מִתּוֹךְ הָעֵדָה וַיִּקַּח רֹמַח בְּיָדוֹ — *Pinchas the son of Elazar son of Aharon the priest saw, and he arose from the community, and he took a spear in his hand* (Bamidbar 25:7).

It is difficult to understand why the Torah had to list Pinchas' ancestors. The reason which *Rashi* gives for the listing of the pedigree *after* he killed Zimri [see *Rashi* in *Parashas Pinchas*] does not explain why the Torah also mentions it prior to telling of his actions.

The answer is that the sole motive, for which נְקָמָה is allowed, is to allow the manifestation of Divine retribution. If the motivations for revenge include any aspects of self-interest such as a desire for personal vengeance, one may very well be considered to be a murderer. This is possibly the reason why a person out to kill a בּוֹעֵל אֲרַמִּית, *one who sins with a gentile woman*, will not be so instructed if he were to ask a *beis din* for permission [הֲלָכָה וְאֵין מוֹרִין כֵּן]. The reason for this may be that *beis din* is never capable of divining a person's motives and therefore cannot tell him to perpetrate נְקָמָה.

נְקָמָה must be an act done solely for motives of קִנְאַת ה׳ צְבָאוֹת, *the revenge for the desecration of Hashem's Name*. This is the reason that the Torah mentions Pinchas' ancestors. Pinchas was the descendent of Aharon the High Priest, the אוֹהֵב שָׁלוֹם וְרוֹדֵף שָׁלוֹם, *the one who loved peace and actively pursued it*. The Torah wished to stress that it was a member of that peace-loving family that undertook this act of vengeance for God's Name. Not blood-thirsty violence but an act of love for the sake of Israel, an act of קִדּוּשׁ הַשֵּׁם, *the sanctification of God's Name*. This motive alone sanctions נְקָמָה.

כְּאִישׁ אֶחָד בְּלֵב אֶחָד

With One Heart

וַיִּחַן שָׁם יִשְׂרָאֵל נֶגֶד הָהָר (שמות יט:ב)

וַיִּחַן — כְּאִישׁ אֶחָד בְּלֵב אֶחָד (רש"י שם).

And Israel encamped there before the mountain (Shemos 19:2).

And Israel encamped — [the singular form denotes that they were united] as one man, with one heart (Rashi).

Torah was not given to the individual. Not even to six hundred thousand individuals. Torah was given only to a single unified nation; their being of one heart transformed six hundred thousand individuals into one entity.

הוֹאִיל וְשָׂנְאוּ יִשְׂרָאֵל אֶת הַמַּחְלֹקֶת וְאָהֲבוּ אֶת הַשָּׁלוֹם וְנַעֲשׂוּ חֲנָיָה אַחַת הֲרֵי הַשָּׁעָה שֶׁאֶתֵּן לָהֶם אֶת תּוֹרָתִי (דרך ארץ זוטא פרק השלום).

Since Israel rejected strife and embraced harmony, dwelling as one, the time is ripe for Me to give them the Torah (Derech Eretz Zuta 11).

This saying of our Sages lends an insight into the fact that קַבָּלַת הַתּוֹרָה, *the receiving of the Torah*, was not realized in its fullest sense until almost a millennium later — during the spiritual renaissance that accompanied the events of *Purim* (see *Shabbos* 88a).

Chazal portray the קַבָּלַת הַתּוֹרָה of Sinai as involuntary and the הָדַר קִבְּלוּהָ, the reacceptance of Torah, on *Purim* as being with alacrity — indicating that the re-acceptance of Torah on *Purim* was of a more profound nature. What brought about this deepened commitment?

The solution is to be found in the fact that the Jewish people at the time of *Purim* were totally united. Haman's decree of genocide — "to massacre, kill and destroy all the Jews" — united the Jewish people as never before. In times of danger, petty quarrels and personal grudges disappear and people focus their concerns on the welfare of the community, not on their personal differences. Therefore, the events of *Purim* led to a kind of genuine unity and hence Israel was able to receive the Torah in its deepest and fullest sense.

With this we can understand the statement of *Arizal* that *Yom Kippur* is "יוֹם כְּפּוּרִים," a day comparable to *Purim*, with the implication that *Purim* is the greater of the two.

Yom Kippur is a day when people cleanse themselves so that they are akin to angels; rising above the human shortcomings of hatred, jealousy and animosity. But *Purim* brings people together through charity, joy and festivity, and therefore surpasses *Yom Kippur* in its ability to unify the community of Israel. It is in this sense that *Purim* overshadows even *Yom Kippur*.

A closer look at *Rashi* reveals that it is not the term אַחְדוּת, *unity*, that is employed but rather the term בְּלֵב אֶחָד, *with one heart*. The term "with one heart" underscores the fact that outward unity is not enough. It was neither the concrete act nor the outward expression that was the prerequisite to the giving of the Torah. It was rather the deep-seated love for one's fellow from a heart cleansed of hatred and ill will that produced the oneness of heart.

The obligation to love and respect one's fellow even in one's heart finds expression in the injunction against enslaving a Jewish servant בַּעֲבוֹדַת פֶּרֶךְ, *with unnecessary labor*.

Rashi explains this עֲבוֹדַת פֶּרֶךְ as follows:

אַל תֹּאמַר לוֹ הָחֵם לִי אֶת הַכּוֹס הַזֶּה וְהוּא אֵינוֹ צָרִיךְ ... שֶׁמָּא תֹּאמַר אֵין מַכִּיר בַּדָּבָר אִם לְצֹרֶךְ אִם לַאו וְאוֹמֵר אֲנִי לוֹ שֶׁהוּא לְצֹרֶךְ הֲרֵי הַדָּבָר הַזֶּה מָסוּר לַלֵּב לְכָךְ נֶאֱמַר וְיָרֵאתָ מֵאֱלֹקֶיךָ (ויקרא כה:מג).

Do not tell [your Jewish servant], 'Warm a drink for

me,' when in fact you do not need it ... perhaps, you will think, 'No one knows whether or not I need it, so I will tell him that I do indeed need it.' This is entrusted to the [master's] heart [and I, Hashem, know what is in the heart]. Therefore [the Torah] declares, 'and you shall fear your God' (Vayikra 25:43).

עֲבוֹדַת פֶּרֶךְ is defined here not as hard labor, but rather as extraneous and futile work. This type of work is degrading and demeaning to the servant. Yet even if the servant feels that his task is necessary — as *Rashi* says, "I will tell him that I need it" — one is prohibited from requesting it of him. The reason is that one is bidden to honor and respect one's fellow even in one's heart. The master is aware of the futility of the task involved and in his mind the servant loses stature. The essence of loving and respecting one's fellow human being is to show him respect and affection not only in deed but in thought as well.

This principle that the level of acceptance of the Torah is in direct proportion to the harmony among the Jewish people will shed a new light on a comparison by *Chazal* of various generations.

שֶׁקֶר הַחֵן — זֶה דוֹרוֹ שֶׁל מֹשֶׁה וִיהוֹשֻׁעַ; וְהֶבֶל הַיֹּפִי — זֶה דוֹרוֹ שֶׁל חִזְקִיָּה; יִרְאַת ה' הִיא תִתְהַלָּל — זֶה דוֹרוֹ שֶׁל ר' יְהוּדָה בְּרַבִּי אִילָעִי ... שֶׁהָיוּ שִׁשָּׁה תַלְמִידִים מִתְכַּסִּין בְּטַלִּית אַחַת וְעוֹסְקִין בַּתּוֹרָה (סנהדרין כ:ע"א).

False is charm — refers to the generation of Moshe and Yehoshua; vain is beauty — refers to the generation of Chizkiyahu; a God-fearing [woman] is praiseworthy — refers to the generation of R' Yehudah bar Ilai ... when six students would cover themselves with one blanket (Sanhedrin 20a).

Rashi explains this as pointing out the exemplary sacrifice for the sake of Torah by the generation of R' Yehudah bar Ilai. It lends itself, however, to another explanation.

Let us ask ourselves: If six people cover themselves with one blanket, can any one of them stay warm? The answer is that if each one pulls the blanket to himself, no one will be covered. But if each one pushes the blanket to his fellow, to ensure that his friend is sufficiently covered, then all six of them will be warm.

Chazal mean to emphasize this specific characteristic of concern for one's fellow. It is this single-minded devotion to the welfare of one's fellow, the true בְּלֵב אֶחָד, that resulted in a generation singular in its scholarly attainments. The generation of Moshe stood at Sinai and witnessed Divine revelation. Yet this was false charm relative to the later generation. Chizkiyahu imbued Israel with a spirit of scholarship so powerful that every man and child knew the most difficult laws of ritual purity. This, too, comparitively speaking, was but empty beauty. It was R' Yehudah bar Ilai's disciples, who lived with such deep-seated unity and cared so much for each other, that was singled out as the God-fearing generation which alone is praiseworthy.

It was their בְּלֵב אֶחָד that allowed them to receive Torah at its highest level.

שְׁלֵמוּת הַמַּעֲשֶׂה

The Complete Mitzvah

אִם כֶּסֶף תַּלְוֶה אֶת עַמִּי אֶת הֶעָנִי עִמָּךְ, לֹא תִהְיֶה לוֹ כְּנֹשֶׁה, לֹא
תְשִׂימוּן עָלָיו נֶשֶׁךְ (שמות כב:כד).

*When you lend money to My people, to the poor that be
with you, do not be to him as a demanding creditor, nor
shall you place any interest upon him (Shemos 22:24).*

Chazal, when expounding on this verse, detailed the various
nuances of kindness that ought to accompany the act of lending
money.

אֶת עַמִּי – לֹא תִנְהַג בּוֹ מִנְהַג בִּזָּיוֹן בְּהַלְוָאָה שֶׁהוּא עַמִּי
*My people — Do not treat him contemptibly in the act
of lending for he is My people.*

אֶת הֶעָנִי עִמָּךְ – הֱוֵי מִסְתַּכֵּל בְּעַצְמְךָ כְּאִלּוּ אַתָּה עָנִי
*The poor that be with you — Imagine yourself to be the
poor man.*

לֹא תִהְיֶה לוֹ כְּנֹשֶׁה – לֹא תִתְבָּעֶנּוּ בְּחָזְקָה אִם אַתָּה יוֹדֵעַ שֶׁאֵין
לוֹ
*Do not be to him as a demanding creditor — Do not
press him for payment if you know that he does not
have (Rashi ibid.).*

All of these directives are intended to shape the act of kindness to be as perfect and as thorough as possible. The lender must perceive the feelings of the borrower and his need for help and comprehend his situation. Yet, even someone who has fulfilled all of these requirements is, in addition, faced with the sternest admonition: לֹא תְשִׂימוּן עָלָיו נֶשֶׁךְ, *You shall not place upon him interest* (*Shemos* 22:24), a prohibition of unusual severity. Yechezkel, when castigating the usurers declares, וָחָי לֹא יִחְיֶה, *He will not live* (*Yechezkel* 18:13), an unusual punishment for a לֹא תַעֲשֶׂה, *a negative commandment*. It would seem that this is not a punishment in the normal sense of the word; rather it is an evaluation that the usurer is unworthy of life. *Chazal* add that he has neither life in this world nor in the World-to-Come (*Shemos Rabbah* 31:13). Why such a severe judgment? Did the lender not act in true kindness fulfilling every nuance and detail prescribed by the Torah and *Chazal*? Did he not treat the borrower with dignity, and show him that he is indebted to his cause, and express his deepest sympathy?

The answer is that the quality of a *mitzvah* is evaluated not only in terms of form, but any accompanying motive such as self-gratification can corrupt the noblest deed. A person who has performed a *mitzvah* perfectly, unswervingly, adhering to the letter of the law, yet did not fulfill the *mitzvah* solely for its own sake, has fallen far short of what is demanded of him. Not being able to do an act of kindness without deriving some personal benefit (e.g., receiving interest) has made that person unworthy of the gift of life.

This idea is reinforced by Yechezkel's usage of the term תַּרְבִּית to denote usury. The word usury is expressed in the Torah by two terms: נֶשֶׁךְ (lit. biting), representing the cost to the borrower, and תַּרְבִּית (lit. increase), representing the gain of the lender (see *Bava Metzia* 60b). The Torah does not fault the lender only for the loss of the borrower. Rather the desire for profit or personal gain, even when doing an act of kindness, indicates that the lender is incapable of fulfilling the *mitzvah* of lending for its own sake.

This demand for the authentic performance of a *mitzvah* is that which distinguishes the Jew's fulfillment of *mitzvos* from that of the non-Jew. *Chazal* determined: וְחֶסֶד לְאֻמִּים חַטָּאת – כָּל צְדָקָה שֶׁעַכּוּ''ם עוֹשִׂין חֵטְא הוּא לָהֶן, שֶׁאֵין עוֹשִׂין אֶלָּא לְהִתְגַּדֵּל בּוֹ, *The kindness of [the other] nations is sin — all the charity and kindness that the nations of the world perform is counted as sin because they do it only to aggrandize themselves* (*Bava Basra* 10b). Nothing lacks in their acts of kindness per se, but it is their motives which are objectionable. Using an act of charity for one's own egoistic pleasure transforms the *mitzvah* into an *aveirah*; it would be far better not to have done it at all. On the other hand, a Jew who performs an act of charity in order to gain merit for a sick child is deemed as righteous, for in his innermost heart his act is performed for philanthropic reasons only (*Bava Basra* ibid. and *Rashi* thereon).

This injunction against using a *mitzvah* for personal pleasure refers not only to an act of kindness but to other Divine pursuits as well. Thus the Torah tells us of Nadav and Avihu the sons of Aharon HaKohen: וְאֶל אֲצִילֵי בְּנֵי יִשְׂרָאֵל לֹא שָׁלַח יָדוֹ וַיֶּחֱזוּ אֶת הָאֱלֹקִים וַיֹּאכְלוּ וַיִּשְׁתּוּ, *[Hashem] did not punish the nobles of the Children of Israel, [though] they beheld Hashem and they ate and drank* (*Shemos* 24:11). *Rashi* explains that Nadav and Avihu deserved punishment, and actually died later, for having eaten and imbibed while beholding the Divine Presence. The food and drink mentioned here does not refer to nourishment in the physical sense, but rather to the pleasure of beholding and understanding that which was Divine (see *Targum Onkelos*). Nadav and Avihu had gained a perception of the *Shechinah* which few people had ever attained — but then allowed themselves to relish it. For this they were later punished. Not so Moshe Rabbeinu, about whom it is written: לֹא כֵן עַבְדִּי מֹשֶׁה בְּכָל בֵּיתִי נֶאֱמָן הוּא, *Not so My servant Moshe, the trusted one in all My house* (*Bamidbar* 12:7).

Moshe is described as the embodiment of the true servant, for a true servant takes nothing for himself; all is for the benefit of the master. Moshe, who perceived and comprehended all that a human being could, and certainly 'beheld Hashem,' did not use that understanding for his intellectual enjoyment. It was done totally לִשְׁמָה, *for the sake of serving Hashem*.

It is in this context that we can understand a story about the Vilna Gaon who one *Succos* did not have an *esrog*. The owner of the only available *esrog* agreed to sell it to him on condition that the reward for the Gaon's *mitzvah* be credited to the seller. Hearing this, the Gaon became filled with joy and immediately agreed. When asked as to the cause of his joy, he replied, "All my life I've looked forward to being able to fulfill the *Mishnah*, הֱווּ כַּעֲבָדִים הַמְשַׁמְּשִׁין אֶת הָרַב שֶׁלֹּא עַל מְנָת לְקַבֵּל פְּרָס, *be as servants serving their master without the expectation of reward* (*Avos* 1:3), and now, I finally have the opportunity!" The Gaon had been looking to perform a *mitzvah* with so pure a motivation, excluding even the reward due in the World-to-Come.

This care to avoid an ulterior motive is not limited to those *mitzvos* which by their very essence are private acts. Even a *mitzvah* as public as endowing a bride and groom or burying the dead should be performed without any self-gratification. Thus Michah proclaimed: הִגִּיד לְךָ אָדָם מַה טּוֹב וּמָה ה' דּוֹרֵשׁ מִמְּךָ כִּי אִם עֲשׂוֹת מִשְׁפָּט וְאַהֲבַת חֶסֶד וְהַצְנֵעַ לֶכֶת עִם אֱלֹקֶיךָ, *He has told you, O man, what is good and what Hashem demands of you; but doing justice, lovingkindness and to walk humbly with your God (Michah 6:8). Chazal* explain (*Succah* 49b) "walking humbly" refers to the *mitzvos* of endowing the bride and groom and properly attending the dead. How does one go about performing such public acts modestly and humbly? It is by elevating one's motivation to be concerned solely with the benefit bestowed and not with the acclamation or reward received.

The *Gemara* (*Avodah Zarah* 18a) demonstrates an awesome example of punishment for tainting one's good deeds with self-gratification. The daughter of R' Chanina ben Tradyon was condemned to live amongst the harlots of Rome. Aghast, the Sages pondered the reason for this terrible punishment. R' Yochanan explained:

פַּעַם אַחַת הָיְתָה בִתּוֹ מְהַלֶּכֶת לִפְנֵי גְדוֹלֵי רוֹמִי, אָמְרוּ כַּמָּה נָאוֹת פְּסִיעוֹתֶיהָ שֶׁל רִיבָה זוֹ, מִיַּד דִּקְדְּקָה בִּפְסִיעוֹתֶיהָ.
Once the daughter [of R' Chanina] was walking before the nobility of Rome. They remarked, "Oh how lovely are the steps of this young woman." Whereupon she took particular care of her steps.

Mesilas Yesharim (Chapter 15) explains that she *was* walking extremely modestly, and this, indeed, is what impressed the Roman aristocrats. When she heard their appreciative remarks she began to walk even more modestly. There was no immodesty in her act; on the contrary, it was the very model of propriety. She was punished, however, for the self-consciousness and for the enjoyment she derived from the compliments she garnered for that modesty.

Shlomo HaMelech sums it up in *Koheles:* וְרָאִיתִי אֲנִי אֶת כָּל עָמָל וְאֵת כָּל כִּשְׁרוֹן הַמַּעֲשֶׂה כִּי הִיא קִנְאַת אִישׁ מֵרֵעֵהוּ גַּם זֶה הֶבֶל וּרְעוּת רוּחַ, *I saw that all labor and all skillful enterprise springs from man's rivalry with his neighbor. This, too, is futility and vexation of the spirit (Koheles 4:4).*

Chazal expanded this to include much more than merely physical pursuits and accomplishments. It also includes Torah and *mitzvos* done with improper motives. Thus, be it even learning Torah, or performing a *mitzvah*, if the motive is 'rivalry with one's neighbor,' the act is deemed vanity and emptiness!

וְעָשׂוּ לִי מִקְדָּשׁ
And Make for Me a Sanctuary

I.

The building of the מִשְׁכָּן, *Mishkan*, *Tabernacle*, is a topic discussed extensively in the Torah. There is the detailed portion describing the command to build the *Mishkan* and the equally lengthy description of the fulfillment of all those commandments.

The key to understanding the lengthy depiction of the building of the *Mishkan* lies in a comment of *Chazal* as to the reason the Torah repeats Eliezer's account of his encounter with Rivkah.

יָפָה שִׂיחָתָן שֶׁל עַבְדֵי אָבוֹת . . . מִתּוֹרָתָן שֶׁל בָּנִים. שֶׁהֲרֵי פָרָשָׁה שֶׁל אֱלִיעֶזֶר כְּפוּלָה בַתּוֹרָה וְהַרְבֵּה גוּפֵי תוֹרָה לֹא נִתְּנוּ אֶלָּא בִּרְמִיזָה (רש״י בראשית כב:מב).

The conversations of the servants of the Patriarchs are more esteemed than the Torah of their descendants. For the portion regarding Eliezer is stated twice in the Torah while many mainstays of the Torah are merely hinted at (Rashi Bereishis 24:42).

This has been explained to us by our Sages as describing the measure of profound Torah lessons inherent in these 'stories' of our Patriarchs. If so many laws could be given to us by mere hints, how many lessons are taught by these 'stories'? These accounts are filled with countless teachings concerning one's relations with and behavior towards one's fellow man.

Even more so is this the case with the repetitious descriptions of the building of the *Mishkan*. The *Mishkan* serves as a dwelling place, as it were, for the Divine Presence. Being so, it is a replica of the Divine abode above, and as *Chazal* tell us, all that is to be found in the Heavens has its counterpart in the *Mishkan*. There are countless Divine mysteries woven into every fiber of the *Mishkan*, and the elaboration of its details contains manifold lessons for us. Let us consider the relevant points.

II.

וְיִקְחוּ לִי תְּרוּמָה . . . וְעָשׂוּ לִי מִקְדָּשׁ (שמות כב:ב,ח).

And they shall set aside for Me . . . and they shall make a Sanctuary for Me (Shemos 25:2,8).

Rashi comments לִי לִשְׁמִי — *solely for My sake.*
The first requirement for building a *Mishkan* properly is that it be constituted solely for Hashem's sake, not containing the slightest trace of self-gratification.

Thus, Shlomo HaMelech informed Hiram king of Tyre, "You know that my father David was not able to build a House for the sake of Hashem, his Lord, due to the wars that surrounded him" (*I Melachim* 5:16).

What was Shlomo HaMelech alluding to in the phrase "The wars that surrounded him"? He could not have been referring to the fact that his energies were occupied with the war efforts and was, therefore, unable to devote himself to building the Temple. The verse itself refutes this interpretation, as it says, *and it came about as the king was sitting in his house and Hashem had given him respite from all his enemies.* And indeed it was then that David began planning to build the Temple. What was it, then, that prevented him from building the Temple "due to the wars that surrounded him"?

To understand this, we must consider Shlomo HaMelech's dedication of the Temple:

כִּי יֵצֵא עַמְּךָ לַמִּלְחָמָה עַל אֹיְבוֹ בַּדֶּרֶךְ אֲשֶׁר תִּשְׁלָחֵם וְהִתְפַּלְלוּ
אֶל ה' דֶּרֶךְ הָעִיר אֲשֶׁר בָּחַרְתָּ בָּהּ וְהַבַּיִת אֲשֶׁר בָּנִתִי לִשְׁמֶךָ
(מלכים א ח:מד).

*When Your people will go out to battle against their
enemy, on the way that You shall send them, they shall
pray to Hashem through the city that You have chosen,
and the House that I have built for Your sake (I
Melachim 8:44).*

Thus the Temple served as a focal point for prayer, especially for
prayers in time of war. Even Haman acknowledged this, observing,
"When they ready themselves for battle, they enter [the Temple],
perform magic, then go out killing and destroying the world" (*Esther
Rabbah* 7:13).

David HaMelech, being so involved in war and battle, would
garner personal benefit from the construction of the Temple, albeit
for the noblest of reasons, the defense and protection of Israel. Yet,
David could not build it, for his motivation fell short of the pure ideal
of לִי לִשְׁמִי, *solely for the sake of Hashem.*

Shlomo HaMelech, when explaining to Hiram the reason for his
father's inability to build the Temple, echoes this theme constantly:
*You know that my father David was unable to build a house 'for the
sake' of Hashem, And I have declared to build a house 'for the sake'
of Hashem,* and again, *Your son whom I will place instead of you
upon the throne will build a house 'for My sake' (I Melachim ibid.).*

The astuteness of this assessment of David's inability to build the
Temple prompted Hiram to remark, "Blessed is Hashem Who has
endowed his servant David with so wise a son."

But purity of motive alone is not a sufficient foundation upon
which to build a Temple. The intensity of one's decision and devotion
is the cornerstone upon which the edifice rests. Thus, the section
describing the materials to be included in the building of the
Mishkan begins כָּל אִישׁ אֲשֶׁר יִדְּבֶנּוּ לִבּוֹ, *Every man whose heart
prompts him to give (Shemos 25:2).*

A striking example where the absence of these qualities detracted
from the value of the contribution, is to be found in the donation of
the נְשִׂיאִים, *princes.* They contributed the valuable stones of the High
Priest's vestments. Their gift was by far the most expensive and yet
it is mentioned last. Why?

Or HaChaim gives two explanations. The princes were last to come forward with their donation. They had decided to wait until everyone else had finished giving for the building of the *Mishkan* and then they would supply all that was missing. The reasoning itself was not faulty, but it pointed to a shortcoming in the quality of their נְדִיבַת הַלֵּב, *generosity of heart*. The person with true נְדִיבַת הַלֵּב cannot bear to wait and will rush forward with his gift, even if reason dictates otherwise. That is why their gift was mentioned last. In addition, the very word נְשִׂיאִם is spelled in the diminutive form — נְשִׂאִם — to underscore this deficiency (*Rashi Shemos* 35:27).

Or HaChaim points to yet another reason why their gift of precious stones is mentioned last. *Chazal* tell us that these precious stones had been given to them by the עֲנְנֵי הַכָּבוֹד, *the clouds of Glory*, hovering above Israel. Seeing that the stones came into their possession effortlessly, they were much less attached to them than most people are attached to their belongings. Consequently, their act of philanthropy was far less meaningful than similar deeds by others. The copper given by people who had labored for it was far more meaningful than the jewels that the נְשִׂיאִם obtained without toil.

A poignant example of what 'giving' means is to be found in the story of R' Chiya and the pauper.

> ר' חִיָּיא לֹא הֲוָה מָצֵי לְמִקְרְבָא לֵיהּ. יוֹמָא חַד אִידְמִי לֵיהּ כְּעַנְיָא אָתָא טָרֵיף אַבָּבָא א"ל אַפֵּיק לִי רִיפְתָּא אַפֵּיקוּ לֵיהּ א"ל וְלֹא קָמְרַחֵם מַר אַעַנְיָא, אַהַהוּא גַּבְרָא אַמַּאי לֹא קָא מְרַחֵם מַר גַּלֵּי לֵיהּ אַחְוֵי לֵיהּ שׁוּטָא דְנוּרָא, אַמְצֵי לֵיהּ נַפְשֵׁיהּ (מועד קטן כח:ע"א).

[The angel of death] could not gain access to R' Chiya. One day the [angel] adopted the guise of a pauper, knocked on his door and asked, "Give me bread." He gave him. [The angel] said, "If you take pity upon a pauper, why do you not take pity on [the angel of death]?" He proved [who he was] by showing him a rod of fire. [R' Chiya] then yielded his life to him (Moed Katan 28a).

This story is incomprehensible. What parallel did the angel of death find between the giving of a morsel of bread to a pauper and the giving up of one's life? The answer is that the angel of death was well aware of R' Chiya's profundity of heart. He knew that when R' Chiya gave even a crust of bread to the beggar, he did not only give it with heart; rather it was his very heart that he gave. Therefore, the angel of death was able to ask him 'to have pity on him' and surrender his life on the basis of the kindness expressed in the act of charity.

Chazal have described each and every person as a miniature Mishkan, wherein the Divine Presence dwells. The focus of the Mishkan was the Torah, embodied in the ark containing the tablets. The housing for this ark was a Mishkan erected upon the twin pillars of לִשְׁמָה, purity of motive and נְדִיבַת הַלֵּב, generosity of heart. A person can make himself into a Mishkan when his essence is Torah and the cornerstones of his deeds are purity of motive and generosity of heart.

דֶּרֶךְ אֶרֶץ

Decency, Respect and Obedience

Chananyah, Mishael and Azaryah were cast into a roaring furnace by Nevuchadnezzar for not worshiping his idols. They remained unscathed as they strolled about with the angel who protected them. Even so, why did they refuse to leave the inferno?

אָמְרוּ: אֵין אָנוּ יוֹצְאִים מִכִּבְשָׁן הָאֵשׁ אֶלָּא בִּרְשׁוּת הַמֶּלֶךְ, שֶׁלֹּא יֹאמַר בָּרְחוּ לָהֶם מִן הַכִּבְשָׁן. אֲנִי פִי מֶלֶךְ אֶשְׁמֹר, בִּרְשׁוּתוֹ הִשְׁלַכְנוּ, וּבִרְשׁוּתוֹ נֵצֵא (תנחומא נח סימן י).

We will not leave the flames without the king's permission, in order that people will not accuse us of running away. "I will keep the king's edicts" — by his dictum we entered the flames, and by his permission we will leave them (Tanchuma Noach 10).

And similarly we find by Noach:

וַיְדַבֵּר אֱלֹקִים אֶל נֹחַ לֵאמֹר: צֵא מִן הַתֵּבָה (בראשית ח:טו).

אָמַר רַבִּי יוּדָן אִלּוּ הָיִיתִי שָׁם הָיִיתִי שׁוֹבְרָהּ וְיוֹצֵא לִי אֶלָּא אָמַר נֹחַ כְּשֵׁם שֶׁלֹּא נִכְנַסְתִּי אֶלָּא בִּרְשׁוּת כַּךְ אֵינִי יוֹצֵא מִמֶּנּוּ אֶלָּא בִּרְשׁוּת (ילקוט שם).

And God spoke to Noach saying. Go out of the Ark (Bereishis 8:15-16).

R' Yuden commented: If I would have been there, I

would have broke down [the door] and left. Noach, however, said, "Since I entered only by [Divine] permission, I will leave only with [Divine] permission" (Yalkut ibid.).

Noach, imprisoned in the Ark and utterly exhausted from the efforts of caring for and feeding the animals (see *Tanchuma Noach* and *Rashi* 7:23), did not take the liberty of leaving without Divine permission. For twelve months he ceaselessly tended to the animals, not even allowing himself the luxury of rest or sleep. Now the land had dried, and there was no need to stay any longer in the Ark. Why wait for permission to leave, when the reason to remain was no longer valid?

The answer is that for Noach to leave without permission would show a lack of דֶּרֶךְ אֶרֶץ, *respect* and *obedience*, and no amount of hardship or suffering can justify a breach in דֶּרֶךְ אֶרֶץ; thus, "I entered [the Ark] with Divine permission, and I will leave only with Divine permission."

The Midrash of Chananyah, Mishael and Azaryah, however, poses a more difficult question, a halachic problem. Every minute that they remained in the furnace constituted a serious danger to their lives, for they remained alive only by a miracle. How were they allowed to risk their lives for such a delicate nuance of דֶּרֶךְ אֶרֶץ? Where do we find an obligation of יֵהָרֵג וְאַל יַעֲבֹר, *martyrdom*, for an act of respect?

The following Midrash sheds some light on the matter.

חֲנַנְיָה מִישָׁאֵל וַעֲזַרְיָה כְּשֶׁיָּרְדוּ לְכִבְשַׁן הָאֵשׁ לֹא יָרְדוּ אֶלָּא בְּסִימָן (שמות רבה פ״ט:א).

Chananyah, Mishael and Azaryah went into the furnace with a portent [that they would be saved] (Shemos Rabbah 89:1).

Thus, they knew beforehand that a miracle would occur and that they would not be consumed by the flames. They reasoned that since the norms of דֶּרֶךְ אֶרֶץ dictated that they wait for royal permission to leave, then that too was considered part of their necessary stay in the furnace and for its duration, as well, they would escape unscathed. Just as one who enters a burning furnace to sanctify God's Name will not be harmed, so too he who remains in the flames on account of דֶּרֶךְ אֶרֶץ would similarly be unharmed. Indeed, the subsequent events confirmed the soundness of their reasoning. No cause, worthy as it may be, can justify disregarding the imperative of דֶּרֶךְ אֶרֶץ.

This principle is borne out by the reaction of Moshe Rabbeinu when he was sent to redeem Israel from Egyptian bondage. He demurred at first because he felt it to be disrespectful of him to assume the leadership of Israel in the presence of his older brother Aharon (*Yalkut Shimoni Shemos* 4:13). Hashem remonstrated with him, not on account of the respect he accorded his brother, but rather for Moshe's suspicion that Aharon would feel slighted by his subordinate role. Therefore, Hashem told him: הֲלֹא אַהֲרֹן אָחִיךָ הַלֵּוִי, *Is not* יָדַעְתִּי כִּי דַבֵּר יְדַבֵּר הוּא, וְגַם הִנֵּה הוּא יֹצֵא לִקְרָאתֶךָ וְרָאֲךָ וְשָׂמַח בְּלִבּוֹ *Aharon the Levite your brother? I know that he will speak [for you] and is also setting out to meet you. When he will see you, he will rejoice in his heart* (*Shemos* 4:14).

The implication is clear. Had Aharon not rejoiced, had he felt hurt or slighted, then Moshe would have been right in refusing the mantle of leadership even at the cost of delaying the redemption of Israel. This all in the name of דֶּרֶךְ אֶרֶץ!

To be more precise, דֶּרֶךְ אֶרֶץ does not and cannot be in contradiction to God's command. Rather, the principles of דֶּרֶךְ אֶרֶץ explain and clarify the manner in which one is to fulfill the Divine command. Thus, Moshe Rabbeinu was commanded to count all the Levites from the age of one month and older. The Torah continues: וַיִּפְקֹד אֹתָם מֹשֶׁה עַל פִּי ה' כַּאֲשֶׁר צֻוָּה, *And Moshe counted them according to the word of God, as he had been commanded* (*Bamidbar* 3:16), stressing Moshe's perfect compliance with his instructions. And yet, Moshe did not fulfill this obligation in its literal sense.

The Midrash relates:

אָמַר מֹשֶׁה לִפְנֵי הַקָּדוֹשׁ בָּרוּךְ הוּא הֵיאַךְ אֲנִי נִכְנָס לְתוֹךְ אָהֳלֵיהֶם לָדַעַת מִנְיַן יוֹנְקֵיהֶם אָמַר לוֹ הַקָּדוֹשׁ בָּרוּךְ הוּא עֲשֵׂה אַתָּה אֶת שֶׁלְּךָ וַאֲנִי אֶעֱשֶׂה שֶׁלִּי. הָלַךְ מֹשֶׁה וְעָמַד עַל פֶּתַח הָאֹהֶל וְהַשְּׁכִינָה מְקַדֶּמֶת לְפָנָיו וּבַת קוֹל יוֹצֵאת מִן הָאֹהֶל וְאוֹמֶרֶת כַּךְ וְכַךְ תִּינוֹקוֹת יֵשׁ בְּאֹהֶל זֶה, לְכַךְ נֶאֱמַר עַל פִּי ה' (רש"י במדבר ג:טז).

Moshe said, "How can I enter their tents [and intrude upon their privacy] to ascertain the number of their babies?" The Holy One replied, "Do your share and I will do Mine." Moshe went and stood in front of each tent and the Divine Presence preceded him and a voice issued from the tent saying, "This is the number of infants in this tent" (*Rashi Bamidbar* 3:16).

The norms of דֶּרֶךְ אֶרֶץ did not permit Moshe to enter private tents. Accordingly, the Divine command *could not* mean that he should enter. Moshe proceeded to fulfill the instructions in a manner in consonance with the requirements of דֶּרֶךְ אֶרֶץ, and the verse describes him as doing so עַל פִּי ה׳ כַּאֲשֶׁר צִוָּה, *as Hashem commanded*. Indeed, this is what Hashem intended for him to do.

וְעָשִׂיתָ עַל שׁוּלָיו רִמּוֹנֵי תְכֵלֶת וכו׳ וּפַעֲמוֹנֵי זָהָב בְּתוֹכָם סָבִיב וכו׳
וְהָיָה עַל אַהֲרֹן לְשָׁרֵת וְנִשְׁמַע קוֹלוֹ בְּבֹאוֹ אֶל הַקֹּדֶשׁ לִפְנֵי ה׳
וּבְצֵאתוֹ וְלֹא יָמוּת (שמות כח:לג-לה).

וּמַה שֶּׁאָמַר לְמַעְלָה וְנִשְׁמַע קוֹלוֹ בְּבֹאוֹ אֶל הַקֹּדֶשׁ . . . וְלֹא
יָמוּת הוּא עַל דַּעְתִּי בֵּאוּר לְמִצְוַת הַפַּעֲמוֹנִים כִּי מִפְּנֵי שֶׁאֵין בָּהֶם
צֹרֶךְ בִּלְבִישָׁה וְאֵין דֶּרֶךְ הַנִּכְבָּדִים לַעֲשׂוֹת לָהֶם כֵּן לְכָךְ אָמַר כִּי
צִוָּה בָהֶם בַּעֲבוּר שֶׁיִּשָּׁמַע קוֹלוֹ בַּקֹּדֶשׁ וְיִכָּנֵס לִפְנֵי אֲדֹנָיו כְּאִלּוּ
בִּרְשׁוּת (רמבן שם לה).

And he shall make around its edges pomegranates of blue wool etc., and golden bells around them etc., and they shall be on Aharon to serve and the sound will be heard when he enters the Holy and when he leaves and thus he will not die (Shemos 28:33-35).

That which it says above "and the sound will be heard when he enters the Holy . . . and he will not die" is in my opinion an explanation for the bells, for there is no need to wear them, nor are they customary among dignitaries. Therefore, he commanded that they be made in order that the sound be heard in the Sanctuary that the priest enter before his Master as if with [His] permission (Ramban ibid.).

The Midrash (quoted by *Rashbam* in *Pesachim*) learns from here that one is obligated to knock before entering his home. The high priest Aharon was clothed in vestments which were a visual embodiment of the principles of דֶּרֶךְ אֶרֶץ. When he entered the *Mishkan* he did so only with permission, as it were, by indicating his imminent entrance. To do so without the accouterments of דֶּרֶךְ אֶרֶץ would be a violation of such severity in the *Mishkan* that it would cause him to be liable for the penalty of death.

The obligation of דֶּרֶךְ אֶרֶץ applies not only to one's relationship with Hashem as evidenced by Noach nor solely to one's dealings with righteous people. Even wicked and evil men must be accorded the דֶּרֶךְ אֶרֶץ due to them. Thus Yosef fled Potiphar's house when accosted by Potiphar's wife and left her clinging to his jacket, which she then used to incriminate him. Why did he not tear from her grasp the jacket that she grabbed from him? *Ramban* (*Bereishis* 39:13) answers that to do so would have been an affront to her honor and dignity, and therefore Yosef preferred to leave it in her hands, even at the risk of her using it as incriminating evidence. Such is the obligation of דֶּרֶךְ אֶרֶץ.

עֶבֶד ה'

Servant of Hashem

I.

חַיָּב אֱנָשׁ לִבְסוּמֵי בְּפוּרַיָּא עַד דְּלֹא יָדַע בֵּין אָרוּר הָמָן לְבָרוּךְ מָרְדְּכַי (אורח חיים תרצה:ב).

A person is required to become intoxicated on Purim until he does not know the difference between the cursing of Haman and the blessing of Mordechai (Orach Chaim 695:2).

The above *halachah* is one of the central aspects of *Purim*. As puzzling as this requirement may seem, we are even more baffled by the implications of the statement of *Shelah* [quoting *Arizal*] that *Purim* is a day that can elevate a person more than *Yom Kippur*: "יוֹם כְּפּוּרִים" — *Yom Kippur* being but a day comparable to *Purim*. It appears that this elevated status of *Purim* is connected to the *halachah* of חַיָּב אֱנָשׁ לִבְסוּמֵי, *the requirement of intoxication*. What is the essence of *Purim* as expressed in this *halachah*?

To understand this, let us examine a few cases where righteous men were punished [for seemingly minor offenses] and find their common denominator.

(a) Moshe Rabbeinu was punished for hitting the rock instead of speaking to it, by not being allowed into *Eretz Yisrael* (*Bamidbar* 19:12). Although he prayed incessantly to have the decree annulled, his request was denied. Yet, while the sin of the golden calf was by far greater, Israel was pardoned after Moshe's persistent prayers. What, then, was the element of sin at the rock that prevented any pardon whatsoever?

(b) *Chazal* tell us that the מְרַגְּלִים, *spies*, were sent by Moshe to reconnoiter *Eretz Yisrael*, with the best of intentions. Their mission was based on the following premise. Hashem promised Israel that the houses in Canaan would be laden with treasures. The Canaanites, knowing that Israel would be coming, would certainly do their utmost to conceal their riches. When Israel would enter the land of Canaan they would not find anything, and the word of Hashem would be desecrated. They felt it therefore imperative to seek out the treasures and make note of their hiding places (*Yalkut Shimoni Bamidbar* 13).

The reasoning seems foolproof; the motive benevolent. The spies themselves were elevated people. Yet, when they returned they were highly critical of *Eretz Yisrael* and went so far as to deny Hashem's omnipotence (see *Bamidbar* 13:31). This is possible only if something was amiss in the original plan. Yet, what can we find wrong with the original idea?

(c) Shaul HaMelech was faulted for not killing Agag, and as a result lost the monarchy. The *Gemara* remarks that although King David erred twice, he retained his monarchy while Shaul lost his after but one misdemeanor (*Yoma* 22b). [It is obvious that Shaul's one sin outweighed David's two transgressions, yet it is hard to discern the severity of Shaul's one sin compared to David's two.]

There is another observation to be made in connection with Shaul's sin. If we peruse the preceding chapters, we find that Shaul was cited for two sins: not killing Agag, and offering the sacrifice without waiting for Shmuel the Prophet to arrive as he had been instructed. Why then are these two mistakes referred to as one?

The key to understanding all this lies in a statement of the *Gemara* concerning Chizkiyahu King of Yehudah:

בַּיָּמִים הָהֵם חָלָה חִזְקִיָּהוּ לָמוּת. וַיָּבֹא אֵלָיו יְשַׁעְיָהוּ בֶן אָמוֹץ
הַנָּבִיא וַיֹּאמֶר אֵלָיו, כֹּה אָמַר ה', צַו לְבֵיתֶךָ כִּי מֵת אַתָּה וְלֹא
תִחְיֶה. מַאי כִּי מֵת אַתָּה וְלֹא תִחְיֶה? מֵת אַתָּה בָּעוֹלָם הַזֶּה וְלֹא
תִחְיֶה לָעוֹלָם הַבָּא. אָמַר לֵיהּ, מַאי כּוּלֵי הַאי? אָמַר לֵיהּ, מִשּׁוּם

דְּלָא עָסְקַהְ בִּפְרִיָה וְרִבְיָה. אָמַר לֵיהּ מִשּׁוּם דְּחַזַאי לִי בְּרוּחַ
הַקֹּדֶשׁ דְּנָפְקֵי מִינַּאי בְּנִין דְּלָא מַעֲלוּ. אָמַר לֵיהּ בַּהֲדֵי כַּבְשֵׁי
דְּרַחֲמָנָא לָמָה לָךְ? מַאי דְּמִיפַּקְּדַתְּ אִיבָּעֵי לָךְ לְמֶעֱבָד, וּמַה
דְּנִיחָא קַמֵּיהּ קֻדְשָׁא בְּרִיךְ הוּא לֶעֱבִיד (ברכות י ע"א).

At that time Chizkiyahu became deathly ill. Yeshayahu ben Amotz the Prophet appeared to him,
saying, "So said Hashem: command your household,
for you shall die and not live" (II Melachim 20:1). What
is meant by 'you shall die and not live?' [It means] you
shall die in this world and not live in the World-to-
Come. [Chizkiyahu] asked, "Why so [severe a punish-
ment]?" He replied, "Because you did not [fulfill the
mitzvah to] bear children." Chizkiyahu said, "It was
because I foresaw that I would bear children who
would not be virtuous." [Yeshayahu] retorted, "Of
what concern to you are the Divine secrets? Do as you
are instructed and God will do as He pleases!"
(Berachos 10a).

This *Gemara* teaches us a new dimension of sin. Chizkiyahu was
not accused solely of not begetting children; that transgression is not
punishable by death. The sin lay principally in the use of his own
reasoning to disobey the Divine command. One's attitude in doing
mitzvos should be that of a servant to a master — he does as he is
told, leaving aside his own reasoning. Trying to use one's own logic
to qualify or bypass the Divine command is a breach in the
relationship between Creator and creature, Master and servant.

This is the essence of the aforementioned incidents. The unforgiv-
able sin of Moshe Rabbeinu was not that he had disobeyed Hashem's
directive; it was that he had used reasoning and logic to reinterpret it.
[*Chazal* explain that the motive for Moshe striking the rock and not
speaking to it was in order to enhance *kiddush Hashem*, sanctification of the Divine Name (see *Bamidbar Rabbah* 19:5).]

The spies, too, were sent on the basis of Israel's own reasoning
which did not stem from complete faith in God. This ultimately led to
their slanderous report about *Eretz Yisrael*.

With this we can understand the dimensions of Shaul's sin. David
sinned terribly, but the transgression was self contained. Nothing
was disrupted in the basic relationship between Hashem and David.
Not so Shaul, who neglected to kill Agag because he felt that it was

not in keeping with the Divine emphasis on the sanctity of life. This constitutes rebellion against the Divine command. There too, Shaul disobeyed Shmuel by dint of his own reasoning. That is why they are considered one sin, for essentially they are one.

This ability to totally subjugate one's own self to the Divine will, forgoing even one's rational conclusions, is the hallmark of Israel's men of greatness.

The pinnacle of our father Avraham's life was the *akeidah*, when he offered his son Yitzchak as a sacrifice. It would be superficial to view the *akeidah* only in its emotional context and see the text merely as the overcoming of a father's love to a son. True, it is superhuman for a father to sacrifice his son, but it is a deed performed many times in the course of Jewish history. Avraham's act was unique in that it was contrary to his life's teachings. Avraham had spent a lifetime teaching people the evils of idolatry and to abhor human sacrifice. Now, he would be going through the same motions as the worship of *Moloch*, by sacrificing his son. All that he had taught mankind about monotheism (and kindness) would be laughed away in a wave of derision. Can there be a greater *chilul Hashem*, desecration of the Divine Name? How easy it would have been for Avraham to disregard or reinterpret the Divine command! Yet he stood fast, following the Divine decree down to its minutest detail. Truly, it could now be said of Avraham, "Now I know that you are a God-fearing man" (*Bereishis* 22:12). Avraham stood by the principle of וַאֲנִי לְתֻמִּי הוֹלֵךְ, *I am a servant who does as told, not deviating at any cost* (see *Sanhedrin* 89b).

Moshe Rabbeinu admitted to forgetting the *halachah* prohibiting the consumption of sacrificial meat while in a state of אֲנִינוּת, *mourning prior to burial*, and was praised for admitting his forgetfulness. The commendation is not for the act of admission per se. One would not imagine Moshe Rabbeinu lying.

The explanation is that Moshe could have worried that if he would be shown fallible, then the very *mesorah*, continuity, of Torah would be endangered. People might think that if Moshe forgot once, who knows how many more times he forgot or misconstrued Hashem's teachings. Yet Moshe did not attempt to rationalize his way out of the obligation to admit his lapse of memory, and for this he was commended. Indeed, it was because of this very quality that the title עֶבֶד ה׳, *servant of Hashem*, was bestowed upon him and enabled him to be the transmitter of Torah, as the verse proclaims, זִכְרוּ תּוֹרַת מֹשֶׁה

עַבְדִּי, *remember the Torah of Moshe My servant* (Malachi 3:22). The person totally devoted to his master is indeed the most trusted to keep the master's heritage intact. It is "Moshe's Torah" and yet, totally Hashem's Torah.

This ideal forms the proclamation of Israel at Sinai, נַעֲשֶׂה וְנִשְׁמָע, *We will obey and we will listen*. Our obligations will be fulfilled even if we do not understand 'why'!

II.

In light of what we have demonstrated, we gain a new perspective regarding the use of חֲקִירָה, *philosophical contemplation*, in the service of God. Even those advocating its use intend it to be but a means toward the ultimate goal of אֱמוּנָה פְּשׁוּטָה, *simple faith*.

Thus the verse enjoins us, דַּע אֶת אֱלֹקֵי אָבִיךָ וְעָבְדֵהוּ, *know the God of your father and serve him* (I Divrei HaYamim 28:9).

Indeed, ponder and use your reason, but ultimately the result must be 'duty' based on utter obedience to Hashem, freed from any personal reasoning.

The *Gemara* demonstrates this point most lucidly:

דְּיָתֵיב רַבִּי יוֹחָנָן וְקָא דָרִישׁ: עָתִיד הַקָּדוֹשׁ בָּרוּךְ הוּא לְהָבִיא אֲבָנִים טוֹבוֹת וּמַרְגָּלִיּוֹת שֶׁהֵן שְׁלֹשִׁים עַל שְׁלֹשִׁים אַמּוֹת וכו' וּמַעֲמִידָן בְּשַׁעַר יְרוּשָׁלַיִם וכו'. לִגְלֵג עָלָיו אוֹתוֹ תַּלְמִיד, אָמַר: הַשְׁתָּא כְּבֵיעֲתָא דְצִיּלְצָלָא לֹא מַשְׁכְּחִינַן כּוּלֵּי הַאי מַשְׁכְּחִינַן. לְיָמִים הִפְלִיגָה סְפִינָתוֹ בַּיָּם. חֲזִינְהוּ לְמַלְאֲכֵי הַשָּׁרֵת דְּקָא מְנַסְּרֵי אֲבָנִים טוֹבוֹת וּמַרְגָּלִיּוֹת. אָמַר לוֹ הַנֵּי לְמַאן. אָמְרֵי עָתִיד הַקָּדוֹשׁ בָּרוּךְ הוּא לְהַעֲמִידָן בְּשַׁעֲרֵי יְרוּשָׁלַיִם. כִּי הָדַר אַשְׁכְּחֵיהּ לְרַבִּי יוֹחָנָן דְּיָתֵיב וְקָא דָרִישׁ אָמַר לֵיהּ, רַבִּי דְּרוֹשׁ, וּלְךָ נָאֶה לִדְרוֹשׁ כְּשֵׁם שֶׁאָמַרְתָּ כַּךְ רָאִיתִי. אָמַר לֵיהּ רֵיקָה, אִם לֹא רָאִיתָ לֹא הֶאֱמַנְתָּ? מְלַגְלֵג עַל דִּבְרֵי חֲכָמִים אַתָּה, יָהַב בֵּיהּ עֵינֵיהּ וַעֲשָׂאוֹ גַּל שֶׁל עֲצָמוֹת (סנהדרין ק' ע"א).

R' Yochanan was sitting and expounding: Hashem will some day bring precious stones thirty cubits by thirty cubits and place them at the gateway of Jerusalem. One of the students [at the lecture] derided this, saying: "If today we cannot find stones as big as an insect's eggs, can we find them as big [as you describe them]?"

One day while journeying on a boat he saw angels cutting gems. He asked them their purpose and they answered, "Hashem will set these in the gateway of Jerusalem." When he returned, he found R' Yochanan sitting and teaching. He said to him, "Expound, my teacher, for you are worthy to do so, for as you have said, so have I seen." R' Yochanan replied, "Wretch! Had you not seen, would you have not believed it? You mock the words of the Sages!" R' Yochanan glared at him and he turned into a heap of bones (Sanhedrin 100a).

This story requires clarification. At the onset when his disciple mocked him, R' Yochanan did not respond nor punish him. It was only after he returned and admitted the veracity of R' Yochanan's statement that R' Yochanan was incensed. The reason is that as long as R' Yochanan's discourse was beyond his disciple's comprehension, he was not to be blamed for his disbelief. It was only after he had seen it, understood it *and still persisted* in emphasizing the role of his rational faculties that R' Yochanan became angry. At this point, *emunah*, faith in God, was called for; anything less was *apikursus*, heresy.

Having explored the uses and limitations of reason in the Divine service, we can begin to understand the essence of *Purim*. Reason is used year-round as a means to *emunah*. Once a year, on *Purim*, we strip away all traces of reasoning (עַד דְּלֹא יָדַע) and serve God with our faith alone.

הַתַּאֲוָה וְהַכָּבוֹד
The Pursuit of Pleasure and Honor

וְכָל זֶה אֵינֶנּוּ שׁוֶה לִי בְּכָל עֵת אֲשֶׁר אֲנִי רֹאֶה אֶת מָרְדְּכַי הַיְּהוּדִי
יוֹשֵׁב בְּשַׁעַר הַמֶּלֶךְ (אסתר ה:יג).
*All this is worthless for me, so long as I see Mordechai
the Jew sitting at the gates of the palace (Esther 5:13).*

H aman, second only to King Achashveirosh, worshiped and deified by all subjects of the vast Persian empire, was dissatisfied with everything he had because of one Jew's refusal to pay homage to him. How could it be that Haman would even notice the lack of that last iota of honor amidst the overwhelming flood of glory that was his? Would someone who had gorged himself on an enormous feast declare that he did not enjoy the entire banquet because of one dish that was missing? Yet, Haman protested that *All this is worthless.*

The explanation lies in understanding the difference between the desire for honor as opposed to physical desires. Someone who craves any of the physical pleasures desires something that is real and exists. Therefore, when he has enjoyed it, his hunger and desire are satiated. Even if he obtains only part of that which he craves, his desires will be requited in direct proportion to that which he has received.

Not so the person who hungers for כָּבוֹד, *honor*. Honor itself is non-existent; it is only a figment of the imagination. There is no tangible pleasure in honor. Its essence lies in the fact that by being accorded it, one's fantasies and desires have been fulfilled. Therefore, if anything is lacking in the fulfillment of one's dreams, then his hunger for honor is not satisfied at all. Thus, Haman's pleasure would have been the total and complete subjugation of the Persian empire in all its components and citizens. If there was but one jot missing from the total realization of that dream, then all the honor bestowed upon him was meaningless, honor in and of itself being incapable of satisfying a human being.

With this understanding that the desire for honor is, in reality, the pursuit of a non-existent pleasure, it is not surprising to observe the seemingly pointless and meaningless honors which people crave. Thus, the story of the woman whose seven children were instructed to bow before the king:

אָמַר לֵיהּ קֵיסָר, אַשְׁדִּי לָךְ גּוּשְׁפַּנְקָא וְנָחִין וְשַׁקְלֵיהּ כִּי הֵיכִי דְּלֵימְרוּ קִיבֵּל עֲלֵיהּ הַרְמָנָא דְּמַלְכָּא. אָמַר לֵיהּ חֲבַל עֲלָךְ קֵיסָר, חֲבַל עֲלָךְ קֵיסָר, עַל כְּבוֹד עַצְמְךָ כָּךְ, עַל כְּבוֹד הַקָּדוֹשׁ בָּרוּךְ הוּא עַל אַחַת כַּמָּה וְכַמָּה (גיטין נז ע"ב).

[When they brought the youngest son before the king,]
the king said to him, "I will toss my signet ring before
you, and you will bend down to pick it up so that people
will say, 'He has accepted the king's rule.' " [The child
replied,] "Woe to you Caesar, woe to you Caesar; if
your own honor is so important, how much more the
honor of the Holy One" (Gittin 57b).

Let us examine the supposed honor here. It was no honor at all, as they both knew that if the boy picked up the ring he meant no obeisance to the king at all. This mighty Roman emperor was so obsessed with honor that he could not do without even the pretended honor of a small child. This was the child's rejoinder to him. "No matter how much honor you will receive you will not succeed in satisfying your obsession with it." As much honor as you will receive, you will find yet more that you must have and so your craving will never be satisfied.

It is in this sense that the *Tanna* says, הַקִּנְאָה וְהַתַּאֲוָה וְהַכָּבוֹד מוֹצִיאִין אֶת הָאָדָם מִן הָעוֹלָם, *Jealousy, physical cravings and honor drive a person from this world* (Avos 4:28).

The need for honor is never filled, the frontiers of its craving being continuously expanded until one becomes a prisoner of the relentless pursuit of honor. This world does not provide satisfaction to such boundless craving.

But, while this is the norm in the desire for prestige, it often applies to the pursuit of other passions as well. Very often a person will develop a desire not for something he really needs but rather for something self induced. For instance, the desire for cigarettes does not normally exist in human beings. A person who has never smoked feels no need to do so. Once, however, someone has begun to smoke, he creates the desire for the cigarette, and in spite of the fact that this craving is self induced he will still be hopelessly caught up in it.

This phenomenon is most pronounced in the case of the desire for money, and it is in this sense that *Rashi* explains the תַּאֲוָה, *desire*, referred to in the aforementioned *mishnah* in *Avos*. *Rashi* supports his explanation by quoting the verse אֹהֵב כֶּסֶף לֹא יִשְׂבַּע כֶּסֶף, *One who loves money will never be satisfied with money* (*Koheles* 5:9). Why?

The answer is that money in and of itself has no pleasure to offer the human being who strives for it. The only satisfaction that one has from accumulating wealth is the fact that one has fulfilled one's self-induced craving to accumulate wealth.

As a person accumulates more wealth, the riches that are already his are now considered necessity rather than luxury and so he craves yet more to assuage his overwhelming desire for wealth. This vicious cycle — of desire for riches, its becoming necessity and the craving for yet more riches — is what drives a person from this world (מוֹצִיאִין אֶת הָאָדָם מִן הָעוֹלָם).

This was the lesson that the people of Afriki taught Alexander the Great. Alexander asked them to bring him bread, and they brought him a loaf of bread made of gold. Astonished, he asked them, *Can one eat bread made of gold?* They replied, *If it is bread that you seek, was there not enough bread where you came from that you had to come here?* (*Tamid* 32a).

The people of Afriki in giving Alexander a gift of 'golden bread' were telling him that gold was no longer a luxury for him, but rather, had become a necessity as indispensable as bread.

This phenomenon is described by *Chazal* as שְׂכַר עֲבֵרָה עֲבֵרָה, *the punishment for a sin is another sin* (*Avos* 4:2). For as soon as a person has committed a sin, his appetite becomes whetted and he will now desire things that he never craved before.

There is a well-known saying, מִי שֶׁיֵּשׁ לוֹ מָנֶה רוֹצֶה מָאתַיִם וּמִי שֶׁיֵּשׁ לוֹ מָאתַיִם רוֹצֶה אַרְבַּע מֵאוֹת, *He who has a hundred desires two hundred and one who has two hundred desires four hundred* (see similar expression in *Koheles Rabbah* 1). It is the hundred that he possesses which creates the desire for the two hundred, and the two hundred which produces the craving for four hundred.

This is the שְׂכַר עֲבֵרָה, the development of new desire creating a still larger appetite. Prior to having one hundred, this person was lacking only that hundred. Now that he has one hundred, he is lacking an additional two hundred, meaning that, in effect, his need is greater than before.

This process works in reverse too. An individual who learns to restrict his desires and to hold them in check slowly frees himself of their shackles, and will find that he has far fewer necessities than he previously thought. This is the meaning of שְׂכַר מִצְוָה מִצְוָה, *the reward of the mitzvah is the mitzvah itself.*

The *Mishnah* says in *Avos* 6:4: פַּת בַּמֶּלַח תֹּאכַל, וּמַיִם בַּמְּשׂוּרָה תִּשְׁתֶּה, *[If one's food ration is] bread with salt, and water in measure,* then, אַשְׁרֶיךָ בָּעוֹלָם הַזֶּה וְטוֹב לָךְ לָעוֹלָם הַבָּא, *You will be happy in this world in addition to the reward of the World-to-Come.* How can the *Mishnah* say that one with such a life will be happy in this world? In the World-to-Come perhaps, but how can such a lifestyle be called happiness here?

In light of the above it becomes clear. When a person refuses to capitulate to the demands of his various appetites he will actually crave less and need less for his sustenance, and as a result be a happier person.

This perhaps is the meaning of Yaakov's request for לֶחֶם לֶאֱכֹל וּבֶגֶד לִלְבֹּשׁ, *bread to eat and clothing to wear* (*Bereishis* 28:20). Yaakov requested that he be given nothing but the barest necessities and that way he was sure to be content, for there is no greater blessing than the ability to sustain oneself on the barest of necessities, free of the imperatives of lust and desire.

מַעֲשֵׂה הָעֵגֶל

The Sin of the Golden Calf

סָרוּ מַהֵר מִן הַדֶּרֶךְ אֲשֶׁר צִוִּיתִם, עָשׂוּ לָהֶם עֵגֶל מַסֵּכָה (שמות
כב:ח).

*They have strayed quickly from the path that I have
commanded them, they have made for themselves a
molten calf (Shemos 32:8).*

The sin of the golden calf is one of the more puzzling events in
Jewish history. While we have elsewhere (see *Parashas Bereishis*)
discussed the ability of Israel to undergo such a rapid downfall
(מֵאִגְּרָא רָמָא לְבֵירָא עֲמִיקְתָּא), it is still difficult to understand the
possibility of the sin itself at such a juncture in Israel's history. Israel
had just witnessed the tremendous miracles in Egypt, and had been
redeemed from the confines of Egyptian bondage. They had 'seen
God' so openly at the sea that they could point a finger and proclaim
זֶה קֵלִי וְאַנְוֵהוּ, *This is my God and I shall beautify Him (Shemos 15:2).*
Chazal tell us: רָאֲתָה שִׁפְחָה עַל הַיָּם מַה שֶׁלֹּא רָאָה יְחֶזְקֵאל בֶּן בּוּזִי, *Even a*
maidservant was able, at the splitting of the Red Sea, to perceive of
the Divine what Yechezkel ben Buzi was unable to grasp.
Subsequently, Israel witnessed the greatest of revelations known to
man: the Divine Revelation at Sinai where they heard Hashem
proclaim, אָנֹכִי ה' אֱלֹקֶיךָ אֲשֶׁר הוֹצֵאתִיךָ מֵאֶרֶץ מִצְרָיִם, *I am Hashem your*

God Who took you out of the land of Egypt (*Shemos* 20:1). How, after all these clear manifestations of the Divine, could Israel become confused and proclaim about a molten calf: אֵלֶּה אֱלֹהֶיךָ יִשְׂרָאֵל אֲשֶׁר הֶעֱלוּךָ מֵאֶרֶץ מִצְרָיִם, *These are your gods O Israel, who brought you up out of the land of Egypt* (*Shemos* 32:4)?

Rashi somewhat softens the question by pointing out that the עֵרֶב רַב, Egyptian proselytes, were the ones who influenced Israel. He stresses these words: אֵלֶּה אֱלֹהֶיךָ יִשְׂרָאֵל — *these are 'your gods* . . .', not 'our gods.' Yet, the question is equally valid as regards the עֵרֶב רַב. Didn't they also witness the miraculous events at the Red Sea and at Mount Sinai? Were they not included in the group about whom it is written, וַיִּירְאוּ הָעָם אֶת ה' וַיַּאֲמִינוּ בַּה' וּבְמֹשֶׁה עַבְדּוֹ, *And the nation feared God, and they believed in God and in Moshe His servant* (*Shemos* 14:31)?

In order to answer this question, we must take a closer look at the statement of *Chazal* describing the events at the sea: *Even a maidservant was able, at the splitting of the Red Sea, to perceive of the Divine what Yechezkel ben Buzi was unable to grasp.* If indeed a maidservant was capable of such lofty understanding, why is she still referred to as a maidservant and not as a prophetess? The answer is that revelations and unique events on their own do not create prophets. A person may experience a lofty awareness, a lucid perception of the Divine, yet remain the same person. His knowledge and awareness will not necessarily effect any change in his personality whatsoever. The maidservant, after her experience at the sea, retained the same humble stature that she possessed before the event. The genuine prophets, on the other hand, had reached prophecy after a long and arduous process of character development and self-perfection. Prophecy per se was but the climax to their efforts and therefore it became an integral part of their personality.

This was the reason why the עֵרֶב רַב turned so quickly to idolatry. They were essentially idol worshipers who had lived through momentous events. These events, being spontaneous and unique, left no lasting impression. No sooner had the revelation at Sinai spent itself, they reverted back to their idolatrous ways, towing Israel in their wake.

Perhaps the most shocking example of the ineffectiveness of Divine Revelation for those unprepared is the story of the statue of Michah:

לְךָ ה' הַצְּדָקָה וְלָנוּ בֹּשֶׁת הַפָּנִים. אָמַר רַבִּי יְהוּדָה בַּר אִילָעָא: עֲבוֹדָה זָרָה עָבְרָה עִם יִשְׂרָאֵל בַּיָּם, וְהַיָּם נִקְרַע לִפְנֵיהֶם.

Yours, O Lord, is the righteousness and ours is shamefacedness (Daniel 9:7). R' Yehudah bar Elai explained: The idol [of Michah] crossed the sea together with Israel, and yet the sea was split (Yalkut Shimoni 74).

Michah clung to his idol through the plagues of Egypt and the splitting of the sea, even while hearing the Divine Voice proclaim, *I am Hashem your God.* Not only did these events fail to leave any impression, but even when these events themselves were occurring, they made no impact whatsoever.

So too, Bilaam, in the midst of a prophecy as great as Moshe's, remained wicked. He attained great heights of prophecy, yet his essence remained as before. It was prophecy obtained effortlessly, without preparation, and consequently it did not raise his moral stature at all.

In the same manner we can understand a certain action of Yeravam which, on the surface, seems incomprehensible.

We find (*I Melachim* 13:1-6) that the prophet came to Yeravam while he was in the middle of offering up a sacrifice to his idol. Yeravam reached out to grab the prophet, but his hand withered. He then pleaded with the prophet to pray to God on his behalf to heal his hand. As soon as his hand was restored to its original condition, he continued immediately with the ceremony of sacrifice to his idol.

It is incomprehensible, that at the very same time when Yeravam felt God's retribution and punishment on his own body and witnessed the total powerlessness of his idols to help him, he changed his actions not one whit. No sooner had he been healed than he turned back to his idols, the preceding events not having affected him one iota. Even in midst of his paralysis Yeravam referred to Hashem as 'your God,' implying his dissociation from Hashem.

This principle is borne out time and again. As overwhelming and as convincing as a Divine Revelation may be, it will often effect no change whatsoever in the beholder. Only through the laborious process of self-improvement and character development does a person become Godly. And only if the development is the result of toil and labor on one's part, rather than a heavenly gift, can he retain those achievements.

וַיִּקְרָא אֶל מֹשֶׁה

And He Called to Moshe

וַיִּקְרָא אֶל מֹשֶׁה (ויקרא א:א).

עֶשֶׂר שֵׁמוֹת נִקְרְאוּ לוֹ לְמֹשֶׁה: יֶרֶד, חֶבֶר, יְקוּתִיאֵל, אֲבִיגְדוֹר,
אֲבִי סוֹכוֹ, אֲבִי זָנוֹחַ וכו'. יֶרֶד, לְפִי שֶׁהוֹרִיד אֶת הַתּוֹרָה מִלְמַעְלָה
לְמַטָּה. אֲבִיגְדוֹר, אֲבִיהֶם שֶׁל גוֹדְרִים. חֶבֶר, שֶׁחִבֵּר אֶת הַבָּנִים
לַאֲבִיהֶם שֶׁבַּשָּׁמַיִם. אֲבִי סוֹכוֹ, אֲבִיהֶם שֶׁל נְבִיאִים שֶׁסּוֹכִים בְּרוּחַ
הַקֹּדֶשׁ (ויקרא רבה פ"א:ג).

And [Hashem] called to Moshe (Vayikra 1:1).

Moshe was called by ten different names: Yered,
Chever, Yekusiel, Avigdor, Avi Socho, Avi Zanoach.
Yered — because he brought down the Torah from
above. Avigdor — the father of those who would build a
protective fence [around the Torah]. Chever — the one
who joined together the children with their father in
Heaven (Vayikra Rabbah 1:3).

A name as used by the Torah is not merely a reference device.
Rather it is an appellation which describes a person's essence and
attributes, a single word which serves to capture the entirety of one's
substance and being. The wisdom needed for establishing the name
of a being is described in the following Midrash:

> When Adam was created, the angels asked, "What will

be the nature of this man?" Hashem replied, "His wisdom will exceed yours." By way of demonstration, Hashem brought them various animals and asked them, "What should be the name of this?" They did not know. He then paraded the animals in front of Adam and Adam responded, "This should be called ox, that should be called donkey," and so on. Hashem asked him, "What is your name?" He replied, "Adam, for I am created from the earth [אֲדָמָה]." God continued, "And what is My Name?" "You are to be called Ado. . . for You are Master [אָדוֹן] of the universe" (Bereishis Rabbah 17:4).

This Midrash describes the profundity of wisdom necessary to accurately give something its true name. It is the highest level of intelligence, higher even than the wisdom of the angels. Man alone was capable of identifying the essence and purpose of each creature and thereby capable of naming it correctly.

Moshe's ten names, then, each indicate a separate dimension of his multifaceted personality. Each name portrayed a facet not described by the others. Yet, it was the name Moshe by which he was known. It is apparent then that the name Moshe described, more than the others, the central feature of his personality.

The Midrash concludes:

> *The Holy One told Moshe, "Of all your names, I will call you only by the name that Bisya the daughter of Pharaoh called you [as it says,] 'and she called him Moshe.'"*

Why did Hashem select the name Moshe? Moreover, while the other names each depict an aspect of Moshe's personality, the name Moshe is nothing more than a description of the fact that Bisya saved him from drowning, defying her father in the process. Of what significance was that to Moshe's essence?

It appears that the saving of Moshe was possible only through the מְסִירַת נֶפֶשׁ, *self-sacrifice*, of Bisya, who defied her father's decree in order to save a life. Since the life of Moshe was accomplished by an act of מְסִירַת נֶפֶשׁ, this power and ability of utter self-sacrifice entered the very body and soul of Moshe, for all that the giver gives to the recipient reaches him and enters him totally. Thus Moshe's מְסִירַת נֶפֶשׁ

was engendered by the self-sacrifice of Bisya, the daughter of Pharaoh, and therefore the name Moshe expresses his essence more than any other name.

Similarly, we find that the attributes with which Hashem relates to Israel become part of Israel's national character.

וְשָׁמַר ה' אֱלֹקֶיךָ לְךָ אֶת הַבְּרִית וְאֶת הַחֶסֶד (דברים ז:יא).

תַּנְיָא שָׁלֹשׁ מַתָּנוֹת טוֹבוֹת נָתַן הַקָּדוֹשׁ בָּרוּךְ הוּא לְיִשְׂרָאֵל:
רַחֲמָנִים בַּיְשָׁנִים גּוֹמְלֵי חֲסָדִים. גּוֹמְלֵי חֲסָדִים מִנַּיִן. דִּכְתִיב וְשָׁמַר
ה' אֱלֹקֶיךָ לְךָ אֶת הַבְּרִית וְאֶת הַחֶסֶד (ירושלמי סנהדרין פ"ו הל'
ז').

And Hashem, your Lord, will keep with you His covenant and lovingkindness (Devarim 7:12).

It was taught: Three precious gifts were bestowed by the Holy One upon Israel, [that Israelites are] merciful, bashful and benevolent, as it says, "and Hashem, your God will keep for you [His] covenant and [His] mercy" (Yerushalmi Sanhedrin 6:7).

The question arises: The mercy referred to in the verse is speaking of God's mercy on His people. Where in this verse is there even a hint that these qualities of mercy and lovingkindness are a part of Israel's national character?

The answer is that the attributes with which God relates to Israel become central features of Israel's essence. The mercy referred to in the verse is indeed God's mercy but it became ingrained in Israel's personality. Thus, by relating to Israel with mercy, He bestowed upon them this precious gift: They themselves became merciful.

There can be no name more fitting for a leader of Israel than the appellation expressing מְסִירַת נֶפֶשׁ, for self-sacrifice is the principal quality necessary for leadership of the Jewish people; self-sacrifice for every individual, not only for the people as a whole.

Moshe's מְסִירַת נֶפֶשׁ for the sake of Israel was a quality that manifested itself long before he assumed the mantle of leadership.

וַיֵּצֵא אֶל אֶחָיו וַיַּרְא בְּסִבְלֹתָם (שמות ב:יא).

הָיָה רוֹאֶה בְסִבְלוֹתָם וּבוֹכֶה וְאוֹמֵר, חֲבָל לִי עֲלֵיכֶם, מִי יִתֵּן
מוּתִי עֲלֵיכֶם שֶׁאֵין לְךָ מְלָאכָה קָשָׁה מִמְּלֶאכֶת הַטִּיט. וְהָיָה נוֹתֵן
כְּתֵפָיו וּמְסַיֵּעַ לְכָל אֶחָד וְאֶחָד מֵהֶן (שמות רבה פ"א:כו).

And he went out to his brethren and observed their suffering (Shemos 2:11).

He would see their suffering and weep, 'Woe is to me for you, would that I could die for you.' There is no labor more strenuous than molding bricks and he used to shoulder the burdens and help each one of them (Shemos Rabbah 1:27).

But it is not מְסִירַת נֶפֶשׁ alone which qualifies one as a leader. Also imperative is the ability to understand the needs and necessities of each and every person as a unique individual.

The Midrash describes this most vividly:

בָּדַק הַקָּדוֹשׁ בָּרוּךְ הוּא לְדָוִד בְּצֹאן, וּמְצָאוֹ רוֹעֶה יָפֶה, וכו'. וְהָיָה מוֹצִיא הַקְּטַנִּים לִרְעוֹת כְּדֵי שֶׁיִּרְעוּ עֵשֶׂב הַבֵּינוֹנִית וְאַחַר כָּךְ מוֹצִיא הַבַּחוּרִים שֶׁיִּהְיוּ אוֹכְלִים עֵשֶׂב הַקָּשֶׁה. אָמַר הַקָּדוֹשׁ בָּרוּךְ הוּא, מִי שֶׁהוּא יוֹדֵעַ לִרְעוֹת הַצֹּאן אִישׁ כְּפִי כֹחוֹ, יָבֹא וְיִרְעֶה בְעַמִּי וכו'. וְאַף מֹשֶׁה לֹא בְחָנוֹ הַקָּדוֹשׁ בָּרוּךְ הוּא אֶלָּא בְצֹאן וכו', בָּרַח מִמֶּנּוּ גְּדִי, וְרָץ אַחֲרָיו וכו', נִזְדַּמְּנָה לוֹ בְרֵכָה שֶׁל מַיִם וְעָמַד הַגְּדִי לִשְׁתּוֹת, כֵּיוָן שֶׁהִגִּיעַ מֹשֶׁה אֶצְלוֹ, אָמַר, אֲנִי לֹא הָיִיתִי יוֹדֵעַ שֶׁרָץ הָיִיתָ מִפְּנֵי צָמָא, עָיֵף אַתָּה, הִרְכִּיבוֹ עַל כְּתֵפוֹ וְהָיָה מְהַלֵּךְ, אָמַר הַקָּדוֹשׁ בָּרוּךְ הוּא, יֵשׁ לְךָ רַחֲמִים לִנְהוֹג צֹאנוֹ שֶׁל בָּשָׂר וָדָם, חַיֶּיךָ אַתָּה תִרְעֶה צֹאנִי יִשְׂרָאֵל (שמות רבה פב:ב).

The Holy One tested David by means of sheep, and found him to be a good shepherd. He would first take out the smaller ones to feed so that they could graze on the tender grass. Afterwards he would take the older sheep out to graze on the ordinary grass. And then the young sheep so that they could feed on the tough grass. Said the Holy One, "He who can tend sheep, each according to his needs, should come and tend My nation."

Moshe too was tested by means of sheep. Once, a sheep escaped, and he ran after it. It reached a pool of water and stopped to drink. When Moshe approached it, he said, "I did not know that you ran away because of thirst; you also must be tired." He placed him over his shoulder and began to walk back. Said the Holy One, "Because you had pity for sheep belonging to mere mortals, by your life, you will tend My flock, Israel" (Shemos Rabbah 2:2).

This gives us an insight into the Torah's explanation of Yehoshua's suitability for the role of leadership. אִישׁ אֲשֶׁר רוּחַ בּוֹ: שֶׁיָּכוֹל לְהַלֵּךְ כְּנֶגֶד רוּחוֹ שֶׁל כָּל אֶחָד וְאֶחָד — *A man infused with spirit: for he can accommodate himself to the spirit of each and every one (Rashi, Bamidbar 27:18).*

This, then, is the essence of leadership: total self-sacrifice for the nation, coupled with an understanding of, and feeling for, the needs of every individual. This was what Bisya instilled in Moshe by saving him with מְסִירַת נֶפֶשׁ and this is what the name Moshe expresses.

And therefore he was called Moshe.

מוֹרֶה הֲלָכָה בִּפְנֵי רַבּוֹ

Disrupting the Chain of Tradition

לֹא מֵתוּ בְּנֵי אַהֲרֹן עַד שֶׁהוֹרוּ הֲלָכָה בִּפְנֵי מֹשֶׁה רַבָּן (ערובין ס״ג
ע״א).

The children of Aharon died because they made halachic decisions without consulting Moshe their teacher (Eruvin 63a).

There are many examples mentioned by *Chazal* of disciples who were disrespectful to their teachers and were subsequently severely punished. We have elsewhere discussed the reasons why such severe punishments were necessary. That, however, relates to the *rebbe-talmid* (master-disciple) relationship in a negative sense. Let us explore more deeply the essence of the positive relationship between *rebbe* and *talmid*.

מְנָא הָא מִלְּתָא דְאָמְרֵי אִינְשֵׁי, חַמְרָא לְמָרֵיהּ, טִיבוּתָא לְשַׁקְיֵהּ.
אָמַר לֵהּ דִּכְתִיב וְסָמַכְתָּ אֶת יָדְךָ עָלָיו, לְמַעַן יִשְׁמְעוּ כָּל עֲדַת בְּנֵי
יִשְׂרָאֵל. וּכְתִיב, וִיהוֹשֻׁעַ בֶּן נוּן מָלֵא רוּחַ חָכְמָה, כִּי סָמַךְ מֹשֶׁה אֶת
יָדָיו עָלָיו וַיִּשְׁמְעוּ אֵלָיו בְּנֵי יִשְׂרָאֵל (בבא קמא צ״ב ע״ב).
ורש״י: הַיַּיִן שֶׁל מֶלֶךְ הוּא, וְהַשׁוֹתִין אוֹתוֹ מַחֲזִיקִים טוֹבָה לְשַׂר
הַמַּשְׁקֶה וְלֹא לַמֶּלֶךְ. כִּי סָמַךְ מֹשֶׁה אֶת יָדָיו עָלָיו. תָּלָה הַחָכְמָה
וְהַגְּדֻלָּה בְּמֹשֶׁה כְּאִלּוּ הוּא נוֹתְנָהּ לִיהוֹשֻׁעַ, וְהִיא אֵינָהּ אֶלָּא מִפִּי
הַקָּדוֹשׁ בָּרוּךְ הוּא.

What is the source of the popular saying, "Though the wine belongs to the owner, thanks are given to the waiter"? For the verse states, "and you [Moshe] shall place your hand upon him ... in order that all of Israel hearken to him." And also it says, "and Yehoshua the son of Nun is filled with the spirit of wisdom, for Moshe had placed his hand upon him and Israel hearkened to him" (Bava Kamma 92b).

Though the wine belongs to the king, those who drink it are grateful nonetheless to the waiter and not to the king, as it says, "for Moshe placed his hands upon him" — the wisdom and greatness [of Yehoshua] are considered as if they were given by Moshe to Yehoshua, while in fact they came from God (Rashi ibid.).

The lesson here is that since the wine previously mentioned belongs to the king, no one can possibly take any himself, rather one is dependent on the waiter to bring it from the wine cellar and serve him. So, too, the wisdom of the Torah is God's but no one can partake of it without a *rebbe* to serve it to him. Thus the *rebbe* is indispensable and one is indebted to him, though the wisdom is Hashem's. Since it was Moshe who "placed his hands" on Yehoshua, it is considered as if he is the one from whom Yehoshua's knowledge came.

Moshe, too, could only take the Torah proffered to him by Hashem. The same applies to the next statement וּמְסָרָהּ לִיהוֹשֻׁעַ, *and [he] transmitted it to Yehoshua*. Just as Sinai was the sole source for the Torah of Moshe, so too Moshe was the sole source for Yehoshua's Torah.

This is the reason for the institution of סְמִיכָה, *ordination*. No person, wise and learned as he may be, can ordain himself. One must be ordained by his *rebbe* who was ordained by his *rebbe* who in turn was ordained by his *rebbe*, and so on, in an unbroken chain reaching back until Moshe.

Rambam — in his introduction to the *Yad HaChazakah* — lists the forty generations from Moshe until חֲתִימַת הַתַּלְמוּד, the era of the completion of the Talmud. He concludes, *thus we find that from Rav Ashi until Moshe there are forty generations and they are Rav Ashi from Rava etc. ... and Yehoshua received from Moshe and Moshe from the Almighty. Therefore in fact all of them received from Hashem God of Israel.*

The Torah knowledge of each and every one of the גְּדוֹלֵי הַדּוֹר, the leading Torah scholars of each generation, is considered as if it was received from Hashem. Why? For every one of them has received his Torah from his *rebbe* and so he becomes a participant in קַבָּלַת הַתּוֹרָה. Only he who has learned his Torah from a transmitter in this unique chain is considered as if he himself received it from the Almighty at Sinai.

Apprenticeship to a Torah scholar is referred to by *Chazal* as שִׁמּוּשׁ תַּלְמִידֵי חֲכָמִים, *serving a talmid chacham. Chazal* declare that even someone who has taught himself all of Torah is considered an עַם הָאָרֶץ, an *ignorant boor*, if he has not served a *talmid chacham*.

The absence of שִׁמּוּשׁ to the self-taught is not the lack of an additional quality. Rather, all his knowledge is flawed. It is not possible to truly understand Torah unless one has been taught by a *rebbe*.

It is for this reason that *Chazal* have determined (*Berachos* 7b) that גְּדוֹלָה שְׁמוּשָׁה יוֹתֵר מִלְּמוּדָהּ, *The apprenticeship to a talmid chacham is more important than the study [of Torah] itself. Chazal* prove this by quoting the verse which describes Elisha the prophet as אֲשֶׁר יָצַק מַיִם עַל יְדֵי אֵלִיָּהוּ, *he who poured water on the hands of Eliyahu.* Although Elisha was Eliyahu's eminent disciple, he is described not as he who learned Torah from Eliyahu, but as he 'who poured water upon Eliyahu's hands.'

It was as a result of his servitude that Yehoshua was designated as Moshe's successor. This — although there were men of greater personal stature [see *Ramban* at the beginning of *Parashas Shelach* and *Baal Haturim* there].

The selection of Yehoshua as successor to Moshe and his qualifications as such are described in the following Midrash:

‏. . . וּמְשָׁרְתוֹ יְהוֹשֻׁעַ בֶּן נוּן נַעַר לֹא יָמִישׁ מִתּוֹךְ הָאֹהֶל (שמות לג:יא).

‏— אָמַר לוֹ הַקָּדוֹשׁ בָּרוּךְ הוּא לְמֹשֶׁה: יְהוֹשֻׁעַ הַרְבֵּה שֵׁרֶתְךָ וְהִרְבֵּה חָלַק לְךָ כָּבוֹד וְהוּא הָיָה מַשְׁכִּים וּמַעֲרִיב בְּבֵית הַוַּעַד שֶׁלְּךָ, וְהוּא הָיָה מְסַדֵּר אֶת הַסַּפְסָלִים וְהוּא פּוֹרֵס אֶת הַמַּחְצְלָאוֹת הוֹאִיל וְהוּא שֵׁרַתְךָ בְּכָל כֹּחוֹ כְּדַאי הוּא שֶׁיְּשַׁמֵּשׁ אֶת יִשְׂרָאֵל שֶׁאֵינוֹ מְאַבֵּד שְׂכָרוֹ. קַח לְךָ אֶת יְהוֹשֻׁעַ בֶּן נוּן לְקַיֵּם מַה שֶׁנֶּאֱמַר נוֹצֵר תְּאֵנָה יֹאכַל פִּרְיָהּ (במדבר רבה פ״כא:יד).

. . . And his attendant Yehoshua son of Nun was a lad who never left the tent (Shemos 33:11).

— *The Holy One said to Moshe: Yehoshua has
served you and honored you greatly; he would arise
early and remain late in your study hall; he would
arrange the benches and spread out the mats. He
served you with all his strength, he therefore is worthy
to serve Israel, for he shall not lose his rightful reward.
Take Yehoshua the son of Nun [and appoint him
leader], as it says, "the keeper of the fig tree shall eat its
fruit" (Bamidbar Rabbah 21:14).*

The Midrash is quite clear in stating that the paramount reason for
the selection of Yehoshua as Moshe's successor was his faithful
service of his master Moshe and it was this attribute that made him
worthy of being his successor.

In addition, the Torah is entrusted to the wise men of the
generation as a group and the individual must subordinate himself to
them, even though he may be the greatest Torah scholar of his
generation. This is clearly demonstrated in the *Gemara*:

כְּשֶׁיָּרַד חֲנִינָא בֶּן אֲחִי ר' יְהוֹשֻׁעַ לַגּוֹלָה הָיָה מְעַבֵּר שָׁנִים וְקוֹבֵעַ
חֳדָשִׁים בְּחוּצָה לָאָרֶץ. שָׁגְרוּ אַחֲרָיו שְׁנֵי ת"ח וכו' ... אָמַר לָהֶם
אַף אֲנִי לֹא הִנַּחְתִּי כְּמוֹתִי בְּאֶרֶץ יִשְׂרָאֵל. אָמְרוּ לוֹ גְּדָיִים שֶׁהִנַּחְתָּ
נַעֲשׂוּ תְיָשִׁים בַּעֲלֵי קַרְנַיִם, וְהֵם שְׁגָרוּנוּ אֶצְלָךְ. וְכַךְ אָמְרוּ לָנוּ לְכוּ
וְאִמְרוּ לוֹ בִּשְׁמֵנוּ אִם שׁוֹמֵעַ מוּטָב וְאִם לָאו יְהֵא בְּנִדּוּי. וְאִמְרוּ
לְאַחֵינוּ בַּגּוֹלָה, אִם שׁוֹמְעָם מוּטָב, וְאִם לָאו יַעֲלוּ לָהָר, אֲחִיָּה
יִבְנֶה מִזְבֵּחַ חֲנַנְיָה יְנַגֵּן בְּכִנּוֹר, וְיִכְפְּרוּ כֻלָּן וְיֹאמְרוּ אֵין לָהֶם חֵלֶק
בֵּאלֹקֵי יִשְׂרָאֵל וכו' (ברכות סג:ע"א).

*When Chanina nephew of R' Yehoshua, went to the
diaspora, he began to calculate years and fix new
moons. So the [Beis Din] sent two Sages to him ... He
replied, "There is no one my equal in Israel." They
replied, "The kids that you left behind have become
goats with horns and they have sent us to you and
instructed us as follows: Tell him in our name that if he
listens, well and good, but if not, he will be excommunicated. And tell our brethren in the diaspora [not to listen
to him]. If they listen to you, well and good, but if not, let
them ascend a mountain; let Achiyah build an altar,
and let Chananyah play a harp and let them say, 'We
have no share in the God of Israel.' " (Berachos 63a).*

This is the ultimate end of all those who break away and separate themselves from the main body of Israel's sages. It is tantamount to proclaiming, "We have no share in the God of Israel," even though, as in the case of Chanina, it was the most prominent of scholars who decided to rely on himself. The *Gemara* further stresses this by explaining that Chanina's mistake was because the verse states כִּי מִצִּיּוֹן תֵּצֵא תוֹרָה וּדְבַר ה' מִירוּשָׁלָיִם, *from Zion Torah shall emanate, and the word of Hashem from Jerusalem.* This verse does not prohibit the setting of leap years in the diaspora (see *Tosafos* ibid.) Rather, it stresses the centrality of *Eretz Yisrael* as the source from where *halachic* decisions are to emanate.

Today, the *yeshivah* is the pulsating center for transmitting Torah and tradition from *rebbe* to *talmid*. He who separates himself from the word of Torah of the *yeshivah* — as prominent and wise as he may be — is separating himself from the truths of Torah. The day will come when he will ascend a mountain and proclaim, "I have no share in the God of Israel." Those who become part of the *yeshivah* become part of Eternity, and merit דַּעַת הַתּוֹרָה from Hashem the God of Israel.

בָּדָד יֵשֵׁב

Alone Shall He Sit

אַל נָא תְהִי כַּמֵּת (במדבר יב:יב).

תַּנְיָא אַרְבָּעָה חֲשׁוּבִים כְּמֵת, עָנִי וּמְצֹרָע וְסוּמָא וּמִי שֶׁאֵין לוֹ
בָּנִים וכו' (נדרים סד:עב).

Let her not be like a dead person (Bamidbar 12:12).

*The Rabbis have taught: Four people are considered
as if they are dead: a pauper, a leper, a blind man and
one who is childless (Nedarim 64b).*

At first glance it would appear that the reason the leper is
"considered as dead" is due to the pain and gravity of his illness.
The physical suffering and incapacitation make his life not worth
living, so to speak. But this is incorrect. We've discussed elsewhere
(see *Parashas Shemos*) that the joy of living in itself overrides the
suffering and anguish of any given moment. Thus the psalmist cries
out in relief, יַסֹּר יִסְּרַנִּי קָּהּ וְלַמָּוֶת לֹא נְתָנָנִי, *God has afflicted me greatly,
but He had not given me over to death* (*Tehillim* 118:18). Yirmiyahu
exclaimed, *Of what can a living man complain* (*Eichah* 3). Chazal
add by way of explanation, *For it is enough that he lives* (*Kedushin*
80b see *Rashi* there). If this is the case, then what is so terrible about
the plight of the leper that he is considered as if dead?

The answer is because he is prohibited from associating with the rest of Israel, as the verse states, בָּדָד יֵשֵׁב מִחוּץ לַמַּחֲנֶה מוֹשָׁבוֹ, *He shall sit alone, outside the camp shall be his habitation* (Vayikra 13:46). One who is disqualified from being with fellow human beings, from giving to or lending a helping hand to a friend is 'considered as dead.' His existence ceases to be meaningful!

A careful analysis of the other three types of people 'considered as dead' will lead us to the same conclusion; it is their inability to relate to and to give to their fellow human beings that renders their lives meaningless.

Let us examine the case of the blind man. The *Gemara* establishes that *One who deafens another person must pay him his entire value* (*Bava Basra* 85b). This is seen as equating the value of hearing to that of all other human faculties combined. Rabbeinu Yonah in *Shaarei Teshuvah Shaar* 2 points out that hearing can *affect* all parts of the body. This may be seen as the source for the evaluation of hearing as being equal to the value of the whole person. Yet *Chazal* do not assert that a deaf person is 'considered as dead.' What makes the gift of sight so unique?

The answer is that although for a person himself, hearing is his most important faculty and this accounts for the high damages assessed when he is deafened, as regards his relationship with fellow man, however, it is the gift of sight which forms a bond. Thus, we find that the Torah says about Moshe,

וַיִּגְדַּל מֹשֶׁה וַיֵּצֵא אֶל אֶחָיו וַיַּרְא בְּסִבְלֹתָם (שמות ב:יא).

And Moshe grew up and he went out to his brethren and he saw their suffering (Shemos 2:11).

Rashi explains, נָתַן עֵינָיו וְלִבּוֹ לִהְיוֹת מֵיצַר עֲלֵיהֶם, *He applied his eyes and heart to share their pain* (Rashi loc cit.).

It was not until Moshe *saw*, that he began to feel for his brethren. Mere knowledge was not enough until he saw; nay, until he *applied* his sight, he could not completely feel for his fellow Jews.

The *Sforno* makes a similar point:

וְעֵינֵי יִשְׂרָאֵל כָּבְדוּ מִזֹּקֶן לֹא יוּכַל לִרְאוֹת, וַיַּגֵּשׁ אֹתָם אֵלָיו וַיִּשַּׁק לָהֶם וַיְחַבֵּק לָהֶם (בראשית מח:ו).

And Israel's eyes were heavy from age and he could not see; Yosef brought [his sons] close to Yaakov and [Yaakov] kissed them and hugged them (Bereishis 48:10).

Sforno explains that it was necessary for Yaakov to kiss and hug them in order to become attached to them, so that his blessing could take effect. This was necessary because he was blind; for if he could see, then he could have blessed them immediately upon seeing them.

Thus, sight is the prime faculty for creating and developing a relationship with one's fellow man. Yaakov could not express his love for his grandchildren; nor Moshe his sympathy for his brethren, without the ability to see. A blind man also sits in isolation — as does the leper — and therefore he is 'considered like dead.'

It is for this reason that a childless person, too, is considered as dead. For a person's fullest instincts of kindness and giving are directed towards one's children. And indeed no one can absorb as much benevolence as a child from his parents. One who has no children is living with a repressed and frustrated instinct of חֶסֶד, and without the possibility to do good for others, one is also considered as dead.

This understanding that one without children is considered dead, being due to one's lack of having someone to whom to give, is borne out by the story of Shlomo HaMelech and the two women. Both claimed that the live child was hers. The woman who was lying and claiming that the other's child was her own knew quite well that it wasn't. What, then, did she stand to gain by snatching it away from its rightful mother and claiming it as her own when she knew that this was not the case?

The answer is that by raising the child as her own, he would come to look upon her as a mother, with the full expectations of a child from his mother. This mother's overwhelming urge to give would be satisfied and she herself would feel 'alive'! So overwhelming and irrepressible is this desire to give and bestow kindness upon another person that she was willing to perform an abominable cruelty and commit a heinous crime, in order to satisfy this urge!

Similarly, the pauper is considered dead not because he doesn't have for himself but because he doesn't have enough to give others.

All four of those mentioned in the *Gemara* have one common denominator. They are crippled in their ability to relate to another person; to share in his suffering; to give and to bestow kindness upon him. They are cursed one way or another with a בָּדָד יֵשֵׁב. The only life worth living is a life of sharing and giving.

הַחִיּוּב לְהִתְעַלּוֹת

The Necessity
for Constant Growth

I.

וַיְדַבֵּר ה׳ אֶל מֹשֶׁה אַחֲרֵי מוֹת שְׁנֵי בְּנֵי אַהֲרֹן (ויקרא טז:א).

Hashem spoke to Moshe after the death of the two sons of Aharon (Vayikra 16:1).

This verse begins the portion read on *Yom Kippur* morning and deals with the sacrifices brought on *Yom Kippur*. The *Zohar* and *Arizal* (cited in *Beer Hetev Orach Chaim* 621:1) comment on the person who, when contemplating the untimely death of Aharon's children, is genuinely filled with sorrow and anguish, to the point of tears. He merits forgiveness for his sins and will not suffer the death of his children during his lifetime.

How does one grieve over an event that occurred thousands of years ago — an event seemingly of a personal nature? What meaning does their death carry for us today, that one should be filled with sorrow when reading of it?

To understand the mourning for the death of Aharon's children we must first understand how a great man affects his surroundings and the spiritual riches he imparts to those with whom he comes in contact. Only if we evaluate the impact of a righteous man on society in the proper manner can we comprehend the magnitude of the loss of a *tzaddik*.

The *Gemara* in *Chulin* (71a) relates that R' Yishmael rebuked Ben Azai saying, *Woe unto [you] Ben Azai for not apprenticing yourself [more conscientiously] to me.* *Rashi* explains the implication of the term *Woe*, חבל, in the sense of *a loss and crippling blow* — חֲבָלָה — to the world as a whole. Thus, R' Yishmael's rebuke was not for Ben Azai's personal loss but for the fact that as a result, society as a whole was the poorer for it. When a person misses the opportunity to grow spiritually or to acquire wisdom, he has deprived not only himself but the world as a whole of a possibility for elevation and improvement.

This rebuke was directed at Ben Azai even though he was greater than R' Yishmael, as he himself said, (*Bechoros* 58a) *All the wise men of Israel are as but a garlic peel compared to [Ben Azai].* Yet there was some dimension of learning that he could have acquired from R' Yishmael and it was for this that he was so harshly criticized. Not only did he squander his chance for knowledge, but the world as a whole suffered.

We see that each great man is the sole bearer of a particular dimension of greatness, imparting it to and sharing it with his surroundings. With his demise that dimension exists no longer.

We find this phenomena by Eliyahu Hanavi as well. The *Tanach* tells of the בְּנֵי הַנְּבִיאִים (lit. children or disciples of prophecy) who confronted Elisha and asked him, *Did you know that Hashem is taking away your master today?* (*II Melachim* 2:3). Yet, when Eliyahu disappeared they forgot the prophecy of his departure and went to look for him! (see ibid. 16:17). *Rashi* comments, *From the time that Eliyahu ascended to Heaven, the spirit of holiness departed from those prophets.* Thus, as long as Eliyahu was alive they were endowed with the ability to prophesize like Eliyahu. Not only were they prophets, but, as *Rashi* (ibid. 3) points out, they were actually his peers. Yet after he departed they lost all prophetic gift, for it was through Eliyahu that they attained and sustained this gift.

In this light we can appreciate the magnitude of the untimely death of Aharon's children. It may have occurred thousands of years ago and there were many other great men, at that time and subsequently, but the particular mission of Nadav and Avihu remains unfulfilled to this very day.

In addition, this understanding makes it imperative for every person to acquire knowledge and grow spiritually in every possible way. For if we fail to do so we deprive not only ourselves but society as well.

II.

We have demonstrated the importance of constant and consistent spiritual growth for each of us. A problem arises, however, when a person is convinced that his capabilities are mediocre. "I can't accomplish much anyway, so why try?"

It would be enlightening to glimpse the manner in which one of Israel's leaders developed his potential to the utmost. Channah, Shmuel's mother, prayed for a child that would be *Average amongst men, . . . neither too smart nor too stupid* (*Berachos* 31b). Her wish was granted as Channah herself acknowledged, אֶל הַנַּעַר הַזֶּה הִתְפַּלָּלְתִּי וַיִּתֵּן ה' לִי אֶת שְׁאֵלָתִי אֲשֶׁר שָׁאַלְתִּי מֵעִמּוֹ, *For this lad have I prayed and Hashem has granted me my request that I have made of Him* (I *Shmuel* 1:27). This very same Shmuel who was comparable to Moshe and Aharon (*Berachos* loc cit.) was but "average amongst men . . . neither too smart nor too stupid." This is what an average man can aspire to and what heights he can attain.

Most startling of all is the statement of our Sages which determines human capacity in relation to the Divine Presence.

> אָמַר ר' שִׁמְעוֹן בֶּן לָקִישׁ: שְׁתֵּי פַרְשִׁיוֹת הִכְתִּיב לָנוּ מֹשֶׁה בַּתּוֹרָה וכו'. כָּתוּב אֶחָד אוֹמֵר וְהָיִיתָ רַק לְמָעְלָה. יָכוֹל כָּמוֹנִי תַּלְמוּד לוֹמַר רַק לְשׁוֹן מְעוּט, גְּדֻלָּתִי לְמַעְלָה מִגְּדֻלַּתְכֶם וכו'. קְדֹשִׁים תִּהְיוּ, יָכוֹל כָּמוֹנִי, תַּלְמוּד לוֹמַר כִּי קָדוֹשׁ אֲנִי קְדֻשָּׁתִי לְמַעְלָה מִקְּדֻשַּׁתְכֶם (ויקרא רבה כד:ט).

> R' Shimon ben Lakish said: Moshe wrote two chapters [needing qualification] in the Torah. One verse reads, "and You will be always elevated." I would think [that this means] "as elevated as Me [Hashem]," therefore the verse uses the term "rak" which is dimunitive, [i.e.,] My elevation is greater than yours.

> Similarly, it says, "You shall be holy." I would think [it means] as holy as Me [Hashem]. Therefore the verse adds, "For I am holy — My holiness is superior to your holiness" (Vayikra Rabbah 24:9).

Chazal appraised human potential and found it comparable even to Hashem's holiness. They concluded not with recognition of limits to human potential but rather with the emphasis on Divine transcendence: "My holiness is superior to yours." Our Sages, in spite of their profound comprehension of Hashem's greatness, dared to compare man's potential for *kedushah*, holiness, with the Divine holiness manifest. This comparison was engendered by their profound evaluation of human capabilities.

But how does one maximize one's potential? What are the means and methods to effect such spiritual development and achievement?

The first step is עֲמֵלוּת בַּתּוֹרָה, *arduous perseverance in Torah study*, a diligence of which our father Yaakov is the paradigm. Yaakov studied with Shem and Ever for fourteen years without sleep, not even on a stone. This is indicated by the fact that his sleeping on stones mentioned in *Parashas Vayeitzei* is described as his first — the implication being that at Shem and Ever he did not even do that.

The reward for עֲמֵלִים בַּתּוֹרָה – שֶׁתִּהְיוּ עֲמֵלִים – אִם בְּחֻקֹּתַי תֵּלֵכוּ, *If you walk in My precepts — that you will toil in Torah* (*Leviticus* 26:3 and *Rashi*), is וְהִתְהַלַּכְתִּי בְּתוֹכְכֶם, *And I will walk in your midst*. Amplified by *Rashi*: אֲטַיֵּל עִמָּכֶם בְּגַן עֵדֶן כְּאֶחָד מִכֶּם וְלֹא תִהְיוּ מִזְדַּעְזְעִים מִמֶּנִּי, *I will stroll with you in Gan Eden like one of you and you will not tremble before Me* (*Vayikra* 26:12).

This closeness to Hashem, walking with Him, as it were, and not trembling before Him, is the climax of constant spiritual progress attained through עֲמֵלוּת בַּתּוֹרָה.

The second prerequisite for developing oneself is abstention from hedonistic indulgence. קְדֹשִׁים תִּהְיוּ – פְּרוּשִׁים תִּהְיוּ, קַדֵּשׁ עַצְמְךָ מִן הַמֻּתָּר לָךְ, *Be holy — be ascetic, sanctify yourself [by refraining] from that which is permitted to you.* It is with regard to this *mitzvah* that *Chazal* compared man to Hashem.

Let us not make the mistake, however, of thinking that these two elements of self-development are optional fulfillments, not included in the mandatory aspects of the service of God.

The Torah states quite clearly that for עָמָל בַּתּוֹרָה one is promised וְלֹא תִגְעַל נַפְשִׁי אֶתְכֶם ... אֵין רוּחִי קָצָה בָכֶם, *And I will not abhor you ... My spirit will not detest you* (*Vayikra* 26:11 and *Rashi*).

The implication is quite clear: One who is slack in his diligence and perseverance is an object of contempt and disgust in the eyes of Hashem. So, too, one who indulges himself excessively eventually degenerates into a בֵּן סוֹרֵר וּמוֹרֶה (a wayward and rebellious son) whose central characteristic, as explained by *Ramban*, is this very lack of self-restraint.

Thus, on the one hand, the diligent person whose life is guided by עֲמֵלוּת and פְּרִישׁוּת is elevated to heights bordering on the Divine. On the other hand, the negligent and lazy person becomes an object of contempt and derision in the eyes of Hashem.

Most remarkably, the *Mishnah* in *Avos* combines these two facets of spiritual growth, stating:

> כָּךְ הִיא דַרְכָּהּ שֶׁל תּוֹרָה: פַּת בַּמֶּלַח תֹּאכַל וּמַיִם בַּמְּשׂוּרָה תִּשְׁתֶּה
> וְעַל הָאָרֶץ תִּישָׁן וְחַיֵּי צַעַר תִּחְיֶה וּבַתּוֹרָה אַתָּה עָמֵל (אבות ו:ב).
> *This is the way of [studying] Torah: Eat bread with salt,*
> *drink water with a measure, sleep on the ground, and*
> *lead a life of hardship and toil in [the study of] Torah*
> *(Avos 6:4).*

While these two elements are the foundations of spiritual growth and elevation, there is an additional factor indispensable to spiritual advancement and that is: prayer. The *Gemara* relates:

> ... מַה יַּעֲשֶׂה אָדָם וְיֶחְכַּם. אָמַר לֵיהּ יַרְבֶּה בִּישִׁיבָה וִימַעֵט
> בִּסְחוֹרָה. אָמְרוּ הַרְבֵּה עָשׂוּ כֵן וְלֹא הוֹעִיל לָהֶם, אֶלָּא יְבַקְשׁוּ
> רַחֲמִים מִמִּי שֶׁהַחָכְמָה שֶׁלּוֹ, שֶׁנֶּאֱמַר כִּי ה' יִתֵּן חָכְמָה מִפִּיו דַּעַת
> וּתְבוּנָה ... מַאי קָא מַשְׁמַע לָן ... הָא בְּלֹא הָא לֹא סַגִּי (נדה
> ע:ע"ב).
> *... What shall a person do to become wise? He replied,*
> *"Let him persevere [in study] and minimize his*
> *commercial affairs." They countered, "Many have*
> *done so and it has not helped them. Rather they should*
> *request wisdom from the One to Whom wisdom*
> *belongs, as it says, "For Hashem grants wisdom; and*
> *from His mouth knowledge and understanding" ...*
> *What is the conclusion? That one without the other does*
> *not suffice (Niddah 70b).*

Prayer alone is not enough. One must toil arduously in the study of Torah, leading a life of self-restraint for כָּךְ הִיא דַרְכָּהּ שֶׁל תּוֹרָה, *This is the way of Torah.* But as with all human endeavor, effort without prayer for assistance from Hashem, the One to Whom wisdom belongs, is futile.

כְּבוֹד הָרַב

Respect for the Teachers and Leaders of Israel

וְהָדַרְתָּ פְּנֵי זָקֵן, וְיָרֵאתָ מֵאֱלֹקֶיךָ (ויקרא יט:לב).

And you shall show respect to elders and fear your God (Vayikra 19:32).

The honor and respect due to the teacher of Torah in Israel is expressed quite clearly by *Chazal*. Thus מוֹרָא רַבְּךָ כְּמוֹרָא שָׁמַיִם, *Let the fear of your teacher be like your fear of Heaven* (*Avos* 4:15). Our Sages have, in addition, depicted quite clearly the punishment meted out to those who show disrespect to their teachers.

וֶהֱוֵי מִתְחַמֵּם כְּנֶגֶד אוּרָן שֶׁל חֲכָמִים וֶהֱוֵי זָהִיר בְּגַחַלְתָּן, שֶׁלֹּא תִכָּוֶה, שֶׁנְּשִׁיכָתָן נְשִׁיכַת שׁוּעָל וַעֲקִיצָתָן עֲקִיצַת עַקְרָב, וּלְחִישָׁתָן לְחִישַׁת שָׂרָף (אבות ב:טו).

Warm yourself by the fire of wise men but beware of their coals, lest you be singed, for their bite is the bite of a fox and their sting is the sting of a scorpion, while their hiss is the hiss of a serpent (*Avos* 2:15).

Chazal describe many people who showed disrespect towards their teachers and their punishment.

The *Gemara* (*Pesachim* 69a) tells of the time that R' Akiva was arguing with his teacher R' Eliezer. To strengthen his position, R' Akiva countered R' Eliezer's point with a facetious reference to the prohibition of slaughtering an animal on *Shabbos* (see *Rashi* there). R' Eliezer replied, "You have replied [to my argument] with 'slaughter,' by slaughter shall you die." Indeed R' Akiva died a terrible death as punishment for having not shown his *rebbi* the proper respect.

What is astonishing about this is that R' Akiva's jesting was not to offend his teacher but rather out of respect! It was his *rebbi* who had taught him this *halachah* but had forgotten it. In order not to embarrass him, R' Akiva had not confronted him directly but looked for a way to jokingly remind him of the ruling that he himself had taught. Was this not a good enough reason for him to reply in the manner that he did? Certainly R' Eliezer understood this too. So why then did he not forgive his student Rabbi Akiva, not even sparing him from a horrible death?

Another example of the severe punishment of a student by his master is to be found in the incident of R' Yochanan and Resh Lakish:

אָמַר לֵיהּ, וּמַאי אַהֲנֵית לִי הָתָם רַבִּי קָרוּ לִי, הָכָא רַבִּי קָרוּ לִי . . . חָלַשׁ דַּעְתֵּיהּ דְּרַ׳ יוֹחָנָן, חָלַשׁ רֵישׁ לָקִישׁ. אָתַאי אַחְתֵיהּ קָא בָּכְיָא, אָמְרָה לֵיהּ עֲשֵׂה בִּשְׁבִיל בָּנַי. אָמַר לָהּ עָזְבָה יְתֹמֶיךָ אֲנִי אֲחַיֶּה. עֲשֵׂה בִּשְׁבִיל אַלְמְנוּתִי. אָמַר לָהּ וְאַלְמְנוֹתֶיךָ עָלַי תִּבְטָחוּ. נָח נַפְשֵׁי דְרַ׳ שִׁמְעוֹן בֶּן לָקִישׁ (בבא מציעה פד:ע״א).

[Resh Lakish] countered, "Wherewith have you bene-fited me? Before they called me 'chief [of robbers]' and here they also call me 'chief.' " R' Yochanan was hurt and [as a result] Resh Lakish fell ill. [R' Yochanan's] sister [i.e., Resh Lakish's wife] came to him crying. She begged, "Do something [forgive him] for the sake of my children." He replied [with a verse], "The orphans that you will leave, I will sustain" (Yirmiyahu 49). [She continued,] "For the sake of my widowhood." He replied, "And your widows shall trust in Me." Resh Lakish died (Bava Metzia 84a).

The punishment meted out by R' Yochanan is astounding in its ferocity. Even if Resh Lakish was wrong in the disrespect he showed R' Yochanan, what had his wife and children done to deserve such pain and suffering? Even more inexplicable is the fact that R' Yochanan himself suffered so much anguish from Resh Lakish's death. The *Gemara* (*Bava Metzia* ibid.) tells that he was so overwrought with grief at the loss of Resh Lakish that he lost his senses and eventually died. Did he want to punish Resh Lakish even at the cost of his own life?

Furthermore, *Chazal* tell us quite clearly what the lot is of he who causes another to be punished on his account. כָּל שֶׁחֲבֵרוֹ נֶעֱנָשׁ עַל יָדוֹ אֵין מַכְנִיסִין אוֹתוֹ בִּמְחִיצָתוֹ שֶׁל הַקָּדוֹשׁ בָּרוּךְ הוּא, *he who causes his fellow to be punished is not permitted to enter into the precincts of the Holy One* (*Shabbos* 149b). Why then did R' Elazar and R' Yochanan allow their disciples to be punished by insisting, as it were, on respect?

The answer is that it was not at all for the sake of their personal honor. Disrespect for the teachers of Israel weakens their leadership and influence in Israel. Lack of respect for the elders of Israel means in effect the elimination of leadership of Israel by their Sages. The avoidance of such a calamity overrode any other consideration.

> כִּי אֲתָא רַב דִּימִי אָמַר: י"ח קְלָלוֹת קִלֵּל יְשַׁעְיָהוּ אֶת יִשְׂרָאֵל וְלֹא נִתְקָרְרָה דַעְתּוֹ עַד שֶׁאָמַר לָהֶם הַמִּקְרָא הַזֶּה, יִרְהֲבוּ הַנַּעַר בַּזָּקֵן וְהַנִּקְלֶה בַּנִּכְבָּד (חגיגה יד:ע"א).
>
> *When R' Dimi came, he said: Yeshayahu cursed Israel with eighteen curses, yet he was not content until he pronounced, "The youngster will behave insolently against the elder, and the base against the honorable"* (*Chagigah* 14a).

Yeshayahu had cursed the Jewish people with eighteen curses affecting every possible stature. He included people with knowledge of Torah and those with the ability to understand its profundities. Also included were; judges, kings, prophets, wise men and counsellors (ibid.). Yet nothing he said compared to the magnitude of the curse that the authority of Israel's elders would be usurped. לֹא נִתְקָרְרָה דַעְתּוֹ, *he was not content*, until this final curse. Why?

The Jewish people are different from other nations in that they cannot survive without the institution of זְקֵנִים, *elders*. Although other nations can exist without being led by the Sages or elders, it is Israel's uniqueness that make their elders a necessity rather than a luxury. This is what R' Akiva meant to express when he said, נִמְשְׁלוּ יִשְׂרָאֵל לְעוֹף מַה הָעוֹף הַזֶּה אֵינוֹ פּוֹרֵחַ בְּלִי כְּנָפַיִם כָּךְ יִשְׂרָאֵל אֵינָם יְכוֹלִים לַעֲשׂוֹת דָּבָר חוּץ מִזִּקְנֵיהֶם, *Israel is compared to a bird. Just as a bird cannot fly without its wings, so too is Israel helpless without its elders* (*Vayikra Rabbah* 11:8).

The comparison is precise. A bird without wings has even less capabilities than that of an animal who never possessed wings in the first place. Rather, he is a helpless and pitiful creature. Israel without elders is similar to that bird, helpless. Other nations survive without elders. For Israel, however, they are the *sine qua non* of survival. Usurping the power of the elders is tantamount to striking a blow at the very core of the life force of the Jewish people.

The understanding of the absolute necessity of the honor and respect which must be the due of our Sages, so as to ensure the existence and survival of Israel, puts the previous stories in their proper perspective. It was not the honor of R' Elazar and R' Yochanan that was at stake. It was the very institution of 'elders' whose leadership was being compromised by jest. This put Israel's survival in jeopardy and the measures called for were severe. Since they were in defense of this important institution, then perhaps it was not considered as if these people were נֶעֱנַשׁ עַל יָדוֹ, *punished on their account.*

Therefore, a *Rav* that causes someone who humiliates him to be punished is thinking in terms of Israel's benefit.

What *is* the proper respect and honor to be accorded the elders of Israel? *Chazal* have given us a glimpse of the majestic honor that will one day be the lot of the elders of Israel.

Although there was a time in Israel's history when even its lowest elements respected the elders of Israel, it is the curse of our generation that this state of affairs no longer exists. A picture of the respect and dignity accorded Israel's leaders is illustrated by the story of the fall of Jerusalem told in *Gittin* 56a. The *Gemara* relates how R' Yochanan ben Zakkai clandestinely left the besieged city of Jerusalem in a coffin so as to be able to negotiate with Vespasian. The rebels, whose job was to ensure that no one left the city, insisted upon inspecting the casket. They wanted to run spears through the coffin or at least to shake it in order to ascertain that R' Yochanan was dead, as his disciples asserted. His disciples countered, יֹאמְרוּ רַבָּן דָּקְרוּ יֹאמְרוּ רַבָּן דָּחֲפוּ, *People will say the Rav was stabbed, people will say that the Rav's coffin was shaken.* Thereupon the rebels desisted. Here we have a glimpse of the honor accorded to Israel's elders. These guards were hardened rebels and among the basest elements of the people. Furthermore, it was their absolute conviction that anyone attempting to make peace with Rome was endangering Israel. Yet, they dared not do anything, not even shake the coffin, which would in any way slight the honor of R' Yochanan ben Zakkai.

It is our shame and disgrace that today's generation no longer listens to its elders. *Mesilas Yesharim* describes this state of affairs most concisely: *This is all the result of the haughtiness which sets wisdom backwards and dulls people's minds. It removes the wise leaders and disciples who have not been sufficiently apprenticed, whose eyes have barely opened, and already consider themselves to be the wisest of the wise* (Mesilas Yesharim ch. 11).

תָּנֵי ר׳ שִׁמְעוֹן בַּר יוֹחָאִי וכו׳: אַף לְעָתִיד לָבוֹא הַקָּדוֹשׁ בָּרוּךְ הוּא חוֹלֵק כָּבוֹד לַזְּקֵנִים הה״ד וְחָפְרָה הַלְּבָנָה וּבוֹשָׁה הַחַמָּה כִּי מָלַךְ ה׳ בְּהַר צִיּוֹן וּבִירוּשָׁלַיִם, וּכְתִיב, וְנֶגֶד זְקֵנָיו כָּבוֹד (ויקרא רבה יא:ח).

R' Shimon bar Yochai taught: Even in the future, the Holy One will accord honor to the elders, as it says, "And the moon will be embarrassed, and the sun put to shame, for God has ruled over Zion and Jerusalem." It continues, "And before his elders there will be honor" (Vayikra Rabbah 11:8).

R' Shimon was speaking of לְעָתִיד לָבֹא, a future epoch when God's eminence will have illuminated the universe, His radiance outshining the brilliance of the sun and the moon. The sun and moon referred to are not the sun and moon of today but rather the sun and moon of the future, whose luminescence will be many times brighter than today's (see *Pesachim* 68a). Yet even in this world of scintillating brilliance, the place of the elders of Israel will be well established. It will be through them that Israel will receive its light and majesty, and "before the elders there will be honor."

The young no longer respect, let alone obey, its elders. What was well understood by the coarsest rebels is no longer common even among the finer elements of Israel. יִרְהֲבוּ הַנַּעַר בַּזָּקֵן, *the younger will behave insolently against the elder.*

May the day speedily come when amidst the great revelation of Hashem we will yet see לִפְנֵי זְקֵנִים כָּבוֹד, *And before his elders there will be honor.*

עַצְלוּת

Laziness

I.

וְהַכֹּהֵן הַגָּדוֹל מֵאֶחָיו (ויקרא כא:י).

לָמָּה נִקְרָא שְׁמוֹ כֹּהֵן גָּדוֹל שֶׁהוּא גָּדוֹל בַּחֲמִשָּׁה דְבָרִים: בְּחָכְמָה בְּכֹחַ וכו'. בְּכֹחַ שֶׁהוּא גִבּוֹר. בֹּא וּרְאֵה אַהֲרֹן כְּשֶׁהֵנִיף אֶת הַלְוִיִּם כ"ב אֶלֶף הֵנִיף בְּיוֹם אֶחָד. כֵּיצַד הָיָה מְנִיפָם מוֹלִיךְ וּמֵבִיא מַעֲלֶה וּמוֹרִיד, הֲרֵי שֶׁהָיָה גָדוֹל בְּכֹחַ (ויקרא רבה כו:ט).

And he that is High Priest among his brethren (Vayikra 21:10).

Why was he called by the name of High Priest? Because he was superior in five different aspects. In wisdom, strength, etc. As regards strength ... when Aharon lifted twenty-two thousand Levites in a single day. How did he lift them? Forward, backward, upward and downward. This proves that he was a strong person (Vayikra Rabbah 26:9).

אֵין הַקָּדוֹשׁ בָּרוּךְ הוּא מַשְׁרֶה שְׁכִינָתוֹ אֶלָּא עַל גִּבּוֹר וכו' (נדרים לח ע"א).

The Holy One bestows His Divine Spirit only on a strong person etc. (Nedarim 38a).

Chazal clearly establish that strength is an essential prerequisite for both the priesthood and prophecy. What is the connection between physical strength and these spiritual vocations?

Rambam (*Yesodei HaTorah* 5:1-2) interprets the strength mentioned here as being of a moral nature: גִּבּוֹר בְּמִדּוֹתָיו וְלֹא יְהֵא יִצְרוֹ מִתְגַּבֵּר עָלָיו בְּדָבָר שֶׁבָּעוֹלָם, *Strong in character, his [evil] inclination holding no sway over him in any aspect.* However, the proof points to a physical strength. Thus Aharon's strength is manifest in his ability to lift the Levites and Moshe's strength is established by virtue of his lifting the tablets which were exceedingly heavy (see כֶּסֶף מִשְׁנֶה and לֶחֶם מִשְׁנֶה). This brings us back to our original question: Why is physical strength a prerequisite for priesthood and prophecy?

The answer is that the גְּבוּרָה referred to is the concentration of all one's skills, strengths and abilities, brought to bear toward the attainment of the goal set and the task to be achieved. It is indeed in a sense the physical strength, but not merely the physical manifestation thereof. It is rather the strength exercised to overcome the body's natural laziness and inertia (עַצְלוּת).

Shlomo HaMelech elaborates in *Mishlei* on the destruction wrought by the sluggard's neglect. From his description we will discern the importance of strength used to prevent the ravages brought on by laziness.

עַל שְׂדֵה אִישׁ עָצֵל עָבַרְתִּי וְעַל כֶּרֶם אָדָם חֲסַר לֵב, וְהִנֵּה עָלָה כֻלּוֹ קִמְּשֹׂנִים כָּסּוּ פָנָיו חֲרֻלִּים וְגֶדֶר אֲבָנָיו נֶהֱרָסָה, וָאֶחֱזֶה אָנֹכִי, אָשִׁית לִבִּי רָאִיתִי לָקַחְתִּי מוּסָר (משלי כד:לב).
I passed by the field of a lazy man, and by the vineyard of a man devoid of understanding, and lo it had become overgrown with thorns, briars had covered it over, and its stone fence had been destroyed. I perceived this and considered it well, I looked upon it and took from it a lesson (Mishlei 24:32).

The slothful person not only forfeits the fruits of his field but grows weeds and briars in their stead.

אָמַר רָבָא לְמַיְמִינִין בָּהּ סַמָּא דְחַיֵּי לְמַשְׂמְאִילִים בַּהּ סַמָּא דְמוֹתָא (שבת פח:ע"ב).
לְמַיְמִינִין בָּהּ, עֲסוּקִים בְּכָל כֹּחָם וּטְרוּדִים לָדַעַת סוֹדָהּ. כְּאָדָם הַמִּשְׁתַּמֵּשׁ בְּיַד יְמִינוֹ שֶׁהִיא עִיקָר (רש"י שם).
Rava stated: For those who use the 'right hand', as it

were, it is an elixir of life, for those who use the 'left hand' it becomes a deadly poison.

'Right hand' — those who study Torah with all their might and are occupied with discovering its secrets, just as a person uses his right hand, which is the prominent one (Rashi).

Doing something left-handedly does not describe a job undone. Rather it points to lethargy in the performance of the act itself. For if a person studies Torah in such a manner, it is not life giving and invigorating; it is deadly. How does this process work? How do the briars and thorns accumulate in the field of the lazy man? How does תּוֹרַת חַיִּים, the Torah of life, metamorphasize into a deadly poison?

Chazal describe this process:

עַל שְׂדֵה אִישׁ עָצֵל עָבַרְתִּי, קָנָה שָׂדֶה וְקָנָה כֶּרֶם וְלֹא עָמַל בָּהֶם נִקְרָא עָצֵל. כֵּן תַּלְמִיד חָכָם אִם אֵינוֹ נוֹשֵׂא וְנוֹתֵן בְּתוֹרָתוֹ, סוֹפוֹ לְהָנִיחַ שְׁנַיִם וּשְׁלֹשָׁה דְבָרִים בְּפָרָשָׁה, וְהִנֵּה עָלָה כֻלּוֹ קִמְּשֹׂנִים. שֶׁמְּבַקֵּשׁ פֵּירוּשָׁהּ שֶׁל פָּרָשָׁה וְאֵינוֹ מוֹצֵא. כָּסוּ פָנָיו חֲרֻלִּים וְגֶדֶר אֲבָנָיו נֶהֱרָסָה, מִתּוֹךְ שֶׁלֹּא עָמַל בָּהֶם, הוּא יוֹשֵׁב וּמְטַמֵּא אֶת הַטָּהוֹר וּמְטַהֵר אֶת הַטָּמֵא וּפוֹרֵץ גִּדְרוֹ שֶׁל תַּלְמִידֵי חֲכָמִים. וּמָה עָנְשׁוֹ שֶׁל זֶה. שְׁלֹמֹה פֵּרַשׁ אוֹתוֹ עָלָיו בְּקַבָּלָה, וּפוֹרֵץ גָּדֵר יִשְׁכֶנּוּ נָחָשׁ (יַלְקוּט משׁלי כד).

"I passed by the field of the lazy man" — He who buys a field or a vineyard and does not work it is considered a sluggard. Similarly, a scholar who does not immerse himself in study will eventually leave two or three things unlearned in the [particular] section. "It had become overgrown with thorns" — meaning, that he tries to divine the meaning of that section but is unable to. "Briars had covered it over and the stone fence had been destroyed" — because he did not study diligently enough, he declares that which is pure as defiled and that which is defiled as pure, thereby breaching the fence of scholars. How is this person punished? Shlomo stated, "He who breaches a fence is bitten by a snake" (Yalkut Mishlei 24).

Thus, the Torah of life becomes a deadly weapon in the hands of he who has learned lackadaisically.

Mesilas Yesharim describes this process: *The evil wrought by the sluggard does not happen at once, but gradually, without his knowledge or awareness. He is dragged from bad to worse, until he is totally ensnared in evil.*

Initially, he decreases the requisite effort which in turn leads to a diminishment of Torah study. Due to this deficiency, when he does study, he lacks the proper understanding. Were the process to stop here it would be bad enough, but he continues to deteriorate. For in an effort to explain a Torah portion, he will explain it falsely, destroying and distorting the truth. He will transgress the rabbinic injunctions. His end is destruction as befalls all those who breach a rabbinic fence.

This, then, is the steady deterioration of the עָצֵל: the transformation of apathy and neglect into a breeding ground of poisonous evil. It is only the גִּבּוֹר, the powerful person who can force his body out of its stupor and lethargy to tend the vineyard, who can utilize the Torah as a source of life. This is why strength is such an essential quality for both the prophet and for the High Priest.

II.

How does עַצְלוּת entrench itself in one's personality? How does it retain its hold on man?

Let us take a closer look at the verse in *Mishlei*: עַל שְׂדֵה אִישׁ עָצֵל עָבַרְתִּי וְעַל כֶּרֶם אָדָם חֲסַר לֵב, *I passed by the field of a lazy man and by the vineyard of a man devoid of understanding.*

The עָצֵל is compared to the person who is חֲסַר לֵב, *devoid of understanding.* Neglect and laziness are the result of apathy and a profound lack of sensitivity. It is only by being totally and completely conscious of the consequences of עַצְלוּת that one can attempt to overcome it. *I passed by the field of a lazy man.* Shlomo HaMelech writes that it is not enough to hear about a situation. One must see with his own eyes in order to be affected. The verse continues to describe the impact being made on Shlomo by the overgrown ruins of the vineyard and field. First Shlomo merely passed by (עָבַרְתִּי). He then pauses to ponder (וָאֶחֱזֶה), and finally the realization strikes him fully (אָשִׁית לִבִּי).

Shlomo then sums up the experience as a whole: רָאִיתִי לָקַחְתִּי מוּסָר, *I looked upon it and took from it a lesson.* The key to self-improvement is the actual perception and understanding of the consequences of עַצְלוּת. Its culmination lies in applying its lessons to one's own deficiencies while the lack of awareness and sensitivity is the root and cause of עַצְלוּת.

There are, in addition, many rationales that a person uses to buttress and reinforce his laziness. The most common pretext to exempt oneself from fulfilling his obligations is the excuse that one lacks the requisite abilities to properly carry out one's tasks in life.

Ramban is perhaps the best rejoinder.

וַיָּבֹאוּ כָל אִישׁ אֲשֶׁר נְשָׂאוֹ לִבּוֹ וגו׳. כִּי לֹא הָיָה בָהֶם שֶׁלָּמַד אֶת הַמְּלָאכוֹת הָאֵלֶּה מִמְלַמֵּד אוֹ מִי שֶׁיְּאַמֵּן בָּהֶם יָדָיו כְּלָל. אֲבָל מָצָא בְּטִבְעוֹ שֶׁיָּדַע לַעֲשׂוֹת כֵּן, וַיִּגְבַּהּ לִבּוֹ בְּדַרְכֵי ה׳ לָבוֹא לִפְנֵי מֹשֶׁה לֵאמֹר לוֹ אֲנִי אֶעֱשֶׂה כָּל אֲשֶׁר אֲדוֹנִי דוֹבֵר (שמות לה:כא).

And they came, everyone whose heart stirred him up. None of [those who came] had learned the craftsmanship from a teacher nor had trained himself. But he discovered within himself the ability to do so. His heart stirred him up in the ways of Hashem to come before Moshe and declare, "I will do whatever my Master commands" (Shemos 35:21).

Building the *Mishkan* required great skills and craftsmanship, skills which these volunteers did not possess. Yet, since they were determined to fulfill Hashem's command and exerted themselves to obey Moshe's instructions, they succeeded in building it. This holds true for every spiritual endeavor; supposed inability does not excuse anyone from any undertaking. If a person but gives his utmost he *will* succeed.

This is the strength demanded of a High Priest and a prophet. Although we are definitely speaking of physical strength, as it appears from the verses, the source of this strength, however, is not in the flesh. It is the concentration and focusing of all of one's energies towards the desired goals. This can apply both to physical powers and to strength in character in overcoming one's evil inclination, as *Ramban* explains.

Both of these strengths are rooted in the concentrated effort of the person. Just as עַצְלוּת brings about the deterioration of a person, זְרִיזוּת, alacrity and zealousness, elevates a person to רוּחַ הַקֹּדֶשׁ and prophecy.

בִּטָחוֹן

Trust in Hashem

בָּרְכוּ ה' מַלְאָכָיו גִּבֹּרֵי כֹחַ עֹשֵׂי דְבָרוֹ לִשְׁמֹעַ בְּקוֹל דְּבָרוֹ (תהלים
קג:כ).

ר' יִצְחָק נַפְחָא אוֹמֵר: אֵלוּ שׁוֹמְרֵי שְׁבִיעִית, בְּנוֹהֵג שֶׁבָּעוֹלָם
אָדָם עֹשֶׂה מִצְוָה לְיוֹם אֶחָד לְשַׁבָּת אֶחָד לְחֹדֶשׁ אֶחָד, שֶׁמָּא לְכָל
יְמוֹת הַשָּׁנָה? וְדֵין חָמֵי חַקְלֵיה בַּיְרָא, כַּרְמֵיה בַּיְרָא וְשָׁתִיק, יֵשׁ לְךָ
גִבּוֹר חַיִל גָּדוֹל מִזֶּה? (ילקוט תהלים תת"ס).

Bless Hashem, O His angels, the strong warriors, who
do His bidding, to obey the voice of His word (Tehillim
103:20).

R' Yitzchak Nafcha said: This refers to those who
observe shmittah. It is customary for a person to
perform a mitzvah for a day, a week or a month. Does
one usually observe a mitzvah for an entire year? Yet
this farmer sees his field lie fallow for a year, his
vineyard lie fallow for a year and he remains silent. Is
there greater strength of character than this? (Yalkut
Tehillim 860).

Chazal find in those who observe shmittah a strength of character
attributed only to angels. The same verse that describes angels
describes shmittah observers as well. In fact greater strength and will

power is required for a man burdened with an evil inclination and greed to reach the heights attained by angels.

What is the nature of this strength? What gives rise to the obedience of angels as well as to the compliance of those farmers who observe *shmittah?*

The *Gemara* says:

בְּשָׁעָה שֶׁהִקְדִּימוּ יִשְׂרָאֵל נַעֲשֶׂה לְנִשְׁמָע יָצְאתָה בַּת קוֹל וְאָמְרָה לָהֶן, מִי גִלָּה לְבָנַי רָז זֶה שֶׁמַּלְאֲכֵי הַשָּׁרֵת מִשְׁתַּמְּשִׁין בּוֹ דִּכְתִיב, בָּרְכוּ ה׳ מַלְאָכָיו גִּבּוֹרֵי כֹחַ עֹשֵׂי דְבָרוֹ לִשְׁמוֹעַ בְּקוֹל דְּבָרוֹ, בְּרֵישָׁא עוֹשֵׂי וְהָדָר לִשְׁמוֹעַ (שבת פח:עא).

When Israel gave precedence to, "We shall do," over "We shall listen," a Heavenly voice exclaimed, "Who has revealed the secret of the angels to My children?" For it is written, "Bless Hashem, all angels, mighty in strength who fulfill God's word, and hearken to His command." [Angels] first 'do' and then 'listen' (Shabbos 88a).

Chazal have revealed to us the source of the strength of angels. It lies in first doing then listening, action before understanding. Since this is the verse used to describe the observers of *shmittah,* we understand this to be the pillar of strength that their faith rests on. If their observance of *shmittah* would have to be the result of logical and rational conclusions, they would not be able to bring themselves to allow their fields to remain fallow. It is only because they can fulfill first and then listen that they can reach a level of strength and faith as great as that of angels, and greater yet.

There is a still deeper point to be made about the necessity of the suprarational observance of *shmittah.* Even if a person were able to attain the requisite commitment necessary to observe *shmittah* by virtue of logic and reason alone, he would, however, be unable to maintain it. The simple faith of first fulfilling and then listening is what maintains this בִּטָחוֹן, *trust,* consistently. *Chazal* have alluded to this by pointing out that *shemittah* is unusual in the fact that it must be observed for an entire year and it is this long duration which is the crux of its difficulty: to keep one's unswerving faith and constant trust in God intact for so long a period of time.

It is a hallmark of the greatness of Israel that they are expected to live with the level of trust that angels have, and if they do not then they are punished through the harshest of national punishments — exile! (see *Vayikra* 27).

My own *Rebbi*, R' Yerucham זצ״ל, stressed this by constantly telling us that when we speak in public on the subject of בִּטָחוֹן we should only speak of it in its simplest terms. He would say, "One must speak about it in public only in tangible and simple language, not with deep philosophical concepts." The reason for this is, as we have explained, that בִּטָחוֹן itself is acquired only through simple faith of doing and then listening, and therefore this is the way in which it should be taught.

The approach of נַעֲשֶׂה וְנִשְׁמָע, *we will do and we will listen*, however, is not only a means for acquiring בִּטָחוֹן but rather reflects the very nature of true בִּטָחוֹן. It is not merely an intellectual recognition of God's providence but first and foremost it is the ability to relate to God's omnipotence as vivid reality.

Chazal give us a few illustrations of people whose בִּטָחוֹן was their sense of reality. The *Gemara* (*Nedarim* 49b) tells of R' Yehudah bar Ilai who was extremely poor. Someone sent him a coat which he refused to accept. To illustrate the reason for not accepting it, he lifted his tablecloth [and demonstrated the "money secreted" there], and told the messenger, "See how much I have, but I do not want to derive benefit from this world."

Although previously there was no money under the tablecloth and it was only through a miracle that he found it there, R' Yehudah nevertheless was nonchalant about the whole matter. He knew with such certainty that money would miraculously appear under the cloth that he could casually lift up the tablecloth and point to the money there — his belief was such that he *knew* it would be there.

The *Gemara* (*Taanis* 24b) tells of R' Chanina ben Dosa's wife who would kindle her empty oven so as to disguise the fact that she was too poor to afford to bake bread. One day a suspicious neighbor entered the house, suddenly, in order to see if there really was bread baking in the oven. When the neighbor saw the oven full of bread, she exclaimed "Quickly, bring a stick to remove the bread for it is burning." R' Chanina's wife replied, "I was just bringing one." The *Gemara* concludes that indeed R' Chanina's wife was bringing a stick for she was accustomed to miracles and was confident that one would occur, in order to save her from humiliation.

The lesson of both these stories is that בִּטָחוֹן is meant to produce a certainty that is identical to our sense of reality. R' Yehudah casually lifted up the tablecloth, while R' Chanina's wife went to bring a stick with which to remove the non-existent bread. This is בִּטָּחוֹן rooted in אֱמוּנָה פְּשׁוּטָה, *simple faith*, not in intellectual speculation.

But it is not only these unique individuals who can rise to such lofty heights of total trust. Every person is expected at times to show such an example of faith. The *Gemara* (*Bava Metzia 42a*), rules that as one enters his granary to measure his produce, he recites a prayer that God send a blessing to increase the produce in the granary. When he is in midst of counting he recites a prayer (according to some opinions, using God's Name) thanking Hashem for having sent a blessing. The blessing referred to is clearly a miraculous phenomenon (see *Rashi* there). Yet every person is expected to pray for it and to thank Hashem for its actualization. The blessing of one who is not certain of a miracle would be a בְּרָכָה לְבַטָּלָה, *a benediction in which one mentions God's Name in vain*. Yet, so sure were *Chazal* about every person's ability to attain such levels that they instituted this blessing for everyone. This is the level of בִּטָּחוֹן demanded of everyone including the simplest farmer.

Another dimension of genuine בִּטָּחוֹן is the total non-reliance on any factor but Hashem. *Chazal* demonstrate this aspect by contrasting the בִּטָּחוֹן of four great kings of Israel:

אַרְבָּעָה מְלָכִים מַה שֶּׁתָּבַע זֶה לֹא תָבַע זֶה, וְאֵלּוּ הֵם דָּוִד וְאָסָא יְהוֹשָׁפָט וְחִזְקִיָּהוּ. דָּוִד אָמַר, אֶרְדּוֹף אוֹיְבַי וְאַשִּׂיגֵם וגו'. אָמַר לֵיהּ הַקָּדוֹשׁ בָּרוּךְ הוּא אֲנִי עוֹשֶׂה כֵן וכו'. עָמַד אָסָא וְאָמַר אֵין בִּי כֹּחַ לַהֲרוֹג אֶלָּא אֲנִי רוֹדֵף וְאַתָּה עוֹשֶׂה. אָמַר הַקָּדוֹשׁ בָּרוּךְ הוּא אֲנִי עוֹשֶׂה כֵן וכו'. עָמַד יְהוֹשָׁפָט וְאָמַר אֵין בִּי כֹּחַ לֹא לַהֲרֹג וְלֹא לִרְדוֹף אֶלָּא אֲנִי הֲרֵינִי אוֹמֵר שִׁירָה וְאַתָּה עוֹשֶׂה, אָמַר לֵיהּ הַקָּדוֹשׁ בָּרוּךְ הוּא אֲנִי עוֹשֶׂה כֵן וכו'. עָמַד חִזְקִיָּהוּ וְאָמַר אֵין בִּי כֹּחַ לֹא לַהֲרוֹג וְלֹא לִרְדֹּף וְלֹא לוֹמַר שִׁירָה אֶלָּא אֲנִי הֲרֵינִי יָשֵׁן בְּמִטָּתִי וְאַתָּה עוֹשֶׂה. אָמַר לֵיהּ הַקָּדוֹשׁ בָּרוּךְ הוּא אֲנִי עוֹשֶׂה כֵן (ילקוט שמואל קס"ג).

There were four kings, each of whom demanded something different. They are: David, Asa, Yehoshaphat and Chizkiyahu. David requested, "Let me chase my enemies and defeat them." The Holy One replied, "I will do so . . ." Asa said, "I have no strength to kill them but I will chase them and You will do the rest." Said the Holy One, "I will do so . . ." Yehoshaphat said, "I have strength neither to kill nor to give chase. Rather I will praise the Almighty and You

*will do the rest." The Holy One said, "I will do so ..."
Chizkiyahu said, "I have no strength to fight, chase, or
even praise the Almighty. Rather, I will sleep in bed
and You will do the rest." The Holy One answered, "I
will do so ..."* (Yalkut Shmuel 163).

Chazal describe here in ascending order the various levels of trust
in God. Even Yehoshaphat who resorted to just praising the
Almighty through song did not quite reach the ultimate in בִּטָּחוֹן. The
very awareness of danger and the recognition of God's intervention
represents a degree of personal involvement and effort. Rather, it is
Chizkiyahu's total non-involvement, his "sleeping in bed," so to
speak, that expresses the total disregard and disavowal of self, the
ability to leave everything to Hashem.

This is perhaps why *Chazal* have taught us, גָּדוֹל הַנֶּהֱנֶה מִיגִיעַ כַּפָּיו
יוֹתֵר מִירְאַת שָׁמַיִם, *He who earns his livelihood by the labor of his own
hands is greater than one who is God fearing* (Berachos 8a). Both of
these individuals are God fearing; one earns his bread by his own
labor, the other one not. Why is the farmer greater? For, by having
worked for his bread he truly sees that it is not his labor which
provides him with his daily bread, but Divine providence, for "he
labors here and finds (his sustenance in another place)." He who had
not worked, even though he may be God fearing, may still labor
under the misconception that it is man's toil which is the cause of his
sustenance.

The *Talmud Yerushalmi* offers a vivid illustration of how, in the
long run, man's efforts do not change his livelihood.

> *The wife of R' Yosi Haglili aggravated him. One day
> R' Elazar ben Azaryah came by and told him, "Divorce
> her for lack of respect; it is not befitting that you live
> with her." He replied, "Her dowry is large." He replied,
> "I will give it to you," whereupon he gave it to her
> and divorced her. She married the town watchman.
> The watchman became poor and blind and she was
> forced to make the rounds and beg. One day they
> did not collect anything. He asked her, "Is there not
> another neighborhood here?" She replied, "There is
> another street here where my first husband lives, but I
> am embarrassed to go there." He began hitting her.
> Just then R' Yosi Haglili passed by and heard her*

humiliation. He put them up in one of his houses and supported them for the rest of their lives. This he did in keeping with the verse, "Do not ignore your kin," which applies even to one's divorcee. Still one could hear her voice at night saying, "Better the beating from my husband which is but an external pain than the humiliation of being supported by R' Yosi Haglili which is an internal one" (Yerushalmi Kesuvos 11:3).

A closer look at this teaches us an outstanding lesson about the effectiveness of human effort. After all her machinations and devices, R' Yosi's wife was back to her original supporter! The same husband who had fed her before fed her now. The difference is only that before she was provided with food in a dignified manner and now she had to bear the humiliation of accepting charity from her former husband. Thus we see that man's sustenance remains unchanged. All that man's deeds can accomplish are a worsening of the conditions of his livelihood. It is, rather, the Provider of the universe who gives to each his needs.

בְּטוּל תּוֹרָה

The Imperative of Torah Study

אִם בְּחֻקֹתַי תֵּלֵכוּ . . . שֶׁתִּהְיוּ עֲמֵלִים בַּתּוֹרָה (ויקרא כו:ג רש״י)
תָּנוּ רַבָּנָן עָנִי וְעָשִׁיר וְרָשָׁע בָּאִין לְדִין. לְעָנִי אוֹמְרִים לוֹ מִפְּנֵי
מַה לֹא עָסַקְתָּ בַּתּוֹרָה, אִם אוֹמֵר עָנִי הָיִיתִי וְטָרוּד בִּמְזוֹנוֹתַי,
אוֹמְרִים לוֹ כְּלוּם עָנִי הָיִיתָ יוֹתֵר מֵהִלֵּל, אָמְרוּ עָלָיו עַל הִלֵּל הַזָּקֵן
שֶׁבְּכָל יוֹם וָיוֹם הָיָה עוֹשֶׂה וּמִשְׂתַּכֵּר בְּטַרְפְּעִיק, חֶצְיוֹ הָיָה נוֹתֵן
לְשׁוֹמֵר בֵּית הַמִּדְרָשׁ, וְחֶצְיוֹ לְפַרְנָסָתוֹ וּלְפַרְנָסַת אַנְשֵׁי בֵיתוֹ וכו׳.
עָשִׁיר אוֹמְרִים לוֹ מִפְּנֵי מַה לֹא עָסַקְתָּ בַּתּוֹרָה, אִם אוֹמֵר עָשִׁיר
הָיִיתִי וְטָרוּד הָיִיתִי בִּנְכָסַי, אוֹמְרִים לוֹ כְּלוּם עָשִׁיר הָיִיתָ יוֹתֵר
מֵרַבִּי אֶלְעָזָר, אָמְרוּ עָלָיו עַל רַבִּי אֶלְעָזָר בֶּן חַרְסוֹם שֶׁהִנִּיחַ לוֹ
אָבִיו אֶלֶף עֲיָרוֹת בַּיַּבָּשָׁה וּכְנֶגְדּוֹ אֶלֶף סְפִינוֹת בַּיָּם, וּבְכָל יוֹם וָיוֹם
נוֹטֵל נֹאד שֶׁל קֶמַח עַל כְּתֵפוֹ, וּמְהַלֵּךְ מֵעִיר לְעִיר וּמִמְּדִינָה
לִמְדִינָה לִלְמוֹד תּוֹרָה וכו׳.
רָשָׁע אוֹמְרִים לוֹ מִפְּנֵי מַה לֹא עָסַקְתָּ בַּתּוֹרָה, אִם אוֹמֵר נָאֶה
הָיִיתִי וְטָרוּד בְּיִצְרִי, אוֹמְרִים לוֹ כְּלוּם נָאֶה הָיִיתָ יוֹתֵר מִיּוֹסֵף וכו׳.
נִמְצָא הִלֵּל מְחַיֵּב אֶת הָעֲנִיִּים, רַבִּי אֶלְעָזָר בֶּן חַרְסוֹם מְחַיֵּב
אֶת הָעֲשִׁירִים, יוֹסֵף מְחַיֵּב אֶת הָרְשָׁעִים (יומא לה:ע״ב).

If you will follow my decrees ... this means you shall
engage in intensive Torah study (Vayikra 26:3 Rashi).

The Rabbis taught: The pauper, the rich man and the
wicked one stand in [heavenly] judgment. The poor
man is asked, "Why did you not study Torah?" If he
replies, "I was poor and busy supporting myself," he is

asked, "Were you poorer than Hillel [who studied Torah despite his poverty]?" It was said about Hillel that he earned a trefik [small coin] each day, half of which he would give to the watchman of the beis midrash and half of which he used to support himself and his family ...

When the rich man comes, he is asked, "Why did you not study Torah?" If he replies, "I was wealthy and occupied with my business affairs," he is asked, "Were you wealthier than R' Elazar?" It was said of R' Elazar ben Charsom that his father bequeathed him a thousand cities on land and a thousand ships at sea. Each day he would take a sack of flour on his shoulder and go from city to city and from province to province to study Torah ...

The wicked man is asked, "Why did you not study Torah?" If he answers, "I was handsome and preoccupied with my evil inclination," he will be questioned, "Were you more handsome than Yosef?" ...

Thus poor people will be held accountable because of Hillel, the rich because of R' Elazar ben Charsom and the wicked because of Yosef (Yoma 35b).

On the Day of Judgment the world is divided into three groups. Each group is judged according to its circumstances and its position in life with the focus directly on the obstacles that prevented them from studying Torah. The pauper in spite of his hardship, the rich man as busy as he may have been, and the wicked man, wallowing in his passions, are all confronted with the question, "Why did you not study Torah?"

What is baffling, though, is that although one's station and position in life is taken into account, no allowance is made for the difference in stature between "Hillel, R' Elazar and Yosef" and the people compared to them. How are we to expect ordinary people to live up to the standards of these giants? Why do their exemplary actions obligate and set the standard for all people in all generations?

The answer is that Torah is the very essence of one's eternal existence. Were the study of Torah to be simply a mitzvah, a good deed or special accomplishment, one can certainly take into account the station in life and the circumstances of the one being judged. But since Torah is the very source of human eternal existence, its demand is equal on all, great and small alike. "Why did you destroy your eternity and your life?"

When a luxury item is unavailable one endeavors to obtain it in proportion to one's refined taste. When bread is lacking, however, rich and poor, wealthy and impoverished will pursue it with equal vigor.

The indispensability of Torah is as *Rambam* puts it: וְחַיֵּי בַעֲלֵי הַחָכְמָה וּמְבַקְשֶׁיהָ בְּלֹא תַלְמוּד תוֹרָה כְּמִיתָה חֲשׁוּבִין, *the life of the masters of wisdom and its seekers without Torah study is considered like death (Rambam Hilchos Rotzeach 7:1).*

When it comes to a matter of life and death, individual stature becomes meaningless. Great men as well as humble people are confronted with the ultimate question of life, "Why did you waste away your time and not use it to its fullest potential for Torah study?"

Let us scrutinize each of the rationalizations given for not studying Torah:

The poor man explains that he was impoverished and had to support his family. His reply is a valid one, for surely one is obligated to support oneself and one's family. The rebuttal lies not in refuting his argument per se, but by showing him how little one needs to support oneself. Hillel was able to support himself on half a *trefik*. How much is a *trefik*? R' Yisrael Salanter once remarked, "If a watchman receives a half a *trefik* for admitting one person, an amount which surely did not make the watchman rich, though he received this amount from everyone entering the *Beis Medrash*, we can well imagine what is its value!" And yet Hillel was able to sustain himself and his family with the other half-*trefik*. It will be against this yardstick that the poor man's excuse will be measured.

What is the rich man's rationalization? "I was rich, occupied in my business." How could one possibly think that this is a valid excuse? One may interpret the meaning of the rich man's rationalization as being that he did not acquire wealth for its own sake and for his personal comfort, but rather for his philanthropic endeavors and worthy charities. The response to this reasoning is the life of R' Elazar ben Charsom who despite his enormous wealth and potential for good deeds spent his life engaged in Torah study, taking for his own needs a sack of flour.

What of the wicked man whose excuse is his involvement with his passions and desires? What kind of an excuse is that? Its meaning is that he claims an inability to overcome the very powerful temptations to which he is subject. The rebuttal to such reasoning is Yosef who was exposed to the greatest of temptations and still spent all his time studying Torah.

What is apparent from these words of our Sages is that besides the judgment on one's deeds in life in general, one is also specifically judged as regards his study of Torah, for Torah study is the root and basis for the observance of the *mitzvos*.

But it is not merely for the amount of time spent in Torah study that one is judged. Even if a person would sit and study Torah day and night, and not waste even a moment, he will be held accountable if he does not attain as deep a level or as profound an understanding as he is capable.

This is illustrated most vividly in the following story of R' Akiva:

כְּשֶׁחָלָה רַבִּי אֱלִיעֶזֶר נִכְנְסוּ ר' עֲקִיבָא וַחֲבֵרָיו לְבַקְּרוֹ וכו'. נִכְנְסוּ וְיָשְׁבוּ לְפָנָיו וכו'. אָמַר לָהֶם לָמָּה בָּאתֶם, אָמְרוּ לוֹ לִלְמוֹד תּוֹרָה בָּאנוּ. אָמַר לָהֶם וְעַד עַכְשָׁיו לָמָּה לֹא בָּאתֶם אָמְרוּ לוֹ לֹא הָיָה לָנוּ פְנַאי. אָמַר לָהֶן תָּמֵהַ אֲנִי אִם יָמוּתוּ מִיתַת עַצְמָן. אָמַר לוֹ ר' עֲקִיבָא שֶׁלִּי מַהוּ; אָמַר לוֹ שֶׁלְּךָ קָשֶׁה מִשֶּׁלָּהֶן (סנהדרין סח:ע"א). מִפְּנֵי שֶׁלִּבְּךָ פָּתוּחַ כְּאוּלָם וְאִלּוּ שִׁמַּשְׁתַּנִי הָיִיתָ לוֹמֵד תּוֹרָה הַרְבֵּה (רש"י שם).

When R' Eliezer fell ill, R' Akiva and his companions went to visit him ... They entered and sat before him. He asked them, "Why did you come?" They replied, "We have come to study Torah." He said to them, "Why did you not come until now?" They replied, "We had no time." He remarked, "I will be surprised if these [i.e., his students] die natural deaths!" R' Akiva asked him, "What about my [death]?" He replied, "Your death will be harsher than theirs" (Sanhedrin 68a).

Rashi explains: For your heart is as open as a great hall and had you apprenticed yourself to me you would have learned much Torah.

R' Akiva was one of the greatest *Tannaim*, a man about whom Moshe said, "If such a man exists in Your world, why do You [God] give the Torah to Israel through me (*Menachos* 29b)?" Yet this towering figure was killed in a most cruel manner (see *Berachos* 61b) for not realizing his fullest potential — for not learning enough from

R' Eliezer [who lived out the last years of his life in a state of excommunication].

There is another dimension to Torah study for which one is held accountable and that is the responsibility to share one's knowledge with one's fellow.

שְׁנֵי תַלְמִידֵי חֲכָמִים הַמְהַלְּכִין בַּדֶּרֶךְ וְאֵין בֵּינֵיהֶם דִּבְרֵי תוֹרָה, רְאוּיִין לְשָׂרֵף בָּאֵשׁ שֶׁנֶא׳ וַיְהִי הֵמָּה הוֹלְכִים הָלוֹךְ וְדַבֵּר וְהִנֵּה רֶכֶב אֵשׁ וגו׳, טַעֲמָא דְאִיכָּא דִּבּוּר, הָא לֵיכָּא דִּבּוּר רְאוּיִן לְשָׂרֵף (סוטה מט:ע״א).

Two scholars who are traveling and do not discuss Torah are deserving of being burnt, as it says, "[Eliyahu and Elisha] were walking and speaking and a chariot of fire ..." The reason was because they discussed [Torah], however, had they not discussed [Torah], they would have deserved to be burnt (Sotah 49a).

It is certain that both Eliyahu and Elisha were each engaged in Torah study. Yet, that would not have been sufficient to protect them from being consumed by fire. It was only because they discussed Torah with each other that they were protected. It is the duty of each person to teach and learn with his fellow man, not to merely worry about his own Torah study. One should be concerned about his friend's growth as well as his own. From the above we learn how obligated we are to learn with our colleagues and to defer to each other in Torah matters, whereby all of us are "teaching each other and learning from one another" (*Rashi Sotah* 49a).

This is the way to acquire Torah. Each person receives from his friend what he himself is lacking spiritually, even if he is the best among his colleagues. By complementing each others shortcomings, each will profit and everyone will benefit.

הַכְּלָל וְהַפְּרָט

The Community and the Individual

I.

אַךְ אֶת מַטֵּה לֵוִי לֹא תִפְקֹד . . . בְּתוֹךְ בְּנֵי יִשְׂרָאֵל (במדבר א:מט).
Only the tribe of Levi you shall not count ... together with the Children of Israel (Bamidbar 1:49).

וְהַלְוִיִּם לְמַטֵּה אֲבֹתָם לֹא הָתְפָּקְדוּ בְּתוֹכָם (במדבר א:מז).
But the Levites according to the tribe of their fathers were not counted among them (ibid. 1:47).

וְהַלְוִיִּם לֹא הָתְפָּקְדוּ בְּתוֹךְ בְּנֵי יִשְׂרָאֵל, כַּאֲשֶׁר צִוָּה ה' אֶת מֹשֶׁה (במדבר ב:לג).
But the Levites were not counted among the Children of Israel as the Lord commanded Moshe (Bamidbar 2:33).

The Torah repeats again and again that the Levites were not counted together with Israel. *Rashi*, in explaining the significance of this repetition, says that Hashem foresaw the decree that all those above the age of twenty would die in the wilderness. He therefore ordered Moshe not to count the Levites, thereby excluding them from this decree.

The Midrash (*Bamidbar Rabbah* 1:1 and 3:7) also makes it clear that had the Levites been included in the census, they would have died together with those aged between twenty and sixty.

This gives us an important insight into the ways in which God rules the world. When a punishment is decreed upon a group as a group, then all members are included, personal merit notwithstanding.

Naturally, there are exceptions to this rule and sometimes a *tzaddik* will be singled out and saved on account of his great merit. But this is the exception rather than the rule. Therefore, the Levites had to be excluded from the counting. Had they been included, then their merits would not have sufficed to exclude them from the main body of the Jewish people.

Or HaChaim also makes use of this principle in explaining the verse, "*and Yehoshua son of Nun and Calev son of Yefunah lived, of all the people who went to explore the land*" (*Bamidbar* 14:38). Yehoshua and Calev were saved from the punishment of dying in the desert only because they were among those "*who went to explore the land*" and hence were excluded from the group that stayed behind. Otherwise they would have been included in the decree even though they had done no wrong, and had not participated in the sin which brought on the decree. On the contrary, they had tried to dissuade Israel from listening to the slander of the spies which was the cause of this decree.

Or HaChaim continues that this is what *Chazal* mean by saying that "*Yair son of Menashe was saved from dying in the desert not on the basis of his greatness (he was equal to the Sanhedrin) but rather because his age excluded him from the group aged twenty to sixty*" (*Bava Basra* 121b). Had he been part of that group he would not have been saved despite his personal greatness.

This principle will help us understand some of the events relating to the killing of the firstborn in Egypt. The Israelites were instructed: "*and no one shall go out of the entrance of his house until the morning*" (*Shemos* 12:22). Had anyone left his house he would have died. It was because of this that the Jewish firstborn were later set aside and given a special sanctity. Hashem said:

כִּי לִי כָל בְּכוֹר בִּבְנֵי יִשְׂרָאֵל בָּאָדָם וּבַבְּהֵמָה בְּיוֹם הַכֹּתִי כָל בְּכוֹר בְּאֶרֶץ מִצְרַיִם הִקְדַּשְׁתִּי אֹתָם לִי (במדבר ח:יז).

For all firstborn in Israel, both men and cattle, became

Mine; on the day that I smote every firstborn in the land of Egypt I have sanctified them for Me (Bamidbar 8:17).

Why would the Jewish firstborn have been punished? What wrong had they done? Were they not part of the people of Israel? *Ran* in one of his dissertations explains this phenomenon:

שֶׁכַּאֲשֶׁר נִתְחַדֵּשׁ שֶׁפַע שׁוֹפֵעַ מַמְשִׁיךְ אֵיזֶה דָבָר מַזִּיק יְקַבֵּל בּוֹ הֶיזֵק גַּם הָאִישׁ אֲשֶׁר אֵינֶנּוּ רָאוּי שֶׁיֵּעָנֵשׁ כְּפִי מַעֲשָׂיו, אִם לֹא שֶׁיִּהְיֶה אֵלָיו זְכוּת פְּרָטִי יָגֵן עָלָיו הַשֵּׁם יִתְבָּרֵךְ בַּעֲדוֹ מֵהַהֶזֵּק הַהוּא (דרשות הר"ן ח')

When a source of destruction opens up, it will harm even one who does not deserve this punishment unless he has very special merit, which will cause Hashem to protect him (Drashos HaRan 8).

There is, however, a complementary aspect to this principle of inclusiveness. While a decree on a group will include every individual, the individual's own due will always coincide with the retribution that he will receive as a member of the group. Thus, the Divine Providence acts on a dual level. Each group is judged as a unit, individuals perforce included; yet each person's personal due 'coincides' with that of the group.

Chazal describes this most clearly with regard to Moshe Rabbeinu's death. On the one hand we are told that his punishment was due to the events of מֵי מְרִיבָה, *the waters of conflict*, where he struck the rock instead of speaking to it (*Bamidbar* 20:12). Yet the Torah also attributes it to the sin of the spies. Thus Moshe tells Israel גַּם בִּי הִתְאַנַּף ה' בִּגְלַלְכֶם לֵאמֹר גַּם אַתָּה לֹא תָבֹא שָׁם, *God also became angry at me, saying, "You too shall not enter there"* (*Devarim* 1:37, see *Ramban* there).

It is in this sense that *Chazal* explained that the verse which details the punishment for the sin of the spies includes Moshe.

אִם יִרְאֶה אִישׁ בָּאֲנָשִׁים הָאֵלֶּה . . . אֶת הָאָרֶץ הַטּוֹבָה (דברים א:לה). אִישׁ זֶה מֹשֶׁה דִּכְתִיב וְהָאִישׁ מֹשֶׁה (תנחומא וישב ד').

If any man among these men will see . . . the good land (Devarim 1:35). 'Man' refers to Moshe as it says "and the man Moshe" (Tanchuma Vayeishev 4).

How do we reconcile this?

The answer is that both reasons are valid. Moshe was part of Israel and therefore perforce had to be included in the punishment of the spies. (Although Moshe was over sixty and a Levite — both reasons *not* to be included in the decree — still it is possible that, being the leader of Israel, he was always considered as part of the nation as a whole). On the other hand, there had to be a personal reason for Moshe not to enter the land of Israel. This was his error at the incident of מֵי מְרִיבָה.

Chazal have described this interplay of personal guilt and preordained punishment.

לְכוּ וּרְאוּ מִפְעֲלוֹת אֱלֹקִים, נוֹרָא עֲלִילָה עַל בְּנֵי אָדָם (תהלים סו:ה). אָמַר רַבִּי יְהוֹשֻׁעַ בֶּן קָרְחָה: אַף הַנּוֹרָאוֹת שֶׁאַתָּה מֵבִיא עָלֵינוּ, בַּעֲלִילָה אַתְּ מְבִיאָן. בֹּא וּרְאֵה, כְּשֶׁבָּרָא הַקָּדוֹשׁ בָּרוּךְ הוּא אֶת הָעוֹלָם מִיוֹם הָרִאשׁוֹן בָּרָא מַלְאַךְ הַמָּוֶת . . . וַעֲלִילָה נִתְלָה בּוֹ שֶׁהוּא הֵבִיא אֶת הַמִּיתָה לָעוֹלָם שֶׁנֶּאֱמַר כִּי בְּיוֹם אֲכָלְךָ מִמֶּנּוּ מוֹת תָּמוּת. וְכֵן אַתָּה מוֹצֵא שֶׁאָמַר לֵיהּ הַקָּדוֹשׁ בָּרוּךְ הוּא לְמֹשֶׁה, אִם יִרְאֶה אִישׁ בָּאֲנָשִׁים וכו', אִישׁ זֶה מֹשֶׁה. וְכֵיוָן שֶׁאָמַר לָהֶם שִׁמְעוּ נָא הַמּוֹרִים אָמַר לֵיהּ הַקָּדוֹשׁ בָּרוּךְ הוּא לָכֵן לֹא תָבִיאוּ אֶת הַקָּהָל הַזֶּה (תנחומא וישב ד').

Go and see the works of God, awesome in deed towards mankind (Tehillim 66:5). R' Yehoshua ben Karcha expounded: [The verse means] that even the awesome things that [God] brings upon us are brought about through a pretext. Come and see, when Hashem created the world He created the angel of death ... yet He pretended that it was Adam that caused death to the world, as it says, "On the day that you eat of the tree you will die."

Similarly, Hashem said to Moshe, "... if one of these men will see the land," and 'men' refers to Moshe ... However, as soon as Moshe said, "Listen to me O rebellious ones," the Holy One declared, "Therefore you will not bring this people" (Tanchuma Vayeshev 4).

This is the 'pretext' which God uses against man. On the one hand, one's fate and destiny are identical to one's people's. On the other hand, one's own merits and faults are rewarded exactly, the two systems coinciding perfectly.

II.

The inclusion of the individual in a group and his being judged, as such, manifests itself in a positive sense as well.

Thus we find that when Elisha asked the Shunamite woman if she needed any favors, she replied, בְּתוֹךְ עַמִּי אָנֹכִי יֹשֶׁבֶת, *Among my people I dwell* (*II Melachim* 4:13).

The *Zohar* [*Noach*] explains that this conversation took place on *Rosh HaShanah*, and its meaning was, "Do you wish for any special mention before the Almighty?" To which she replied, "I wish to be judged among my people and not singled out as an individual." One who is judged as part of the community is granted the same benefits as the entire community, regardless of lack of personal merit.

This is also the basis for the admonition of *Chazal* that לְעוֹלָם לְשַׁתֵּף אֱנָשׁ נַפְשֵׁיהּ בַּהֲדֵי צִבּוּרָא, *A person should always associate himself with the community* (*Berachos* 30a). *Rashi* explains this as meaning that one's prayers should be in the plural form rather than in the singular. By praying for the public welfare, one is automatically included with them and does not need personal merits in order to benefit from one's prayers.

The reason for this is that the community is not seen as a mere collection of individuals but rather a new entity exceeding the combination of the merits and strengths of the individuals of which it is composed.

Ran (*Drashos* 1) points this out in the case of Moshe who was punished for calling Israel 'the rebellious people.' He explains that although as individuals each one of them deserved to be called 'rebellious,' the people as a whole, however, did not deserve to be described as such. Accordingly, Moshe was unjustified in so labeling them.

The exhortations of *Chazal* to be part of the community at large apply not only to prayer but to the entire gamut of human activity. It is the *yeitzer hara's* ploy to isolate individuals from the community, thus making them easy prey to temptation. Even Yaakov, as soon as וַיִּוָּתֵר יַעֲקֹב לְבַדּוֹ, "*And Yaakov was left alone,*" וַיֵּאָבֵק אִישׁ עִמּוֹ, "*a man came and fought with him*" (*Bereishis* 32:25). *Chazal* (see *Rashi* there) point out that this was Esav's angel. As long as Yaakov was with his family he was safe; his isolation attracted the forces of evil.

This then forms the essence of the advice of *Chazal*, אִם פָּגַע בְּךָ מְנֻוָּל

זֶה מָשְׁכֵהוּ לְבֵית הַמִּדְרָשׁ, *if this despicable one has begun bothering you, draw him into the house of study* (Kedushin 30b). The בֵּית הַמִּדְרָשׁ is a place of the community, and there the 'despicable one' is helpless. The best protection for the individual is to steadfastly remain part of the community. לְעוֹלָם אַל יִמְנַע אָדָם עַצְמוֹ מִבֵּית הַמִּדְרָשׁ אֲפִלּוּ שָׁעָה אֶחָת, *one should not absent oneself from the Beis Hamedrash even for a little while* (Beitzah 24b), for there the 'merit of the many' encompasses all who are found there.

שְׁבִירַת הַמִּדּוֹת

Overcoming One's Faults

בְּיוֹמֵי דְּרַבִּי תַּנְחוּמָא הָיוּ צְרִיכִין יִשְׂרָאֵל לְמִטְרָא. אָתוּן לְגַבֵּיה
וְאָמְרִין לֵיהּ רַבִּי גְּזַר תַּעֲנִיתָא דְּיֵיחוּת מִטְרָא. גְּזַר תַּעֲנִיתָא פַּעַם
רִאשׁוֹנָה וּשְׁנִיָּה וְלֹא יָרְדוּ גְּשָׁמִים. פַּעַם שְׁלִישִׁית קָם וְדָרַשׁ, אָמַר
לוֹן כָּל עַמָּא יִפְלְגוּן מִצְוָה. קָם חַד גְּבַר וְנָסַב מַה דַּהֲוָה לֵיהּ בְּגוֹ
בֵּיתֵיהּ וְנָפַק לְמִפְלְגָהּ. פָּגְעָה בֵּיהּ מְשַׁבַּקְתֵּיהּ וְאָמְרָה לֵיהּ זְכִי
בְּהַהִיא אִיתְּתָא דְּמִן יוֹמָא דְּמַפְּקִית מִן בֵּיתָךְ לֹא חָמִית טַב. כֵּיוָן
שֶׁרָאָה אוֹתָהּ עֲרָמָּה וּבְצָרָה גְּדוֹלָה נִתְמַלֵּא עָלֶיהָ רַחֲמִים וְנָתַן לָהּ
... שָׁלַח רַבִּי תַּנְחוּמָא וְאַיְתֵיתֵיהּ ... בְּאוֹתָהּ שָׁעָה הִגְבִּיהַּ ר'
תַּנְחוּמָא פָּנָיו לַשָּׁמַיִם וְאָמַר לִפְנֵי הַקָּדוֹשׁ בָּרוּךְ הוּא, רִבּוֹנוֹ שֶׁל
עוֹלָם מַה אִם זֶה שֶׁהוּא בָּשָׂר וְדָם וְאַכְזָרִי וְלֹא הָיוּ עָלָיו מְזוֹנוֹתֶיהָ
נִתְמַלֵּא עָלֶיהָ רַחֲמִים וְנָתַן לָהּ, אָנוּ שֶׁאָנוּ בְּנֵי בָנֶיךָ בְּנֵי אַבְרָהָם
יִצְחָק וְיַעֲקֹב וּמְזוֹנוֹתֵינוּ עָלֶיךָ עַל אַחַת כַּמָּה וְכַמָּה שֶׁתִּתְמַלֵּא
עָלֵינוּ רַחֲמִים. בְּאוֹתָהּ שָׁעָה יָרְדוּ גְּשָׁמִים וְנִתְרַוַּח הָעוֹלָם (ויקרא
רבה לד:יד).

In the days of R' Tanchuma, Israel was in need of rain.
The people came to him and said, "Rebbi, declare a fast
day so that it should rain." He declared a fast once and
a second time but the rain did not fall. The third time he
announced, "Let each person perform a mitzvah (i.e.,
charity)." One man went and gathered all that he had
in his house and went to distribute it. He met his former
wife who pleaded with him, "Have mercy upon me, for

*no good has befallen me since I left your house." Seeing
that she was in great distress, he became compassionate and gave her [charity]...R' Tanchuma sent for him
...and the man told him the entire story. R' Tanchuma
lifted his eyes towards heaven and exclaimed, "Master
of the world, if this man — who is of flesh and blood and
is [by nature] cruel, and is not responsible for her
maintenance — showed mercy and gave her [what she
needed]; how much more should You be filled with
compassion for us Your children, the children of
Avraham, Yitzchak, and Yaakov whom You are
obligated to support." It began to rain immediately and
the world was relieved [from drought] (Vayikra
Rabbah 34:14).*

C*hazal* have demonstrated here the power of שְׁבִירַת הַמִּדּוֹת, the
overcoming of one's natural disposition and character traits.
Neither R' Tanchuma's prayers nor the community's fast days had
any effect on the drought. It was one man's שְׁבִירַת הַמִּדּוֹת, one man's
overcoming the bitter enmity and raging hatred, towards his former
wife, that brought about the much-needed rain for Israel. Perhaps, if
we bear in mind R' Yisrael Salanter's appraisal that the successful
conquest of even one bad character trait is more difficult than
mastering the entire Talmud, we can understand its great merit and
value.

We find again and again that the שְׁבִירַת הַמִּדּוֹת of an individual
can protect an entire generation or even generations of Israel. Thus,
R' Shimon bar Yochai exclaimed that in the combined merit of his
son, himself and King Yosam, they would be able to protect the entire
world from the ravages of judgment from the time of creation until
the end of days.

The singular achievement of Yosam was that he resisted the
temptation of honor and for decades refused to assume his living
father's monarchy, despite the fact that he was indeed the king
(*Succah* 45b).

Similarly, we are told of R' Preida who had a disciple who was
exceedingly difficult to teach. R' Preida would have to repeat the
lesson four hundred times before his student would understand. One
day R' Preida finished repeating the lesson the usual amount of times

when he noticed that his student had still not understood. The student excused himself saying that he had been distracted, whereupon R' Preida explained the lesson another four hundred times! Let us put ourselves in R' Preida's position and imagine if it would be possible for us to overcome our impatience and anguish at the loss of precious time. If after all one's efforts to teach the student he would admit that he didn't understand 'because he was distracted,' surely we would become angry and justifiably so. Yet R' Preida patiently urged him to concentrate again and taught him another four hundred times. Can we imagine a greater example of שְׁבִירַת הַמִּדּוֹת? His reward was, "a heavenly voice rang out and queried, 'Would you prefer four hundred years added to your life or that you and your generation merit the World-to-Come?' He replied that he would prefer that he and his generation merit the World-to-Come to which the Holy One replied, 'Give him both rewards' " (*Eruvin* 54b).

In both the aforementioned events we find that the שְׁבִירַת הַמִּדּוֹת of an individual affected an entire generation or generations of people.

We also find that Queen Esther initiated an act of שְׁבִירַת הַמִּדּוֹת, whose merit was to serve as the basis for Israel's rescue from Haman's decree. The entire Jewish people, in danger of annihilation, fasted and prayed for three days. Yet they did not depend on this.

> תָּנוּ רַבָּנָן מָה רָאֲתָה אֶסְתֵּר שֶׁזִּמְּנָה אֶת הָמָן. ר' שִׁמְעוֹן בֶּן מְנַסְיָא
> אוֹמֵר אוּלַי יַרְגִּישׁ הַמָּקוֹם וְיַעֲשֶׂה לָנוּ נֵס (מגילה ט"ו ע"ב).
> יַרְגִּישׁ שֶׁאֲנִי צְרִיכָה לְהַחֲנִיף לָרָשָׁע זֶה וּלְזַלְזֵל כְּבוֹדִי (רש"י שם).
> *The Rabbis have taught: Why did Esther see fit to*
> *invite Haman? ... R' Shimon ben Menassia said:*
> *[Esther said:] Perhaps God will take pity on me and*
> *perform a miracle (Megillah 15b).*
>
> *Take pity: That I must flatter a wicked person and*
> *demean myself (Rashi ibid.).*

Thus in the final analysis, the event which brought about the miracle that indeed saved Israel was an act of שְׁבִירַת הַמִּדּוֹת.

Perhaps this is the essence of *Yom Kippur* and the reason that it is a day of forgiveness and atonement. *Arizal* states that *Yom Kippur* is יוֹם כְּפּוּרִים, a day like *Purim*. *Shelah* explains this comparison as follows. Just as the essence of *Purim* is the fraternal love and kinship expressed in and engendered by מִשְׁלוֹחַ מָנוֹת, *mishloach manos*, sending presents to one's friends, and by מַתָּנוֹת לָאֶבְיוֹנִים, *gifts to the needy*, so too on *Yom Kippur* one is without jealousy, enmity or ill will towards one's fellow man, similar to an angel. It is for this reason that *Yom Kippur* is a day when our sins are forgiven.

Although שְׁבִירַת הַמִּדוֹת is extremely important in its own right, it has, in addition, another dimension. It is a prerequisite for the true understanding of Torah. *Chazal* refer to *Purim* as being a day on which קַבָּלַת הַתּוֹרָה, Israel's acceptance of the Torah, was renewed and intensified (קִיְּמוּ וְקִבְּלוּ).

As a result of the great danger Haman's decree posed to the entire Jewish people, they were spurred on to overcome their differences and enmities and it was this that gave Israel the moral strength to renew and intensify their commitment to Torah. And indeed this elimination of differences and enmities through מַתָּנוֹת לָאֶבְיוֹנִים, מִשְׁלוֹחַ מָנוֹת and מִשְׁתֶּה וְשִׂמְחָה has remained an integral dimension of *Purim*.

The *Gemara* relates how Avimi, an *amora*, enhanced his acquisition of Torah through שְׁבִירַת הַמִּדוֹת:

אֲבִימִי מַסֶּכְתָּא אִתְעֲקוּרֵי אִתְעֲקַרָא לֵיהּ וְאָתָא קַמֵּיהּ דְּרַב חִסְדָּא לְאַדְכּוּרֵי גְּמָרֵיהּ ... וְלִשְׁלַח לֵיהּ וְלֵיתֵי לְגַבֵּיהּ ... סָבַר הָכִי מִסְתַּיְּעָא מִלְתָא טְפֵי (מנחות ז׳ ע״א).

Avimi could not recall one of the tractates. He went to R' Chisda [his disciple] so that [R' Chisda] should remind him. Why did he not send for [R' Chisda]? He felt that [if he went to his disciple] he would be more successful (Menachos 7a).

It would seem that Avimi felt that not only would going to his student and not vice versa constitute יְגִיעָה בַּתּוֹרָה, *extra effort to study Torah*, but in addition, the שְׁבִירַת הַמִּדוֹת, in which he went to his disciple and not the reverse, would assist Avimi in his learning and enhance his comprehension of Torah. This teaches us that שְׁבִירַת הַמִּדוֹת is the proper preparation for Torah study and brings greater סִיַּעְתָּא דִּשְׁמַיָּא to the person studying.

Chazal describe quite clearly the severity of the punishment of those Torah scholars who allow bad character traits to create enmity among them. Thus, שְׁנֵי תַלְמִידֵי חֲכָמִים הַדָּרִין בְּעִיר אַחַת וְאֵין נוֹחִין זֶה לָזֶה בַּהֲלָכָה, אֶחָד מֵת וְאֶחָד גּוֹלֶה (סוטה מ״ט ע״א), *Two Sages who live in one city and do not consult each other in matters of halachah, one will die and the other will be exiled (Sotah 49a).*

Torah finds its place in people capable of controlling their מִדוֹת in order to associate with their fellow human beings.

There is another point. *Chazal* make it quite clear that it is always
the fault of *both* parties involved. True, the blame is not necessarily
evenly shared as evidenced by uneven punishment, death vs. exile, but
both parties are culpable. No one can excuse his inability to get along
with his fellow human being by blaming the other person. If a person
feels that there is a distance between himself and his fellow man, he
must work tirelessly to rectify his *own* מִדּוֹת in order to bridge the gap.
bridge the gap.

Moreover, אֵינָם נוֹחִים זֶה לָזֶה, *not consulting each other*, is not to be
interpreted in its active sense, i.e., a positive enmity between the two.
Rather, the absence of Torah study between the two people, is
enough to deem them אֵינָם נוֹחִים זֶה לָזֶה. This interpretation is borne
out by *Rashi* who explains מְלַמְּדִים זֶה אֶת זֶה וּלְמֵדִים זֶה לָזֶה as נוֹחִים זֶה לָזֶה
מִזֶּה, *teaching each other and learning from one another (Sotah* 49). It
follows then the אֵינָם נוֹחִים is simply the lack of such cooperation.

The *Gemara* in *Sotah* (ibid.) also bears out this point. The *Gemara*
quotes a verse to prove that if two Torah scholars are journeying
together and are not actively engaged in studying together they are
deserving of punishment.

The retribution for this lack of cooperation is not only an external
punishment not related to his Torah knowledge. It affects, in
addition, one's Torah knowledge itself. Thus,

רָשׁ וְאִישׁ תְּכָכִים נִפְגָּשׁוּ מֵאִיר עֵינֵי שְׁנֵיהֶם ה' עָשִׁיר וָרָשׁ נִפְגָּשׁוּ
עוֹשֵׂה כֻלָּם ה'.

רָשׁ — זֶהוּ רָשׁ בַּתּוֹרָה, וְאִישׁ תְּכָכִים — זֶה שֶׁשּׁוֹנֶה סֵדֶר אוֹ שְׁנֵי
סְדָרִים. עָמַד רָשׁ עִם אִישׁ תְּכָכִים וְאָמַר לִי' הַשְׁנֵנִי פֶּרֶק אֶחָד
וְהִשְׁנָהוּ, מֵאִיר עֵינֵי שְׁנֵיהֶם ה' וכו'. עָשִׁיר וָרָשׁ נִפְגָּשׁוּ — עָשִׁיר
בַּתּוֹרָה וְרָשׁ בַּתּוֹרָה. אָמַר אוֹתוֹ רָשׁ לְאוֹתוֹ עָשִׁיר, הַשְׁנֵנִי פֶּרֶק
אֶחָד וְלֹא הִשְׁנָהוּ. אָמַר לוֹ מָה אֲנָא בָּעֵי מֵיתַב וּמַתְנִיתָךְ, בְּמַשְׁקִין
אוֹ בְמֵאֵימָתַי, קְרֵי וּתְנֵי עִם דִּכְנָתָךְ. עוֹשֵׂה כֻלָּם ה' — מִי שֶׁעָשָׂה
לָזֶה חָכָם יָכוֹל לַעֲשׂוֹתוֹ טִפֵּשׁ. וּמִי שֶׁעָשָׂה לָזֶה טִפֵּשׁ יָכוֹל לַעֲשׂוֹתוֹ
חָכָם (ויקרא רבה לד:ד).

When a pauper and a crafty person meet, Hashem
enlightens the two of them. When a wealthy man and a
pauper meet, Hashem has made them both.

A pauper — that refers to one who is poor in the
knowledge of Torah. A crafty person — that refers to
one who has studied a section or two. If the pauper tells
the crafty one, "Teach me a chapter," and he taught

him, then Hashem enlightens both of them.

A pauper and a wealthy man meet, namely 'poor' and 'wealthy' in knowledge of Torah. The 'pauper' tells the 'rich man,' "Teach me a chapter," and he refuses, saying, "What do I want to sit down for and teach you מֵאֵימָתַי *(i.e., the first chapter of the Talmud) or Mashkin (one of the last tractates)? Go instead and learn with people of your own standard." Then, "Hashem has made them both" — i.e., the One who has made the rich man learned can make him stupid, and He can also make the ignorant one learned (Vayikra Rabbah 34:4).*

This is the proper care and concern that a Torah scholar should have for his fellow human being. If he is unwilling to spend time or overcome his מִדּוֹת in order to teach the lesser one, then he risks losing the Torah that he has accumulated. Let him reach out to his less capable fellow human being and Hashem will grant him an even greater knowledge of Torah.

עָבִיד אֱנַשׁ לְאַחֲזוּקֵי בְּדִבּוּרֵיהּ
Prejudices and Preconceptions

לֹא תִשָּׂא שֵׁמַע שָׁוְא (שמות כג:א).

...וּלְדַיָּין שֶׁלֹּא יִשְׁמַע דִּבְרֵי בַעַל דִּין עַד שֶׁיָּבֹא בַעַל דִּין חֲבֵרוֹ (רש"י שם).

You shall not raise a false report (Shemos 23:1).

[And it is a warning] to a judge that he not listen to the testimony of one claimant until the other claimant appears before the court (Rashi ibid.).

The Torah prohibits a judge from listening to one side of a case until the other litigant is also present in court. The *Rishonim* explain that the reason for this prohibition is *in order that the judge not be influenced by slanted or false testimony (Rambam, Sefer Hamitzvos).* Ralbag (Mishlei 18:17) explains, *For the judge believes the person who appears before him first, while the other person's claim will be believed by the judge only after extensive investigation.*

The *Gemara* refers to one engaged in prejudicing a judge as a cunning rogue (רָשָׁע עָרוּם) (*Sotah* 21b). Rashi explains, *For when he has fixed his claims in the heart of the judge it becomes difficult for the judge to remove them, and this is his cunning.*

Let us take a closer look at this prohibition for a judge to hear one side of a case without the presence of the other litigant. The law is obviously referring to a judge who understands the process of litigation and knows that he is only hearing one side of the story. He realizes that the other litigant will appear and may well totally deny and contradict the story he has just heard. Still, once the judge has heard one side without challenge he becomes prejudiced and will not really change his mind even after listening to the other side. His mind has been set to believe his initial perspective on the case.

If this is true of a judge, an objective outsider, certainly it holds true of a person's attitude towards his own opinions and statements. Once a human being has stated a position, he becomes inwardly bound to that stand and remains obstinately intransigent and it is difficult for him to admit otherwise.

This ability to admit error and to see another's viewpoint was the reason why, with rare exception, the *halachah* was fixed in accordance with the opinion of Beis Hillel. As the *mishnah* explains:

מִפְּנֵי מַה זָכוּ בֵּית הִלֵּל לִקְבּוֹעַ הֲלָכָה כְּמוֹתָן, מִפְּנֵי שֶׁנּוֹחִין וַעֲלוּבִין הֵם וְשׁוֹנִים דִּבְרֵיהֶם וְדִבְרֵי בֵּית שַׁמַּאי וְלֹא עוֹד אֶלָּא שֶׁמַּקְדִּימִין דִּבְרֵי בֵּית שַׁמַּאי לְדִבְרֵיהֶם (עירובין י"ג ע"ב).

What was it that entitled Beis Hillel to have the halachah established in accordance with their rulings? For they were humble and forgiving and they studied their own rulings and those of Beis Shammai. In addition, they mentioned Beis Shammai's words before their own (Eruvin 13b).

Not only the merit of a fine character, as it would seem at first, was the reason that the *halachah* was decided like Beis Hillel. Rather, their placing *Beis Shammai's words before their own* gave them the opportunity to objectively appraise all sides of the question before coming to a decision. They were not biased, in favor of their own opinions, but rather were open to consider the case from every angle and perspective. Such a ruling is therefore objective and true. It is for this reason that the *halachah* is determined according to their opinion.

Likewise, the false prophet, Chananyah ben Azur, was told by Yirmiyahu that he would die before the end of the year, as a punishment for prophesying falsely (*Yirmiyahu* 28:16-17). *Chazal* tell us that Chananyah died on the eve of *Rosh Hashanah*, and that he instructed his children not to bury him before *Rosh Hashanah* in order to conceal his death until the end of the year. Chananyah saw in the most unmistakable way that Yirmiyahu's prophecy was proving true. He stood at the threshold of death and he saw clearly that the truth was with Yirmiyahu. On his own flesh he was suffering the consequences of his lies and deceit. Yet, he would not make a public concession to that fact by allowing himself to be buried. His last act was a petty lie to 'prove' his 'being right' before the world.

Chiel (see *I Melachim* 16) rebuilt Yericho in defiance of Yehoshua's prophecy that he who would rebuild Yericho would see his children die in his lifetime. Chiel's first son died when he laid the foundation of Yericho and as he continued building, his sons died one by one. His last child died when he put up the gates of Yericho.

It is incomprehensible how Chiel could witness the demise of his entire family before his very eyes and not immediately stop what he was doing. Yet so strong is a person's unwillingness to admit error, so powerful the inability to admit one's mistake. Better to bury one's children with one's own hands than to admit error!

Thus we find that the *sotah*, the woman whose fidelity is in doubt, was brought before the High Court — not because it was necessary in a legal sense but rather in order to frighten her into confessing. A woman in that position is well aware of the fate that awaits her if she does not confess her sin. She knows how horrible and ignoble a death will be her lot upon drinking the 'bitter waters.' She can spare herself this fate by confessing her sin. Why then does the Torah mandate going to such great lengths in an effort to convince her to confess? Wouldn't simple logic dictate that she would herself take any opportunity to spare herself such a horrible death? The answer is that once this woman has declared her innocence she finds it unbearably difficult to retreat from her stand, even at the price of so horrible a death.

Perhaps this is the reason that עֲבֵרָה גוֹרֶרֶת עֲבֵרָה, *Sin brings more sin in its wake.* For after a person has committed a sin, he is loath to admit that he was wrong. He will, therefore, continue to sin rather than retreat and thereby acknowledge his shortcomings.

On the other hand, the person who can rise above his natural obstinacy and admit his failure is able to extricate himself from the morass of sin in which he wallows. Thus כָּל הָעוֹשֶׂה עֲבֵרָה וּמִתְבַּיֵּשׁ בָּהּ מוֹחֲלִין לוֹ עַל כָּל עֲוֹנוֹתָיו (ברכות י״ב ע״ב), *He who sins and is ashamed of it, all his sins are forgiven (Berachos 12b).*

One who has the strength and courage to overcome one's natural inclination to rationalization is forgiven his sins.

The paradigm of such behavior is Achan who defied Yehoshua's injunction against taking booty from the enemy. Because of his actions, Israel suffered losses in battle. The *Gemara* in *Sanhedrin* 44 elaborates on Achan's misdeeds. In a moment of rare inspiration he confessed his sins before the entire community of Israel. The words with which Achan gave expression to this unique moment of spiritual elevation is the prayer of עַל כֵּן נְקַוֶּה which is recited thrice daily, a prayer in which Achan did not request anything for himself. Instead he yearns that the knowledge of Hashem be spread throughout the world. This is a very high level indeed to which he became elevated by the confession of his sin, for the one who rises above himself and admits his wrongdoing will find himself on a high and elevated spiritual level.

הַכָּרַת הַטּוֹב

Gratitude

I.

לָמָּה נִסְמְכָה פָּרָשַׁת הַמְּנוֹרָה לְפָרָשַׁת הַנְּשִׂאִים? לְפִי שֶׁכְּשֶׁרָאָה אַהֲרֹן חֲנֻכַּת הַנְּשִׂיאִים חָלְשָׁה אָז דַּעְתּוֹ כְּשֶׁלֹּא הָיָה עִמָּהֶם בַּחֲנֻכָּה, לֹא הוּא וְלֹא שִׁבְטוֹ. אָמַר לוֹ הַקָּדוֹשׁ בָּרוּךְ הוּא, חַיֶּיךָ, שֶׁלְּךָ גְדוֹלָה מִשֶּׁלָּהֶם, שֶׁאַתָּה מַדְלִיק וּמֵטִיב אֶת הַנֵּרוֹת (רש"י במדבר ח:ב).

Why is the portion dealing with the candelabra juxtaposed to the portion [dealing with the sacrifice] of the princes? Because when Aharon saw the princes [bringing] inaugural sacrifices, he was upset that neither he nor his tribe were among them. The Holy One told him, "By your life, your [Divine service] will be of greater importance than theirs, for you will light and prepare the lamps [of the menorah] (Rashi Bamidbar 8:2).

Ramban comments that the above reassurance strikes us as being strangely specific. Aharon HaKohen had been granted the priesthood in its entirety, burning incense, bringing sacrifices, etc. If it was the priesthood that he was being comforted with, then there was no need to specify the lighting of the *menorah*, ignoring the full range of duties performed solely by the *Kohen*. It would seem then that the lighting of the *menorah* was not intended to represent priestly duties in general, but that it had a special significance not found in burning the incense nor in any other priestly duties. Let us take a closer look at the essence of the lighting of the *menorah*.

The concept that we will have to explore in order to understand this Midrash is that of הַכָּרַת הַטּוֹב, *the expression of gratitude*. This concept has been misconstrued to mean merely a repayment of someone else's benevolent deed. Yet a look at many of the words of *Chazal* associated with this obligation will show us its true dimensions.

וַיִּשְׁמַע רְאוּבֵן וַיַּצִּלֵהוּ מִיָּדָם (בראשית לז:כא).

וְהֵיכָן הָיָה? רַבָּנָן אָמְרֵי, אָמַר רְאוּבֵן, הוּא מוֹנֶה אוֹתִי עִם אַחַי, וְאֵינִי מַצִּילוֹ? אֲנִי הָיִיתִי סָבוּר שֶׁנִּדְחֵיתִי מִכֹּחַ אוֹתוֹ מַעֲשֶׂה וְהוּא מוֹנֶה אוֹתִי עִם אַחַי, שֶׁנֶּאֱמַר וְאַחַד עָשָׂר כּוֹכָבִים מִשְׁתַּחֲוִים לִי, וְאֵינִי מַצִּילוֹ? (בראשית רבה פד:טו).

And Reuven heard and saved him from their hands (Bereishis 37:22).

Where indeed was [Reuven]? The Rabbis said: Reuven reasoned, "He included me with my brothers, shall I not save him? I thought that I was excluded [from the tribes] on account of my interference [concerning Bilhah], yet he listed me together with my brothers, as it says, 'and eleven stars are bowing down to me.' Shall I not save him?" (Bereishis Rabbah 84:15).

Chazal here interpret the word "heard" not as implying that he was far away, but rather in the sense of realization. Reuven realized that he owed Yosef a debt of gratitude and proceeded to act accordingly. Yosef was tried by his brothers and they concluded that he deserved to be killed. Reuven did not question the fairness of the trial nor the justice of the verdict, yet he felt that *hakaras hatov* required him to extricate Yosef from the pit. But what had Yosef done for him? His role was merely passive, being the bearer of a message. It was not Yosef's own declaration that included him in the family circle, but a Divine revelation repeated by Yosef, contained in a dream whose content was an enhancement of Yosef's prestige. Yet the very fact that he served as an agent of Reuven's relief made him deserving of recognition and repayment. This act of *hakaras hatov* was noteworthy enough for the Torah to allude to it by stating וַיִּשְׁמַע רְאוּבֵן, *and Reuven heard.*

This debt extends not only to human beings, but even if we benefit from mere objects we are obligated to show our appreciation as well. In that very chapter we read that Yaakov instructed Yosef to *go and inquire as to the welfare of your brothers and the welfare of the sheep (Bereishis 37:14). Chazal* ask: We understand the inquiry as to his brother's welfare, but why ask about the sheep's welfare?

"This teaches that one is to inquire about the welfare of that from which he had derived benefit [even if it be but sheep]" (*Bereishis Rabbah* 84:13). Is it not astonishing that he inquired about the sheep in the same breath that he asked about his children's welfare!

This was demonstrated to an extreme by R' Chiya who suffered greatly from a shrewish wife. Yet whenever he found something she liked, he would wrap it up and bring it to her as a gift. Rav asked him, "Doesn't she mistreat you?" To which he replied, דַּיֵּינוּ שֶׁמְּגַדְּלוֹת בָּנֵינוּ וּמַצִּילוֹת אוֹתָנוּ מִן הַחֵטְא, *It is enough that they [our wives] raise our children and protect us from sin [by keeping themselves attractive]* (*Yevamos* 63a).

The first half of the reply is plausible enough; the bearing and raising of children are the most difficult tasks a woman performs, and certainly they deserve appreciation for that. But what is the favor of "protecting us from sin"? Is it not a woman's nature and vanity that drive her to beautify herself? Yet R' Chiya uttered it in the same breath as raising children! The answer is that as far as R' Chiya's obligation to be grateful was concerned, both were equal and both were equally valid reasons for *hakaras hatov* — the disparity of effort expended notwithstanding.

Moreover, *hakaras hatov* is an obligation not only to the immediate source of benefit, but we are even duty bound to discern that which brought about the action of our benefactors, and to acknowledge their role in our gain. Therefore we learn,

אִישׁ מִצְרִי הִצִּילָנוּ (שמות ב:יט).

מָשָׁל לְאֶחָד שֶׁנְּשָׁכוֹ הָעָרוֹד וְהָיָה רָץ לִתֵּן רַגְלָיו בְּמַיִם. נָתַן לְנָהָר וְרָאָה תִּינוֹק אֶחָד שֶׁהוּא שׁוֹקֵעַ בַּמַּיִם וְשָׁלַח יָדוֹ וְהִצִּילוֹ. אָמַר לוֹ הַתִּינוֹק, אִלּוּלֵא אַתָּה, כְּבָר הָיִיתִי מֵת. אָמַר לוֹ, לֹא אֲנִי הִצַּלְתִּיךָ אֶלָּא הָעָרוֹד שֶׁנְּשָׁכַנִי וּבָרַחְתִּי הֵימֶנּוּ. הוּא הִצִּילְךָ. כַּךְ אָמְרוּ בְּנוֹת יִתְרוֹ לְמֹשֶׁה יִישַׁר כֹּחַךְ שֶׁהִצַּלְתָּנוּ מִיַּד הָרוֹעִים. אָמַר לָהֶם מֹשֶׁה, אוֹתוֹ מִצְרִי שֶׁהָרַגְתִּי הוּא הִצִּיל אֶתְכֶם. וּלְכַךְ אָמְרוּ

לַאֲבִיהֶן אִישׁ מִצְרִי (שמות רבה א:לב).

An Egyptian man saved us (Shemos 2:19).

This is to be compared to a man bitten by a lizard who ran to place his feet in water (a purported remedy). When he put them in the river he saw a child drowning. He reached out and saved him. The child exclaimed, "If not for you, I would have drowned." To which the man replied, "It was not I who saved you, but the lizard who bit me and from which I escaped." Thus, the daughters of Yisro told Moshe, "Thank you for saving us." To which Moshe replied, "It is the Egyptian whom I killed [and on whose account I was subsequently forced to run away] who saved you." Therefore they said to their father, "An Egyptian saved us" (Shemos Rabbah 1:32).

It did not suffice for them to be thankful to Moshe alone, as it is not enough to thank only the man who did the actual rescuing. So too, it is incumbent upon us to discover the causes and drives behind the act and acknowledge them accordingly, even if the one who caused it had no intention whatsoever to do us any good, and even if they be as far removed from any intended benevolence as the Egyptian or the lizard.

Having described various dimensions of *hakaras hatov* to man and beast, let us acknowledge the ultimate benefactor of man — Hashem. All that is ours is the gift of God. Yet man stands helpless, unable to acknowledge it with more than words, for with what action can one "repay" Hashem? However, one act alone has been described as an expression of *hakaras hatov*, as it were, and it was this sublime deed that was offered to Aharon: lighting the *menorah*. Thus,

אָמְרוּ יִשְׂרָאֵל לִפְנֵי הַקָּדוֹשׁ בָּרוּךְ הוּא, רִבּוֹנוֹ שֶׁל עוֹלָם לָנוּ אַתָּה אוֹמֵר שֶׁנָּאִיר לְפָנֶיךָ אַתָּה הוּא אוֹרוֹ שֶׁל עוֹלָם וכו'. אָמַר לָהֶם הַקָּדוֹשׁ בָּרוּךְ הוּא, לֹא שֶׁאֲנִי צָרִיךְ לָכֶם אֶלָּא שֶׁתָּאִירוּ לִי בִּדְרֶךְ שֶׁהֶאַרְתִּי לָכֶם. לָמָּה? לְעַלּוֹת אֶתְכֶם בִּפְנֵי הָאֻמּוֹת שֶׁיִּהְיוּ אוֹמְרִים, רְאוּ הֵיךְ יִשְׂרָאֵל מְאִירִין לְמִי שֶׁהוּא מֵאִיר לְכָל הָעוֹלָם. מָשָׁל לְמָה הַדָּבָר דּוֹמֶה? לְפִקֵּחַ וְסוּמָא שֶׁהָיוּ מְהַלְּכִים בַּדֶּרֶךְ. אָמַר לוֹ פִּקֵּחַ לְסוּמָא, כְּשֶׁנִּכָּנֵס לְתוֹךְ הַבַּיִת, צֵא וְהַדְלֵק לִי אֶת הַנֵּר הַזֶּה וְהָאֵר לִי. אָמַר לוֹ הַסּוּמָא, בְּטוֹבָתְךָ, כְּשֶׁהָיִיתִי בַּדֶּרֶךְ אַתָּה הָיִיתָ מְסַמְּכֵנִי, עַד שֶׁנִּכְנַסְנוּ לְתוֹךְ הַבַּיִת אַתָּה הָיִיתָ מְלַוֶּה אוֹתִי, וְעַכְשָׁיו

אַתָּה אוֹמֵר הַדְלֵק לִי אֶת הַגֵּר הַזֶּה וְהָאֵר לִי? אָמַר לוֹ הַפִּקֵּחַ, שֶׁלֹּא
תְּהֵא מַחֲזִיק לִי טוֹבָה שֶׁהָיִיתִי מְלַוְּךָ בַּדֶּרֶךְ, לְכָךְ אָמַרְתִּי לְךָ הָאֵר
לִי. כַּךְ הַפִּקֵּחַ זֶה הַקָּדוֹשׁ בָּרוּךְ הוּא וכו', וְהַסּוּמָא אֵלּוּ יִשְׂרָאֵל וכו'.
הָיָה הַקָּדוֹשׁ בָּרוּךְ הוּא מַנְהִיגָן וּמֵאִיר לָהֶם שֶׁנֶּאֱמַר וַה' הוֹלֵךְ
לִפְנֵיהֶם יוֹמָם, כֵּיוָן שֶׁעָמַד הַמִּשְׁכָּן קָרָא הַקָּדוֹשׁ בָּרוּךְ הוּא לְמֹשֶׁה
וְאָמַר לוֹ תָּאִירוּ לִי שֶׁנֶּאֱמַר בְּהַעֲלֹתְךָ אֶת הַנֵּרוֹת בִּשְׁבִיל לְעָלוֹת
לָכֶם (במדבר רבה טו:ה).

*Israel said to the Holy One, "Master of the universe, do
You ask us to give light before You? Are You not the
light of the world . . .?" The Holy One replied, "It is not
that I require your [light] but rather [the purpose of the
menorah is] to illuminate before Me as I have
illuminated for you. For what purpose? To raise you in
front of the nations who will say, 'See how Israel
illuminates before the One Who gives light to the whole
world.'"*

*This may be illustrated by a parable. A person,
capable of seeing, traveled together with a blind man.
The seeing man turned to the blind one [saying], "When
we enter the house, light this candle for me and give me
light." The blind man replied, "Be good enough to
explain that while on the road you supported me, and
until we entered the house you accompanied me, and
now you tell me to light this candle and give you light?"
The other man replied, "In order that you should not be
under an obligation to me for having accompanied you
on the journey, therefore I told you to light before me."
Thus, the man capable of seeing is Hashem . . . and the
blind man is Israel . . . Hashem led [Israel] and lit the
way for them as it says, "and Hashem went before
them in the day . . ." But as soon as the Mishkan was
erected, Hashem called Moshe and said, "Illuminate
before Me as it says, 'When you light up the candles.'"*
(Bamidbar Rabbah 15:5).

This Midrash describes the act of lighting the *menorah* not just as
another form of Divine service, but rather as an act that embodies
hakaras hatov. It was this sublime expression of gratitude that was
able to comfort Aharon for not participating actively in the
inauguration of the *Mishkan*. For *hakaras hatov* is an obligation

which weighs heavily upon the recipient, allowing him no rest until he has made some acknowledgment. Indeed this is one of the greatest gifts of Hashem to Israel, the possibility to offer some token repayment, as it were, for all they receive from God.

II.

וּבְשָׁעָה שֶׁאָמַר לוֹ הַקָּדוֹשׁ בָּרוּךְ הוּא וְעַתָּה לְכָה וְאֶשְׁלָחַךָ אֶל פַּרְעֹה אָמַר לוֹ רִבּוֹן הָעוֹלָם אֵינִי יָכוֹל מִפְּנֵי שֶׁקִּבְּלַנִי יִתְרוֹ וּפָתַח לִי בֵּיתוֹ וַאֲנִי עִמּוֹ כְּבֵן וּמִי שֶׁהוּא פוֹתֵחַ פִּתְחוֹ לַחֲבֵרוֹ נַפְשׁוֹ חַיָּב לוֹ. וְכֵן אַתָּה מוֹצֵא בְּאֵלִיָּהוּ בְּשָׁעָה שֶׁהָלַךְ אֵצֶל צָרְפִית הָאַלְמָנָה מֵת בְּנָהּ. הִתְחִיל מִתְחַנֵּן וְאוֹמֵר, הֲגַם עַל הָאַלְמָנָה אֲשֶׁר אֲנִי מִתְגּוֹרֵר עִמָּהּ הֲרֵעוֹתָ לְהָמִית אֶת בְּנָהּ. וּכְתִיב, וַיִּשְׁמַע ה' בְּקוֹל אֵלִיָּהוּ וַתָּשָׁב נֶפֶשׁ הַיֶּלֶד וכו' (שמות רבה ד:ב).

When Hashem said to him, "Go now and I will send you to Pharaoh," he [Moshe] said, "Master of the universe, I cannot, for Yisro received me and opened his home to me and I am to him like a son, and to one who opens his door [home] to his friend, he [the guest] owes him his life." [This is truly outstanding! Moshe is being sent by Hashem to fulfill a mission. The mission is to save Israel. Yet, until he has permission from the one to whom he owes hakaras hatov, Yisro, he will not go! Obviously Moshe knew that this indeed must be God's will.] And so you find in the case of Eliyahu when he went to the widow of Tzarfas when her son died. [Eliyahu] began to beseech [God], "Even to the widow by whom I reside have You brought evil, [by] killing her son," and it says, "And God listened to the voice of Eliyahu and the soul of the child returned" [I Melachim 17:20,22] (Shemos Rabbah 4:2).

Eliyahu HaNavi succeeded in performing the most outstanding miracle — the resurrection of the dead. The question then arises: If he was capable of doing it, why did he not do the same for his beloved ones?

The answer is that the power and ability to resurrect this child was a result of the tremendous need he felt to repay the kindness he had received. Indeed he felt that he owed a 'life,' as it were, to those that had sustained him and it was this imperative that enabled him to break the bonds of death. True, there were close ones that he would have wanted to see alive, but the urgency, the 'debt of life', did not press on him (see Midrash ibid.).

When one lives with the total realization of the debt of *hakaras hatov*, there is very little that one is unable to do to repay it!

This motif for the miracle is expressed in Eliyahu's plea, הֲגַם עַל הָאַלְמָנָה אֲשֶׁר אֲנִי מִתְגּוֹרֵר עִמָּהּ הֲרֵעוֹתָ לְהָמִית אֶת בְּנָהּ, *Even to the widow by whom I reside have you brought evil, [by] killing her son.* And it was in reply to this cry that וַיִּשְׁמַע ה' בְּקוֹל אֵלִיָּהוּ וַתָּשָׁב נֶפֶשׁ הַיֶּלֶד, *and Hashem heard the voice of Eliyahu and returned the soul of the child.*

The *Yefeh Toar* explains that it was in this point that Eliyahu and Moshe are compared to each other. Each one was ready to give his life in order to repay their gratitude: Moshe did not leave his father-in-law without permission even to fulfill so important a mission, and Eliyahu brought about the ultimate miracle, the resurrection of the dead.

III.

We have so far described the obligation of *hakaras hatov* upon every person to any benefactor. There is, in addition, a much finer point involved in this debt of gratitude. We shall see that *hakaras hatov* is so obligatory and binding that even the Divine command takes on a different meaning when one takes into account his debts of gratitude. The Midrash cites a striking example in the command to Moshe to fight Midian: נְקֹם נִקְמַת בְּנֵי יִשְׂרָאֵל מֵאֵת הַמִּדְיָנִים, *Avenge Israel against the Midianites (Bamidbar 31:2).* Yet Moshe did not do so, but sent Pinchas instead. How did he dare deviate from God's command? The Midrash replies: ע"י שֶׁנִּתְגַּדֵּל בְּמִדְיָן אָמַר אֵינוֹ בְדִין שֶׁאֲנִי מֵצַר לְמִי שֶׁעָשׂוּ לִי טוֹבָה, *Since I was made great in Midian, it is not right to harm those that have been good to me (Yalkut Bamidbar 31).*

The question, however, remains. True, Moshe had reason for not harming Midian, but had he not been explicitly instructed to avenge Israel? How does Moshe, the faithful servant of God, pit his own reason against the Divine word? The answer is that the duty of *hakaras hatov* was the medium for *interpreting* God's word. The contradiction between the instruction and the Divine command was resolved by understanding it to mean 'avenge Israel through an agent.' Moshe made this interpretation as resolutely as if he had used one of the י"ג מִדּוֹת שֶׁהַתּוֹרָה נִדְרֶשֶׁת, *thirteen hermeneutic rules of expounding the Torah*. The obligation of *hakaras hatov* gave Moshe an understanding of the true meaning of God's word. *Hakaras hatov* did not negate God's word; on the contrary, it illuminated and revealed its true meaning.

How did Moshe know this? This lesson had been taught to him while still in Egypt. All of the plagues had been performed by Moshe except for that of the blood, frogs and lice — the plagues originating from the water and from the earth. The reason these plagues were evoked by Aharon was that Moshe owed a debt of gratitude to the river which had served him in time of need — when he was in the basket — to evade the decree of death, and to the earth which hid the body of the Egyptian that he had killed. Even though the river and earth are inanimate, and neither know nor understand, still Moshe owed them *hakaras hatov*. It was then that Moshe realized that no command of Hashem could be taken to mean a denial of *hakaras hatov* (see *Rashi Shemos* 7:19).

Hakaras hatov demands that a person acknowledge every benefactor, no matter how remotely connected. Nor is his motive a consideration. So great is the obligation for *hakaras hatov* that no effort is seen as too difficult. But most important, it is not a mere burden, an obligatory debt, but rather it is the will of Hashem. It is a perspective in understanding the word of Hashem!

זְכִירַת מַעֲשֵׂה מִרְיָם

The Lesson of Miriam

שְׁלַח לְךָ אֲנָשִׁים וְיָתֻרוּ אֶת אֶרֶץ כְּנַעַן (במדבר יג:ב).
לָמָּה נִסְמְכָה פָּרָשַׁת מְרַגְּלִים לְפָרָשַׁת מִרְיָם? לְפִי שֶׁלָּקְתָה עַל
עִסְקֵי דִבָּה שֶׁדִּבְּרָה בְּאָחִיהָ, וּרְשָׁעִים הַלָּלוּ רָאוּ וְלֹא לָקְחוּ מוּסָר
(רש"י שם).

Send out men for you that they may scout out the land of Canaan (Bamidbar 13:2).

Why was the portion [discussing] the spies juxtaposed to the portion [discussing] the story of Miriam? [To show the grievousness of their sin] that although Miriam was punished for slandering her brother, these sinners observed this and did not take a lesson [from her] (Rashi).

The lesson of this saying of our Sages is that the purpose of God's punishment is corrective, to notify the recipient that he must mend his ways. Thus, the מְרַגְּלִים, *spies*, were taken to task for having witnessed punishment for a deed similar to theirs, the sin of לָשׁוֹן הָרָע, *slander*, and for having failed to take this lesson to heart. This is also the reason why Divine retribution is meted out מִדָּה כְּנֶגֶד מִדָּה, *measure for measure*. It is to enable a person to pinpoint his sin and to improve that which needs correction.

With this in mind we can understand the nature of the punishments meted out to Yosef for slandering his brothers:

וַיָּבֵא יוֹסֵף אֶת דִּבָּתָם רָעָה אֶל אֲבִיהֶם (בראשית לז:ב).

כָּל רָעָה שֶׁהָיָה רוֹאֶה בְּאֶחָיו בְּנֵי לֵאָה הָיָה מַגִּיד לְאָבִיו, שֶׁהָיוּ
אוֹכְלִים אֵבֶר מִן הַחַי, וּמְזַלְזְלִין בִּבְנֵי הַשְּׁפָחוֹת לִקְרוֹתָן עֲבָדִים,
וַחֲשׁוּדִים עַל הָעֲרָיוֹת. וּבִשְׁלָשְׁתָּן לָקָה. עַל אֵבֶר מִן הַחַי –
„וַיִּשְׁחֲטוּ שְׂעִיר עִזִּים,“ בִּמְכִירָתָן וְלֹא אֲכָלוּהוּ חַי כְּדֵי שֶׁיִּלָּקֶה
בִּשְׁחִיטָה. וְעַל דִּבָּה שֶׁסִּפֵּר עֲלֵיהֶם שֶׁקּוֹרִין לַאֲחֵיהֶם עֲבָדִים
„לְעֶבֶד נִמְכַּר יוֹסֵף,“ וְעַל הָעֲרָיוֹת שֶׁסִּפֵּר עֲלֵיהֶם „וַתִּשָּׂא אֵשֶׁת
אֲדֹנָיו“ (רש"י שם).

And Yosef brought their evil report to their father (Bereishis 37:2).

He would report to his father all the evil [deeds] that he noticed by his brothers: They eat unslaughtered meat, degrade the children of the maids, and are morally suspect. He was punished for all three. For saying that they ate unslaughtered meat — "They slaughtered a goat,"when they sold him, and did not eat it live. On the slander that they call their brothers "servants" — "Yosef was sold as a slave." For slandering them concerning their morals — "and the wife of his master etc." (Rashi ibid.).

The last two punishments are truly severe. A slave is at the lowest social stratum and belongs totally to his master. This was Yosef's punishment for saying that his brothers, Leah's sons, called their brothers servants. The difficulties that Yosef experienced in the affair with Potiphar's wife endangered his portion in the World-to-Come. But of what significance is the fact that the brothers slaughtered the goat after they sold him as a slave? In what sense was this a punishment as expressed in the term לָקָה employed by Chazal?

The purpose of punishment is not to afflict the recipient but rather to demonstrate to the recipient the area in which he erred. The essence of punishment is rebuke, telling the sinner, "This is your error; correct it." No rebuke could be greater than the fact that Yosef's brothers were meticulous in slaughtering the goat at the very same time that they were engaged in selling Yosef. This demonstrated clearly the untruth of his accusation.

Since the purpose of punishment is not affliction per se but rather rebuke, we often find that Hashem's choice of punishment is intended for another person's benefit.

Thus, even the form of a sinner's death, although no longer useful to rectify the ways of the sinner, serves as a lesson and reminder to those around him. The מְרַגְּלִים, spies sent by Moshe, were punished with death by a plague, as the Torah says, וַיָּמֻתוּ הָאֲנָשִׁים מוֹצִאֵי דִבַּת הָאָרֶץ רָעָה בַּמַּגֵּפָה לִפְנֵי ה', and the men who slandered the land died in a plague before Hashem (Bamidbar 14:37). Rashi explains the nature of their death: They died in a manner befitting them, 'measure for measure.' They sinned with their tongues, and consequently, their tongues protruded from their mouths reaching their stomachs and worms crawled to and from their tongues. Hence it says, "before Hashem," meaning by the manner in which Hashem inflicts punishment: 'measure for measure.'

This 'measure for measure' was not meant for the benefit of the spies. They were already dead. What additional lesson could they have learned? It was rather for the sake of pointing out their sin to the nation of Israel as a whole so that they would not repeat the grave error of the spies.

Similarly, we find the story of the Sadducee High Priest who altered the Yom Kippur service and consequently died:

מַעֲשֶׂה בִצְדוּקִי אֶחָד שֶׁהִתְקִין מִבַּחוּץ וְהִכְנִיס. בִּיצִיאָתוֹ הָיָה שָׂמֵחַ שִׂמְחָה גְדוֹלָה . . . אָמְרוּ, לֹא הָיוּ יָמִים מוּעָטִים עַד שֶׁמֵּת וְהוּטַל בָּאַשְׁפָּה, וְהָיוּ תוֹלָעִין יוֹצְאִין מֵחֹטְמוֹ (יומא י"ט ע"ב).

There was a Sadducee who prepared the [incense] outside [the Holy of Holies] and then brought it in [as the Sadducees believed to be right]. When he left the Holy of Holies he was extremely happy ... It is reported that it took only a few days before he died. His body lay in the refuse pile, and worms crawled out of his nose (Yoma 19b).

Rashi explains that his nose was the organ singled out for punishment, for that is the first organ of the body to enter a room and his sin was illegal entry into the Holy of Holies. Here again, we have a punishment which cannot be meant as an object lesson to the one afflicted. It was rather meant to serve as a reminder and warning to others.

Although the purpose of punishment is to educate and pinpoint the areas where one has erred, it is hard for the recipient to accept it as such. It is human to rationalize and explain away. Even if one is forced to admit that one is being punished, one would rather attribute it to some sin rather than the one for which he is being punished.

A story is told about the wife of a famous Torah personality of a previous generation who differed with her husband about a prospective son-in-law. The prospective groom was one of the greatest scholars of his time but he limped, and this displeased her. One morning while bringing a glass of warm milk to her frail husband before his prayers, she slipped and broke her leg. "Woe unto me," she exclaimed, "I have sinned by forcing my husband to drink before his prayers." She could not admit to herself the real reason for which she was being punished, and substituted a virtuous deed in its stead.

Chazal paint before us a powerful and vivid picture of a man clearly aware of the reason for his impending death yet unwilling to admit it, going to great lengths to deny it even at the moment of truth. Chananyah ben Azur was a נְבִיא שֶׁקֶר, *a false prophet*, who lived at the time of Yirmiyahu. Yirmiyahu told him, "This very year you will die for you have spoken falsely concerning Hashem." *Chazal* cited by *Rashi,*

בְּאוֹתָהּ שָׁנָה בְּעֶרֶב רֹאשׁ הַשָּׁנָה מֵת חֲנַנְיָה בֶּן עַזּוּר וְצִוָּה לְבָנָיו אַל
תִּקְבְּרוּנִי אֶלָּא לְאַחַר ר״ה, כְּדֵי לַעֲשׂוֹת אֶת דְּבָרָיו שֶׁל יִרְמְיָה
בַּדָּאִים (רש״י ירמיהו כח:יז).

That year, on the eve of Rosh HaShanah, Chananyah ben Azur died. He instructed his children, "Do not bury me until after Rosh Hashanah so as to put the lie to Yirmiyahu's prophecy" (see Rashi Yirmiyahu 28:17).

Here we have a man being shown in the most vivid and lucid manner that his own prophecy was a grievous error, yet he struggled to find some way of 'disproving' Yirmiyahu. So unrelenting and so impassive is the human heart! [See *Parashas Naso.*]

This then is the purpose of remembering the episode of Miriam. It is for us to learn how evil לָשׁוֹן הָרָע is, and how excluded from the community will be the one who spreads it. It is a מִצְוַת עֲשֵׂה, *positive command*, to remember this daily (according to various *rishonim*). Let us not fall under the category of לֹא לָקְחוּ מוּסָר, *those who didn't accept mussar*.

מִדָּה כְּנֶגֶד מִדָּה
Measure for Measure

רַב לָכֶם (במדבר טז:ז).

It is enough (Bamidbar 16:7).

The Torah's narrative dealing with the sale of Yosef into slavery and his travails in Egypt is abruptly interrupted with the story of Yehudah and Tamar. R' Yochanan explains the reason for this in the following manner,

> וּמִפְּנֵי מַה הִיסְמִיךְ פָּרָשָׁה זוּ לְזוּ וכו' ר' יוֹחָנָן אָמַר כְּדֵי לְסָמוֹךְ הַכֵּר לְהַכֵּר (בראשית רבה פה:ב).
>
> *Why is this portion juxtaposed with the other? R' Yochanan explained: So as to juxtapose the word "recognize" (הַכֵּר) [said by Yehudah to his father] to the word "recognize" (הַכֵּר) [said by Tamar to Yehudah] (Bereishis Rabbah 85:2).*

The Midrash is perplexing. Granted that *Chazal* are pointing out that Yehudah's predicament was in retribution for the anguish he caused his father by being actively involved in selling Yosef into slavery, but of what significance is the similarity of the word "recognize"? Would Yehudah have suffered less humiliation had Tamar not used that word?

Similarly, we find *Chazal* pointing out the recurrence of the word
רַב לָךְ by Moshe. Thus,

וַיֹּאמֶר ה׳ אֵלַי רַב לָךְ (דברים ג:כו).

אָמַר רַבִּי לֵוִי, בְּ"רַב" בְּשֵׂר בְּ"רַב" בְּשׂרוּהוּ. בְּ"רַב" בְּשֵׂר – רַב
לָכֶם בְּרַב בְּשׂרוּהוּ, רַב לָךְ (סוטה י"ג ע"ב).

R' Levi said, Moshe told [Korach], "Enough," and he
was told by Hashem [when he pleaded to enter Eretz
Yisrael], "Enough" (Sotah 13b).

Rashi explains that *Chazal* mean to point out the מִדָּה כְּנֶגֶד מִדָּה,
measure for measure, by which Moshe was punished. Due to the fact
that he had been overly harsh with Korach and his assembly, he was
denied permission to enter *Eretz Yisrael*.

The *Yalkut Shimoni* [*Vayeilech*] attributed the fact that Moshe
was denied permission to enter *Eretz Yisrael* to the fact that he
unnecessarily scolded Israel by the waters of Merivah. We find a
similar stress on identical expressions: "because Moshe said, הֵן לֹא
יַאֲמִינוּ, therefore, Hashem told him, הֵן קָרְבוּ יָמֶיךָ לָמוּת, *Your days are
coming close to death."* In both these references to 'key words' the
question is obvious. Would Moshe's death have been any less of a
punishment had the very same words not have been used to inform
him of it?

Let us analyze a similar statement regarding Yosef.

וַיָּבֵא יוֹסֵף אֶת דִּבָּתָם רָעָה אֶל אֲבִיהֶם (בראשית לז:ב).

כָּל רָעָה שֶׁהָיָה רוֹאֶה בְּאֶחָיו בְּנֵי לֵאָה הָיָה מַגִּיד לְאָבִיו, שֶׁהָיוּ
אוֹכְלִים אֵבֶר מִן הַחַי, וּמְזַלְזְלִין בִּבְנֵי הַשְּׁפָחוֹת לִקְרוֹתָן עֲבָדִים,
וַחֲשׁוּדִים עַל הָעֲרָיוֹת. וּבִשְׁלָשְׁתָּן לָקָה. עַל אֵבֶר מִן הַחַי –
"וַיִּשְׁחֲטוּ שְׂעִיר עִזִּים," בִּמְכִירָתָן וְלֹא אֲכָלוּהוּ חַי כְּדֵי שֶׁיִּלְקֶה
בִּשְׁחִיטָה. וְעַל דִּבָּה שֶׁסִּפֵּר עֲלֵיהֶם שֶׁקּוֹרִין לַאֲחֵיהֶם עֲבָדִים
"לְעֶבֶד נִמְכַּר יוֹסֵף," וְעַל הָעֲרָיוֹת שֶׁסִּפֵּר עֲלֵיהֶם "וַתִּשָּׂא אֵשֶׁת
אֲדֹנָיו" (רש"י שם).

And Yosef brought their evil report to their father
(Bereishis 37:2).

He would report to his father all the evil [deeds] that
he noticed by his brothers: They eat unslaughtered
meat, degrade the children of the maids, and are
morally suspect. He was punished for all three. For
saying that they ate unslaughtered meat — "They
slaughtered a goat,"when they sold him, and did not

*eat it live. On the slander that they call their brothers
"servants" — "Yosef was sold as a slave." For
slandering them concerning their morals — "and the
wife of his master etc." (Rashi ibid.).*

If we take a closer look at the מִדָּה כְּנֶגֶד מִדָּה, *the measure for
measure*, meted out to Yosef we can readily understand the latter two
points. Being sold as a slave is a terrible punishment. The seduction
attempted by Potiphar's wife and his near brush with temptation
could have cost him his portion in the World-to-Come. But in what
way was Yosef punished by the fact that his brothers "dipped his
cloak in blood" and indeed slaughtered the animal before partaking
of it? Was he at all affected by this incident? Can we in any way
compare it to the latter two examples where he was truly punished?

The answer to the above is grounded in a clear understanding of
Divine justice. We have mentioned on many occasions [see *Parashas
Shelach*] that the purpose of punishment is not to 'avenge' a sin but
rather to instruct and educate. It is for this reason that מִדָּה כְּנֶגֶד מִדָּה
is the form used for Divine punishment, for מִדָּה כְּנֶגֶד מִדָּה pinpoints
the reason for the punishment, and the actions that led to it. As a
result the one being punished is made aware of the areas in which his
actions need to be rectified.

Thus, Yosef was punished for each act of wrongdoing through an
event and experience that pointed out his error to him. Even though
the brothers' partaking of the goat — only after they slaughtered it —
did not harm him in any way, it accomplished its educational
mission. It vividly pointed out how wrong Yosef had been when he
had slandered his brothers. And he was stricken in that he became
painfully aware of his error.

Even today when *beis din* is no longer empowered to mete out a
sentence of capital punishment, it still exists — within the framework
of מִדָּה כְּנֶגֶד מִדָּה. Thus, our Sages say,

אַף עַל פִּי שֶׁבָּטְלוּ ד׳ מִיתוֹת בֵּית דִּין, דִּין ד׳ מִיתוֹת לֹא בָטֵל. מִי
שֶׁנִּתְחַיֵּב סְקִילָה אוֹ נוֹפֵל מִן הַגַּג אוֹ חַיָּה אוֹ דוֹרַסְתּוֹ (כתובות ל׳
ע״א).

*Even though the death penalty [administered by the
Sanhedrin] no longer exists, the death penalty per se
does exist. Thus, a person who deserves the penalty of
stoning either falls from a roof or is devoured by a beast
(Kesubos 30a).*

A further look at this *Gemara* in *Sotah* 8b shows us that the punishment meted out is in the nature of מִדָּה כְּנֶגֶד מִדָּה rather than an outright punishment. *Tosafos* (ibid.) points out that at times the punishment a person receives is not at all related to the punishment that he deserves but is rather strikingly similar to the misdeed perpetrated. That is to say that מִדָּה כְּנֶגֶד מִדָּה can manifest itself either by the punishment being similar to the punishment which would be meted out to the sinner in court at the time of the *Beis HaMikdash*, or it can be similar to the sin itself. It is evident from *Tosfos* that the significance of דִּין ד׳ מִיתוֹת, *the law of the four types of capital punishment,* is not the retributive aspect of the capital punishment, but rather the educational aspect of the punishment. Thus when people witness the מִדָּה כְּנֶגֶד מִדָּה of the sinner's death, they learn to avoid the person's mistakes.

With this understanding we can comprehend the significance of the similarity of words. When Yehudah heard the familiar ring of ״הַכֶּר נָא״ he was reminded that the humiliation that he was suffering at Tamar's hands was due to his callousness in dealing with Yosef.

Moshe, too, realized his error in dealing with Korach. For although Korach was a man of strife and contentiousness, there lay a grain of spiritual yearning in his desire for priesthood. Moshe was therefore wrong in telling him, "Enough" (רַב לָכֶם). And therefore when he himself prayed for spiritual elevation through entering the land of Israel, he was refused in kind, רַב לָךְ — Enough!

Since the goal of מִדָּה כְּנֶגֶד מִדָּה is its educational dimension, the punishment must correspond exactly to the sin. Thus the *Gemara Chullin* 7b explains that when a person injures his finger it is atonement in the manner of a קָרְבַּן עוֹלָה, *a burnt offering.* The *Gemara* and *Rishonim* go into detailed explanation of the circumstance of the injury. The reason for all of the detail as to the circumstance is that it must correspond (conceptually) exactly to a burnt offering in order to be מִדָּה כְּנֶגֶד מִדָּה.

Since the purpose of the punishment is to force upon a person a recognition of his misdeeds, it follows therefore that if a person comes to this recognition on his own, as evidenced by his embarrassment, his sins are forgiven. Therefore we find *Chazal* stating כָּל הָעוֹשֶׂה עֲבֵרָה וּמִתְבַּיֵּשׁ בָּהּ מוֹחֲלִין לוֹ כָּל עֲוֹנוֹתָיו, *He who sins and is embarrassed has all his sins forgiven* (*Berachos* 12b). [See the *Meiri* who explains this as referring only to that particular sin.] He has realized his shortcoming and no further punishment is necessary.

The purpose of pain and suffering is to educate and rehabilitate man. Fortunate is the person who recognizes his faults on his own, and through his embarrassment is spared this suffering!

עֶבֶד ה׳

Servant of God

זֹאת חֻקַּת הַתּוֹרָה (במדבר יט:א).

This is the statute of the Torah (Bamidbar 19:1).

With this as an introduction, the Torah proceeds to delineate the laws of פָּרָה אֲדֻמָּה, *the red cow.* The question arises: Why are the laws of פָּרָה אֲדֻמָּה described as חֻקַּת הַתּוֹרָה, the universal statute of Torah?

Or HaChaim explains: "Performance of a *mitzvah* despite the fact that it has no apparent human rational basis is tantamount to the observance of the entire Torah. The fulfillment of a seemingly non-rational *mitzvah* bears testimony to one's unswerving faith and desire to fulfill Hashem's commandments."

This means that a person fulfilling a rational *mitzvah* has not yet demonstrated his commitment to fulfill the dictates of the Divine Will as such. It could very well be that he is performing the *mitzvah* by dint of his own reasoning. It is only through the performance of a commandment such as פָּרָה אֲדֻמָּה that one demonstrates absolute commitment to fulfilling Hashem's will. Thus, it is indeed פָּרָה אֲדֻמָּה which is rightfully considered חֻקַּת הַתּוֹרָה, the quintessential statute of Torah.

Important as this principle may be to the proper fulfillment of Torah, it is, however, most difficult to observe. The human psyche finds it difficult to accept the notion that one is a servant to God, and must perform his commands purely as an obligation. Man, even while performing a *mitzvah*, would prefer to do so as a result of his own understanding and cognitive intellect.

This gives us an understanding of a very perplexing Midrash.

וַיּוֹאֶל מֹשֶׁה לָשֶׁבֶת אֶת הָאִישׁ, בְּשָׁעָה שֶׁאָמַר מֹשֶׁה לְיִתְרוֹ תְּנָה לִי אֶת צִפּוֹרָה בִּתְּךָ לְאִשָּׁה, אָמַר לוֹ קַבֵּל עָלֶיךָ דָּבָר אֶחָד שֶׁאֲנִי אֹמֵר לָךְ, וַאֲנִי נוֹתְנָהּ לְךָ לְאִשָּׁה, אָמַר לוֹ מֹשֶׁה מַה הוּא, אָמַר לוֹ הַבֵּן שֶׁיִּהְיֶה לְךָ תְּחִלָּה יִהְיֶה לַעֲבוֹדָה זָרָה, מִכַּאן וָאֵילַךְ לְשֵׁם שָׁמַיִם, וְקִבֵּל עָלָיו (ילקוט שמעוני קס״ט).

Moshe consented to dwell together with the man.

When Moshe said to Yisro, "Give me your daughter Tzipporah for a wife," he replied, "Consent to one condition that I will make with you, and I will give her to you as a wife." Moshe asked, "What is [the condition]?" He replied, "The first son you will beget must [be raised as an] idolater. The others will be raised for the sake of Heaven." Moshe accepted [the condition] (Yalkut Shimoni Shemos 169).

This is the same Yisro who once served as an idolatrous priest and came to the recognition of the true Deity, and rejected all forms of idol worship. He was excommunicated by his former community and his children were harassed and molested (see *Shemos Rabbah* 1:32). Yet, he stood fast in his recognition of the Almighty. How then could this same Yisro possibly lay down this condition for the marriage of his daughter? What reason could he possibly have had to insist that his grandson should serve the very idols that he himself had rejected? Even more mystifying is the fact that Moshe himself agreed to this condition.

The answer is that Yisro himself came to recognize Hashem by virtue of his own reason and understanding. He did not want his eldest grandson to be forced into accepting the Torah merely because it was a family tradition. Rather, he would raise him as an idolater, and only if he would come to the decision himself would he become an עוֹבֵד ה׳, *a worshiper of Hashem*. However, what Yisro did not realize is that the ideal service of God is that one's personal recognition and awareness of God be but the prelude to service of

God as a Divinely mandated subservience. We therefore understand, as *Baal HaTurim* points out, that Moshe consented only in hope of eventually convincing Yisro to the contrary.

A human being finds it very difficult to be a מְחֻיָב, to be obligated to do, or to be prohibited from doing something. So much so, that he will at all costs break the bonds restraining him, even if it means risking his life. This is demonstrated most vividly in the story of Shimi ben Geira and Shlomo HaMelech.

Shimi ben Geira had vilified and cursed David HaMelech during his lifetime. On his deathbed David HaMelech instructed his son Shlomo,

וְעַתָּה אַל תְּנַקֵּהוּ כִּי אִישׁ חָכָם אָתָּה, וְיָדַעְתָּ אֵת אֲשֶׁר תַּעֲשֶׂה לּוֹ, וְהוֹרַדְתָּ אֶת שֵׂיבָתוֹ בְּדָם שְׁאוֹל (מלכים א ב:ט).

Now, therefore, do not hold him guiltless for you are a wise man, and you will know what you ought to do to him and you shall bring him to the grave with blood (I Melachim 2:9).

Shlomo, in compliance with his father's instructions, called Shimi ben Geira and warned him:

בְּנֵה לְךָ בַיִת בִּירוּשָׁלַם וְיָשַׁבְתָּ שָׁם, וְלֹא תֵצֵא מִשָּׁם אָנֶה וָאָנָה. וְהָיָה בְּיוֹם צֵאתְךָ וְעָבַרְתָּ אֶת נַחַל קִדְרוֹן יָדֹעַ תֵּדַע כִּי מוֹת תָּמוּת, דָּמְךָ יִהְיֶה בְרֹאשֶׁךָ (מלכים א ב:לו-לז).

Build yourself a house in Jerusalem and dwell therein, and do not leave it neither to here nor to there. For on the day that you will leave and cross the valley of Kidron, know that you will die, your blood is on your head (I Melachim 2:36-37).

Not only did Shlomo administer this solemn warning to Shimi, but in addition, he reinforced it with a stern vow. What was his intent? Where does Shlomo's legendary wisdom manifest itself? There are many old men who have lived all their lives in Jerusalem, not finding any imperative to leave. Certainly Shimi, who had solemnly sworn to remain there, and knew that he would be killed if he left, would not leave. And how, indeed, is it that for the loss of a mere two servants, Shimi would forfeit his life?

The answer is that certainly it is possible to live in Jerusalem, the joy of the entire earth (*Tehillim* 48), without ever leaving. However, on the day that a person is forced to stay, Jerusalem becomes for him an unbearable prison. His efforts to free himself from this jail will know no bounds. This is what Shlomo perceived in his profound wisdom, and this was the trap that ensnared Shimi. He knew that by forcing Shimi to stay in Jerusalem with so severe a penalty, reinforced yet with a solemn vow, Shimi would eventually be compelled to break these iron shackles in an attempt at freedom.

This powerful drive for the dissolution of restrictions that bind and fetter people adds a new dimension to the following description of Lot.

The *Gemara* (*Nazir* 23a) explains that Lot was aware of the fact that his daughters induced him to become intoxicated in order to bring him to sin with them. He assented to become drunk to enable himself to sin without his usual restraint. *Rosh* explains that although according to many opinions a gentile is permitted to live with his daughter, the gentiles themselves decided to refrain from incest. The question arises, if Lot had accepted these restrictions, why would he drink and transgress these self-accepted constraints? Secondly, what pleasure would he derive from an act performed in a state of drunken stupor?

The answer is that it was not the pleasure of the act itself that drove Lot. Rather, having placed a restraint upon himself he was now impelled to somehow break his self-imposed restraints. While he would not do so in a state of sobriety, he knew, however, that as soon as he would drink and lose his normal inhibitions, he would be free to do as his heart desired and break the bonds restraining him.

To accept barriers and to carry out orders because they are decreed by Hashem, זֹאת חֻקַּת הַתּוֹרָה, this is the true service.

The *Gemara* (*Sanhedrin* 26b) states that even a promiscuous individual is believed if he testifies that a woman is married. The *Gemara* then asks, "*Of course his testimony is accepted; why would we think otherwise?*" To which the *Gemara* replies, מַהוּ דְּתֵימָא הָא עֲדִיפָא לֵי דִּכְתִיב מַיִם גְּנוּבִים יִמְתָּקוּ, *I would think that he prefers her status this way, [so that when he sins with her, he has the added enjoyment] of 'stolen waters are sweet' [a phrase meaning that forbiddenness gives added pleasure].*

Here we have a person who has deliberately lied to create an illusionary barrier to make this woman forbidden to him. He is well aware that she is not married at all and hence permissible. Yet being that society in general accepts her as married, he would perversely enjoy the illusionary adultery! [The conclusion of the *Gemara* is that even though this is the case, still his testimony is accepted.]

So great is this compulsion, so perverse is this pleasure, so powerful is this drive to break restraints that a person will build illusionary barriers only in order to enjoy breaching them. The true עֶבֶד ה', however, will rejoice in fulfilling the Divine commands and strictures, out of pure and unconditional obedience to God.

כְּבוֹדוֹ שֶׁל אָדָם

The Dignity of Man

וַיֹּאמֶר אֶל שָׂרֵי בָלָק לְכוּ אֶל אַרְצְכֶם כִּי מֵאֵן ה' לְתִתִּי לַהֲלֹךְ עִמָּכֶם (במדבר כב:יג).

And [Bilaam] said to the princes of Balak: Go back to your country for God has refused to permit me to go with you (Bamidbar 22:13).

Rashi comments that Bilaam based his rejection of these emissaries of Balak on the fact that they were not high ranking enough to associate with. This does not mean that *Rashi* is stating that Bilaam lied to them and gave them a false reason. Rather, a careful reading of the verse shows that Hashem gave Bilaam two reasons for dissociating himself from Balak's emissaries. The first was indeed to protect Bilaam's dignity, while only the second was that he should not curse Israel. *Or HaChaim* explicitly interprets the verse in this vein.

מִי הָאֲנָשִׁים הָאֵלֶּה עִמָּךְ. כְּמוֹ כֵן, אָמְרוּ מִי הָאֲנָשִׁים הָאֵלֶּה שֶׁהִכְנַסְתָּ אוֹתָם לְמָקוֹם זֶה עִמָּךְ בַּחֶדֶר הַמְיֻחָד לְךָ, לְדַבֵּר עִמְּךָ מַלְאַךְ אֱלֹקִים. כִּי יַקְפִּיד ה' עַל כְּבוֹד בִּלְעָם וּכְמוֹ שֶׁמָּצִינוּ שֶׁהָרַג אֶת הָאָתוֹן מִשׁוּם כְּבוֹדוֹ שֶׁל בִּלְעָם (במדבר כב:ט).

Who are these people with you? For Hashem told him,

*"Are these people worthy of being with you that you
have taken them into your special chamber to
speak with you, a messenger of God?' For God was
concerned for Bilaam's dignity as we see that He killed
the donkey on account of Bilaam's dignity (Bamidbar
22:9).*

But who is this Bilaam that Hashem is so concerned about his
dignity? Is this not the same Bilaam who planned Israel's destruction?
Is this not the very Bilaam who the *Mishnah* described as the
paradigm of haughtiness and conceit? Is this not the same Bilaam to
whom our Sages attribute (*Sanhedrin* 105a) the most immoral and
disgusting behavior, to the extent of sinning with animals?

Yet, even this most low and decadent individual is not to be
humiliated more than is necessary. The stature and importance of an
אָדָם, *a man* — created in God's image — is so great, that extreme care
must be taken to prevent any unnecessary degradation even of one as
wicked as Bilaam.

Hashem even went so far as to set aside His own honor in order to
preserve the dignity of Bilaam. We are told that Bilaam's donkey was
slain so that people would not point to it saying, *This is the donkey
that brought about Bilaam's downfall (Rashi Bamidbar* 22:22). This
in spite of the fact that had the donkey remained alive it would have
constituted a tremendous קִדּוּשׁ הַשֵׁם, *sanctification of God's Name.*
People would have pointed to the donkey and proclaimed God's
wonders and justice. It would have been living testimony to
Hashem's creation and control of the universe. The humiliation that
Bilaam would have suffered would itself be honoring God's Name.
Yet, the dignity of a human being, even of a Bilaam, is so valuable
that Hashem preferred that His own honor be set aside for the sake of
Bilaam's.

The same principle holds true for any person killed for bestiality.
Chazal are puzzled by the injunction "and the animal shall be killed"
(*Vayikra* 20:15).

אִם אָדָם חָטָא בְּהֵמָה מֶה חָטְאָה, וכו' דָּבָר אַחֵר שֶׁלֹּא תְהֵא
בְּהֵמָה עוֹבֶרֶת בְּשׁוּק וְיֹאמְרוּ זוֹ הִיא שֶׁנִּסְקַל פְּלוֹנִי עַל יָדָהּ
(סנהדרין נד:ע"א).

*If the person sinned, what offense did the animal
commit? ... So that the animal should not pass in the
street and people will say, "This is the animal on*

account of which that person was stoned" (Sanhedrin 54a).

Thus, the Torah demands that we go through the trouble of convening a Sanhedrin of twenty-three judges in order to sentence the animal to death, so as to prevent the humiliation of a human being. This, although we are dealing with a lowly transgressor of the most abominable sort.

Similarly, we find Hashem protecting the dignity of Korach and his entourage. *Meiri (Berachos* 28a) explains that the reason that Eliezer and not Aharon was instructed to gather Korach's pans was that Aharon had been Korach's opponent. Korach was entirely wrong and had provoked the entire altercation. Yet the disgrace and shame of having his prime opponent gather the 'spoils' was unwarranted; Korach did not deserve that, so Hashem told Aharon's son Eliezer to collect them instead. [Still more fascinating is that *Meiri* cites this in conjunction with the protection of R' Gamliel's dignity when he was replaced as *Rosh Yeshivah.* He was replaced by R' Elazar ben Azaryah and not the more prominent R' Yehoshua, because it was his disagreement with R' Yehoshua which brought about his dismissal. Although the qualities of these two people — one a great saint, the other a sinner — are hardly comparable, they nevertheless deserve the same basic human dignity.]

The exalted status of a human being also prompts an extreme effort to attempt to rectify his wrongdoings. Thus, in order to save Bilaam, Hashem *created* the donkey's ability to speak.

עֲשָׂרָה דְבָרִים נִבְרְאוּ בְּעֶרֶב שַׁבָּת בֵּין הַשְּׁמָשׁוֹת וְאֵלוּ הֵן: פִּי הָאָרֶץ וּפִי הַבְּאֵר וּפִי הָאָתוֹן (אבות ה:ח).

Ten things were created on [Friday] at twilight and they are: the mouth of the land, the mouth of the well and the mouth of [Bilaam's] donkey, etc. (Avos 5:8).

This last-minute creation* was not needed to protect Israel from the effects of Bilaam's curse; they were protected by Hashem's annulment of Bilaam's curse. Rather, it was for the sake of Bilaam, the ultimate attempt to have Bilaam turn back from his evil path. In the last fleeting moments of creation, a special attempt was made to save this despicable would-be-annihilator of Israel. So great and important

---

* [A special act of creation was necessary at this last minute as nothing new is created after the seven days of creation.]

is every human being, no matter what his particular situation at the moment might be.

The same is true of the *sotah*, the unfaithful wife, who would deserve death had there been witnesses to her sin. Yet, when there are no witnesses, every attempt is made to have her confess and be saved. She is harassed continuously and moved from place to place in the Temple courtyard, all for the purpose of causing her to confess and be saved from a horrible death. Even the Sanhedrin is convened in order to frighten her into confessing (see *Tos. Sotah* 7a).

We are enjoined to emulate Hashem in all his ways. This concern for the dignity of every person is an attribute of Hashem which we must follow. We must make every possible effort to prevent sinners from falling even further, regardless of how wicked and depraved they may be, and similarly must make every effort to prevent the unwarranted humiliation of every human being regardless of his station in life.

אוֹהֵב שָׁלוֹם וְרוֹדֵף שָׁלוֹם
One Who Loves and Pursues Peace

וַיַּרְא פִּינְחָס בֶּן אֶלְעָזָר בֶּן אַהֲרֹן הַכֹּהֵן וַיָּקָם מִתּוֹךְ הָעֵדָה וַיִּקַּח
רֹמַח בְּיָדוֹ (במדבר כה:ז).

*Pinchas, son of Elazar, son of Aharon the priest, saw
[what happened], and he arose from the midst of the
community and he took a spear in his hand (Bamidbar
25:7).*

The Torah depicts Pinchas with two almost contradictory
descriptions. On the one hand, Pinchas is described as the
ultimate zealot who killed Zimri, the prince of the tribe of Shimon,
for having sinned with Kazbi. Yet, simultaneously he is identified as
"son of Aharon," the son of the supreme example of an אוֹהֵב שָׁלוֹם
וְרוֹדֵף שָׁלוֹם — *one who loves and pursues peace* (see *Rashi*, ibid.).
How are we to reconcile these two opposing descriptions: the
zealousness on the one hand and the peace-lovingness on the other?

We find a similar contradiction regarding the feelings of our father
Avraham to his son Yishmael. When Avraham was instructed to
drive Yishmael out of his home, he provided him with nothing but a
loaf of bread and a jug of water, despite the fact that Yishmael was

dangerously ill at the time. *Rashi* explains that Avraham did not give him gold and silver because he loathed him for being a sinner (*Bereishis* 21:11). Yet, when God told Avraham, "Take your son (for a sacrifice)," he replied, "I have two children." Hashem elaborated, "Your only [son]." Avraham replied, "Both are only sons (of their mothers)." God continued, "Whom you love." Avraham replied that he could not differentiate between his love for each of them. This Avraham said to the Omniscient, Who penetrates the heart of man and before Whom no thought is concealed. It is clear, then, that his love for Yishmael was indeed genuine. How do we resolve these conflicting descriptions of Avraham's feelings towards Yishmael?

The apparent contradiction between these two descriptions reflects the fact that his emotions were governed by his sense of right and wrong; he was able to use both of these feelings when needed, even towards the same person. We either love a person or we hate him; love and hate being to our mind mutually exclusive. Avraham, however, was not controlled by his emotions. Nor were his feelings a reflection of his personal bias. He was capable of feeling at the same time the love of a father towards his son Yishmael, and the proper animosity for his many shortcomings. Moreover, here the Torah demonstrates more than just the greatness that enabled Avraham to maintain dual feelings towards Yishmael. The Torah means to teach us that it was only *because* he loved Yishmael so deeply that he permitted himself to punish him so severely.

One who metes out punishment must first and foremost be filled with love and compassion to the one being punished. Only then is he permitted to administer justice. Pinchas, filled with righteous indignation at Zimri's shameful act, could punish Zimri precisely because he was the son of Elazar, the son of Aharon the priest, who was the אוֹהֵב שָׁלוֹם וְרוֹדֵף שָׁלוֹם par excellence.

This lesson is to be learned from Divine justice itself.

The *Gemara* tells us: בְּשָׁעָה שֶׁנִּכְנְסוּ נָכְרִים לַהֵיכָל רָאוּ כְּרוּבִים מְעֹרִים זֶה בָּזֶה (יומא נ״ד ע״ב), *When the gentiles entered the Temple [to destroy it], they found the cherubs in embrace* (Yoma 54b).

The *Maharsha* questions this. The embrace of the cherubs is an expression of Hashem's love and closeness to Israel (*Bava Basra* 99a). How can it be that at a moment of severe punishment and destruction the cherubs would be in embrace?

The answer is that it is *because* Israel was being so severely punished that there had to be this expression of utter closeness and love. At the moment of embrace, then and only then, could Hashem decree the destruction of the Temple and Israel's subsequent exile.

Even when Hashem destroyed the wicked Sodom and Amorrah he did so only within the context of his love for them.

Lot was instructed: אַל תַּבִּיט אַחֲרֶיךָ וְאַל תַּעֲמֹד בְּכָל הַכִּכָּר, *Do not look behind you and do not stay in the entire district* (*Bereishis* 19:17). The Midrash quoted by *Ramban* explains the reason for this as follows.

אָמְרוּ לָהֶם אַל תַּבִּיטוּ לַאֲחוֹרֵיכֶם, שֶׁהֲרֵי יָרְדָה שְׁכִינָתוֹ שֶׁל הַקָּדוֹשׁ בָּרוּךְ הוּא לְהַמְטִיר עַל סְדוֹם וְעַל עֲמוֹרָה גָּפְרִית וָאֵשׁ. עִירִית אִשְׁתּוֹ שֶׁל לוֹט . . . הִבִּיטָה לְאַחֲרֶיהָ . . . וְרָאֲתָה אֲחוֹרֵי שְׁכִינָה וְנַעֲשֵׂית נְצִיב מֶלַח.

The [angels] told them not to look back, for the Divine Presence descended on Sodom and Amorrah, raining fire and brimstone. Iris, the wife of Lot, looked behind . . . and became a pillar of salt for she perceived the back of the Divine Presence.

At the very moment that Hashem was raining fire and brimstone upon the most wicked of peoples, He revealed Himself to them in His fullest grandeur. So fully did He reveal himself, so close was He to those present, that all those looking back were consumed, for לֹא יִרְאַנִי הָאָדָם וָחָי, *no man may see Me and remain alive* (*Shemos* 33:20). It was only by being so close to them and descending in their midst that Hashem would inflict so terrible a punishment.

We are enjoined to follow Hashem's ways. מָה הוּא רַחוּם אַף אַתָּה רַחוּם, *Just as He is compassionate, be compassionate as well* (*Shabbos* 133b). We must therefore bear in mind that even in instances when we must punish somebody, we must do so not from hate or spite, but out of a love and closeness that resembles the embrace of the cherubs, and the Divine revelation at Sodom. When we can say that someone is as close to us as an only child, then and only then are we permitted to punish him for his wrongdoings and misdeeds.

גְּנוּת הַכַּעַס

The Disgrace of Anger

*C*hazal have described countless times the shortcomings of and the consequences suffered by a person who becomes angry or enraged. Thus, *He who becomes angry does not respect even the Divine Presence, ... becoming angry is a sign that one's sins are greater than one's merits, ... He who becomes angry is possessed by all sorts of purgatory (Nedarim 22b).*

The most striking effect of כַּעַס, *anger*, however, is that one loses all one's wisdom and spiritual stature. *Chazal* cite many examples to prove this point. Subsequent to Israel's victory over Midian, Moshe Rabbeinu became angry and as a result forgot the law.

רֵישׁ לָקִישׁ אָמַר, כָּל אָדָם שֶׁכּוֹעֵס אִם חָכָם הוּא חָכְמָתוֹ מִסְתַּלֶּקֶת מִמֶּנּוּ . . . מִמֹּשֶׁה, דִּכְתִיב וַיִּקְצֹף מֹשֶׁה עַל פְּקוּדֵי הֶחָיִל (במדבר לא:יד) וּכְתִיב, וַיֹּאמֶר אֶלְעָזָר הַכֹּהֵן אֶל אַנְשֵׁי הַצָּבָא הַבָּאִים לַמִּלְחָמָה, זֹאת חֻקַּת הַתּוֹרָה אֲשֶׁר צִוָּה ה' אֶת מֹשֶׁה, מִכְּלַל דְּמֹשֶׁה אִיעֲלַם מִנֵּי וכו'.

אָמַר רַבִּי מָנִי בַּר פַּטִּישׁ, כָּל שֶׁכּוֹעֵס אֲפִלּוּ פּוֹסְקִים עָלָיו גְּדֻלָּה מִן הַשָּׁמַיִם מוֹרִידִים אוֹתוֹ, מִנַּלָן מֵאֱלִיאָב שֶׁנֶּאֱמַר וַיִּחַר אַף אֱלִיאָב בְּדָוִד (שמואל א' יז:כח), וְכִי אָזִיל שְׁמוּאֵל לְמִמְשְׁחַנְהוּ בְּכֻלְּהוּ כְּתִיב ,,גַּם בָּזֶה בָּחַר ה'.'' וּבֶאֱלִיאָב כְּתִיב ,,כִּי מְאַסְתִּיהוּ,'' מִכְּלַל דַּהֲוָה רָחִים לֵיהּ עַד הָאִידָנָא (פסחים סו:ע''ב).

Reish Lakish said: Any person who becomes angry, if he is wise, he loses his wisdom ... [we see this from]

> Moshe, as it says, "and Moshe became angry at the officers of the army" (Bamidbar 31:14), and it says, "and Elazar the priest told the soldiers going to war, "This is the statute of the Torah that God told Moshe." The implication being that Moshe forgot it . . .
>
> R' Mani bar Patish said: He who becomes angry, even if he had been destined for greatness, it is taken from him. This we see from Eliav, as it says, "and Eliav beame upset at David" (I Shmuel 17:28), and when Shmuel went to anoint him by all of them it says, "Hashem did not choose him," but by Eliav it says, ". . . I have despised him," implying that until then [God] favored him (Pesachim 66b).

The way to control one's anger would appear to be by focusing on those statements of our Sages which vividly describe the pitfalls of כַּעַס and the loss of one's stature in its wake. There remains, however, the problem that unlike other character traits and transgressions, one who is angry usually feels that his anger is justified. Such is the effect of כַּעַס, that a person's thinking becomes distorted to the extent that he is convinced that his reaction is altogether proper and justified.

The way to overcome this problem is by understanding that even justified anger has a detrimental effect on a person, causing a loss of wisdom and stature. This is apparent from the following Midrash.

> אָמַר רַב הוּנָא בִּשְׁלֹשָׁה מְקוֹמוֹת כָּעַס מֹשֶׁה רַבֵּנוּ וְנִתְעַלְמָה מִמֶּנּוּ הֲלָכָה, וְאֵלּוּ הֵן, בְּשַׁבָּת, וּבִכְלֵי מַתָכוֹת וּבְאוֹנֵן (ויקרא רבה יג:א).
> R' Huna said: There were three instances when Moshe became angry and each time he forgot the halachah: Shabbos, metal vessels, and mourning (Vayikra Rabbah 13:1).

In each of these three instances, Moshe's anger was justified. The people were given manna on the condition that they do not put any aside for the next day. Dassan and Aviram purposely set aside manna for the next day and Moshe castigated them angrily. There certainly was justification for Moshe's anger, yet as a direct consequence he forgot the laws of Shabbos that he was supposed to teach to Israel.

Similarly, during the war against Midian, Moshe's anger was fully justified. The very reason that Israel waged war against Midian was because the latter had sent their daughters to entice Israel to sin and yet Israel left the females of Midian unharmed. Surely Moshe's anger was justified. Yet Moshe forgot the *halachah* pertaining to the cleansing of metal dishes, the righteousness of his anger notwithstanding.

The third incident was when Moshe was upset with Aharon for deciding on his own with regards to the sacrifice (see *Or HaChaim, Vayikra* 10:16). Moshe was correct in that Aharon was wrong in ruling on this matter. Yet, as a result, he himself forgot some of the very laws of the sacrifice about which he was angry at Aharon.

We see from all three incidents that anger affects a person not only when it is unjustified. This is due to the fact that anger's effect is not to be viewed only in the framework of a punishment for a sin, but rather as a 'natural' consequence of anger. Moshe may have been entirely correct in all three incidents — but the anger caused some of his wisdom to disappear, nonetheless.

Or HaChaim explains that Moshe had known the laws of mourning *before* he became angry and *forgot* them. This aspect of the effect of anger is puzzling. We can readily understand how anger affects a person so that after the fact he is of lesser stature and wisdom than before. But how does anger make one's previously acquired knowledge disappear? How does one lose wisdom which one already possesses?

The answer is that Torah differs from other forms of wisdom. Other forms of wisdom do not relate to the personality or character of its possessor. A person may be wicked or obnoxious and yet retain a storehouse of knowledge and wisdom. Not so the Torah, which esconces itself and finds its place only in the personality of the *talmid chacham*. A person who becomes unfit to retain Torah loses it; even the knowledge that he had already acquired leaves him. The prerequisite for the study, acquisition and retention of Torah is a personality untainted by base character traits. When one's character becomes sullied — for whatever reason — one loses the ability to be a vessel for Torah. Thus, it is not the knowledge itself that is affected, but rather the individual who ceases to possess it.

We can explain this further by drawing a parallel from the acquisition of prophecy to the acquisition of Torah. When Eliyahu ascended to the Heavens in a fiery chariot, the בְּנֵי הַנְּבִיאִים, *disciples of the prophet*, came to Elisha and suggested that they search for the missing Eliyahu (see *II Melachim* 2:3). *Rashi* asks, "Is it possible that these same prophets, who had foretold that Eliyahu would be taken, would forget and ask as to his whereabouts? This teaches us that from the day that Eliyahu was taken, the Holy Spirit left the prophets."

Rashi's answer is startling. True, the spirit of prophecy had left them and they were no longer prophets. But how did they forget that which they already knew? The answer is that prophetic knowledge is not knowledge in the mundane sense of the world. A person must be a prophet in order to *know* these things; if he falls in stature he no longer knows those facts of which he was aware only yesterday.

This is true of prophecy and true of Torah as well. It is a knowledge that must integrate itself into a person. Let one's character become sullied or blemished, and resultantly his Torah knowledge will vanish as well.

כְּבוֹד הַבְּרִיּוֹת

Human Dignity

אֵלֶּה הַדְּבָרִים אֲשֶׁר דִּבֶּר מֹשֶׁה אֶל כָּל יִשְׂרָאֵל בְּעֵבֶר הַיַּרְדֵּן וגו'.
וַחֲצֵרֹת וְדִי זָהָב (דברים א:א).
וּמָנָה כַּאן כָּל הַמְּקוֹמוֹת שֶׁהִכְעִיסוּ לִפְנֵי הַמָּקוֹם בָּהֶן, לְפִיכָךְ
סָתַם אֶת הַדְּבָרִים וְהִזְכִּירָם בְּרֶמֶז מִפְּנֵי כְּבוֹדָן שֶׁל יִשְׂרָאֵל (רש"י
שם).

*These are the words that Moshe spoke to all of Israel on
the other side of the Jordan [River] . . . between Tofel
and Lavan and Chatzeros and Di-Zahav (Devarim 1:1).*

*[Moshe] enumerated all the places where [Israel] had
angered Hashem. Therefore he did not mention them by
name but only alluded to them to preserve Israel's
dignity (Rashi ibid.).*

The sins alluded to in this verse were very much public knowledge.
They included the affair of the spies, sent by Moshe, who
delivered a slanderous report, a sin for which Israel suffered for 40
years, causing the death of an entire generation in the desert and
denying them the merit to enter *Eretz Yisrael*. The sin of the golden
calf continues to plague Israel to this day, yet Moshe would not
mention it by name.

Furthermore, the purpose was to rebuke Israel and to induce them to *teshuvah*. Would it not have been more effective if he had clearly stated each incident?

The answer is that Moshe felt that to do so was an unnecessary embarrassment to the Jewish people and was not permissible even for the purpose of a public rebuke. The dignity of every person is sacred, and Moshe carefully weighed each word so as not to shame or embarrass a community or an individual more than was absolutely necessary.

This obligation to protect the feeling and dignity of our fellow man refers not only to righteous people or even to merely simple people but rather it applies to even the lowliest and coarsest parts of *Klal Yisrael*.

אָמַר רַבִּי אֶלְעָזָר: בֹּא וּרְאֵה כַּמָּה גְדוֹלָה כֹּחָה שֶׁל בּוּשָׁה, שֶׁהֲרֵי סִיַּע הַקָּדוֹשׁ בָּרוּךְ הוּא אֶת בַּר קַמְצָא וְהֶחֱרִיב אֶת בֵּיתוֹ וְשָׂרַף אֶת הֵיכָלוֹ (גיטין נ״ז ע״א).

R' Elazar said: Note the seriousness of putting a man to shame. For Hashem espoused the cause of Bar Kamtza [who had been humiliated] and destroyed His House and burnt His Temple (Gittin 57a).

Bar Kamtza was a man of exceptionally low character, a man who stooped so low as to slander his own people before the Roman emperor and as a result brought death and destruction upon them. Yet, his dignity, too, was sacred. The humiliation of this miscreant brought upon Israel the loss of its Temple and the destruction of its holiest shrine — indeed סִיַּע הַקָּדוֹשׁ בָּרוּךְ הוּא אֶת בַּר קַמְצָא, *Hashem espoused the cause of Bar Kamtza.*

This principle that one may not embarrass his fellow man goes even further. Hashem protected the dignity of even a person as wicked as Bilaam who is considered the 'patriarch' of evil (see *Avos* 5:19 and *Rabbeinu Yonah*).

Rashi relates that the donkey who rebuked Bilaam died immediately afterwards, so that people would not point to the donkey and exclaim, "This is the donkey that rebuked Bilaam and left him speechless." The humiliation of Bilaam by the donkey remaining alive would not have been in keeping with the dictates of כְּבוֹד הַבְּרִיּוֹת, *human dignity*, and so it died.

Consider the קִדּוּשׁ ה׳, *the sanctification of God's Name*, which would have ensued had the donkey remained alive. People everywhere would have pointed at the donkey as testimony to the wonders of Hashem. Indeed this wondrous donkey was created during the twilight of the sixth day of creation. Yet, so as not to embarrass a man, although of such low character, the donkey was not allowed to remain alive. [See in greater detail: essay on *Parashas Balak*.]

This principle finds halachic expression in the law of גָּדוֹל כְּבוֹד הַבְּרִיּוֹת שֶׁדוֹחָה לֹא תַעֲשֶׂה שֶׁבַּתּוֹרָה, *Rabbinic enactments and various scriptural prohibitions are set aside when they conflict with human respect and dignity* (*Berachos* 19b). Those cases which do require one to forfeit his self-respect or dignity in order not to transgress a prohibition are described as אֵין חָכְמָה וְאֵין תְּבוּנָה וְאֵין עֵצָה לְנֶגֶד ה׳, *There is no wisdom, nor counsel nor understanding when facing Hashem* (*Mishlei* 21:30). The implication of this concept is that reason and wisdom would indeed dictate that the preservation of כְּבוֹד הַבְּרִיּוֹת is more important. It is in spite of this, that the law declares that the *mitzvah* takes precedence.

The concept of כְּבוֹד הַבְּרִיּוֹת does not, however, stop at refraining from insulting or degrading one's fellow human being. One is also obligated to enhance and magnify the prestige and honor of one's fellow. This we see from the *Gemara* (*Chullin* 6b) which comments on the destruction by Chizkiyahu of the copper snake which Moshe had fashioned. Chizkiyahu destroyed it because the Jewish people had come to worship it as an idol. The *Gemara* asks, "Could it be that neither Asa or Yehoshafat, his predecessors, destroyed it? They had destroyed all other idols." The *Gemara* answers, מָקוֹם הִנִּיחוּ לוֹ לְהִתְגַּדֵּר, that Chizkiyahu's ancestors left him room for accomplishment! *Rashi* explains: Had his predecessors not done so he would not have been able to make a reputation for himself [see *Maharam* who explains that *Rashi* and *Tosafos* argue only whether this was a conscious decision on their part or an act of Providence for this purpose].

It was so important to enhance Chizkiyahu's prestige and to give him lasting fame that a troublesome idol was left around for generations, even at the price of the desecration of God's Name.

Having apprehended the overriding importance of human dignity it becomes understandable why shame and embarrassment are the substance of punishment in the World-to-Come.

The *Gemara* (*Yevamos* 105b) depicts the punishment suffered by Avdan: the loss of his sons, their not being brought to burial, their widows' plight. The *Gemara* sums up this terrible suffering with one statement: בְּרִיךְ רַחֲמָנָא דְּכַסְפֵּי לְאַבְדָן בְּהַאי עָלְמָא, *Blessed is the Holy*

One who humiliated Avdan in this world [and not in the World-to-Come]! The essential dimension of all his physical pain was the anguish of humiliation — כַּסְפֵּי. And it was humiliation intensified many a time — that would have been his punishment in the World-to-Come!

Our astonishment at the overwhelming importance attached to כְּבוֹד הַבְּרִיּוֹת is due to the fact that we do not truly comprehend the towering stature of the human being. Were we to recognize the potential inherent in a mere mortal, we would not wonder at the honor that is his due. An example of the appraisal of human potential can be found in the following Midrash:

קְדֹשִׁים תִּהְיוּ (ויקרא יט:ב).

יָכוֹל כָּמוֹנִי? תַּלְמוּד לוֹמַר כִּי קָדוֹשׁ אָנִי, קְדֻשָׁתִי לְמַעְלָה מִקְּדֻשַׁתְכֶם.

וְהָיִיתָ רַק לְמַעְלָה (דברים כח:י"ג).

יָכוֹל כָּמוֹנִי? תַּלְמוּד לוֹמַר רַק . . . גְּדֻלָּתִי לְמַעְלָה מִגְּדֻלַּתְכֶם (ויקרא רבה כד:ט).

You shall be holy (Vayikra 19:2).

I would think that this means as holy as [God] Himself, therefore it says, "for I am Holy," i.e., My holiness is superior to yours.

And you will be elevated (Devarim 28:13).

I would think that this means "as exalted as God Himself," therefore [the dimunitive] רק, only, (a limitation) God's elevation is higher than man's (Vayikra Rabbah 24:9).

These two statements compare human potential achievement and attainment to the Divine, as it were. To us, this comparison is unfathomable. It is only *Chazal*, who fully appreciated the vastness of human ability, who raised the possibility of comparing it with the Divine, until an indication was found to distinguish between the two. It must be noted that *Chazal* did not distinguish between the two by lowering their evaluation of man — but rather by declaring that as great as man's potential may be, the Divine is greater yet.

This then is the true stature of a human being, created in the image of God, with the ability to scale heights beyond our conception. It is this loftiness which obligates us to the extreme of כְּבוֹד הַבְּרִיּוֹת.

תּוֹכָחָה

Rebuke

אֵלֶּה הַדְּבָרִים אֲשֶׁר דִּבֶּר מֹשֶׁה אֶל כָּל יִשְׂרָאֵל בְּעֵבֶר הַיַּרְדֵּן
(דברים א:א)

These are the words that Moshe spoke to all of Israel on the other side of the Jordan ... (Devarim 1:1).

Rashi, citing the *Sifri*, explains that these were words of rebuke which Moshe spoke to Israel, reminding them of the various sins they had committed during the forty years of wandering in the wilderness. The events Moshe alluded to were expressed in strong terms, as the word דְּבָרִים implies, (as opposed to אֲמִירָה which alludes to soft terms) yet the references are veiled and are not stated clearly. Why?

Rashi explains, מִפְּנֵי כְּבוֹדוֹ שֶׁל יִשְׂרָאֵל, "for the sake of preserving Israel's dignity." The Torah teaches us here that even when the תּוֹכָחָה must be delivered in the strongest of terms, one must be careful not to degrade the person being rebuked. If תּוֹכָחָה, *rebuke*, can be made less humiliating by being in veiled terms, then it must be expressed in that manner, so as to minimize the humiliation of the sinner.

One of the many aspects of the necessary care when delivering תּוֹכָחָה is that one must also be aware of the chance the rebuke has of being effective. Thus:

וְהַנִּמְלָט מֵחֶרֶב יֵהוּא יָמִית אֱלִישָׁע (מלכים א יט:יז).
And he who will escape Yehu's sword will be killed by Elisha (I Melachim 19:17).

Radak explains that although Elisha did not in fact put anyone to death, the prophet is making reference here to his remonstrations with Israel. The prophet declares that when Israel sinned despite the fact that they were chastised by Elisha, they were punished far more severely than if he had not rebuked them at all. It was, so to speak, *his* sword that killed them! Since the punishment for sinning in spite of rebuke increases the sinner's punishment, a heavy burden of discretion rests upon one who wishes to reprove another. One must decide if rebuke will cause the sinner to mend his ways and be spared punishment, or if that person will continue despite one's admonitions and be subject to even more severe punishment.

Another aspect which the מוֹכִיחַ, *the one delivering the rebuke*, must consider, is the possibility that his תּוֹכָחָה might cause the sinner to leave the fold entirely as a result of the rebuke. It was for this reason that Yaakov waited all his life for the opportunity to rebuke Reuven. Only when Yaakov was on his deathbed did he feel it proper to chastise Reuven. The reason given in the Midrash is "so that Reuven does not desert me and go instead to Esav" (*Rashi Devarim* 1:3)!! He who gives תּוֹכָחָה must be very careful to take this point into consideration. This, too, the מוֹכִיחַ must carefully consider: "Will, God forbid, my rebuke bring the sinner to total despair and loss of any hope for rehabilitation?"

The essence of the תּוֹכָחָה can be gleaned from the following Midrash:

אָמַר רַבִּי שִׁמְעוֹן בֶּן אֶלְעָזָר אוֹי לָנוּ מִיּוֹם הַדִּין, אוֹי לָנוּ מִיּוֹם הַתּוֹכָחָה. יוֹסֵף קְטַנָּם שֶׁל שְׁבָטִים הָיָה וְלֹא יָכְלוּ אֶחָיו לַעֲנוֹת אוֹתוֹ כִּי נִבְהֲלוּ מִפָּנָיו. לִכְשֶׁיָּבוֹא הַקָּדוֹשׁ בָּרוּךְ הוּא וְיוֹכִיחַ כָּל אֶחָד וְאֶחָד לְפִי מַעֲשָׂיו עַל אַחַת כַּמָּה וְכַמָּה (ילקוט שמעוני ויגש קנב).

R' Shimon ben Elazar said: Woe to us from the day of judgment, woe to us from the day of rebuke. Yosef was the youngest of the tribes, and yet his brothers [were overwhelmed] and could not answer him. Certainly this will be the case when the Holy One will rebuke each and every one of us according to his deeds (Yalkut Shimoni Vayigash 152).

This Midrash is puzzling in its allusion to the תּוֹכָחָה of Yosef. How did he rebuke his brothers? In vain will we search for a powerful word of criticism to his brothers who had sold him into slavery. The Torah mentions no rebuke whatsoever. All we find is the simple pronouncement, "I am Yosef."

The explanation is that the crux of תּוֹכָחָה is not a tongue-lashing. It is rather making one's fellow aware that he has erred. When the sinner becomes aware that his actions were wrong, then תּוֹכָחָה has been realized. Thus, Yosef's brothers had felt that his dreams were but idle dreams. When Yosef made the simple statement, "I am Yosef," it brought home the fact that the dreams were a Divine prophecy come true; the brothers were overwhelmed. They recognized the truth in an instant. That was profound תּוֹכָחָה! They realized that all their actions in this matter were erroneous and therefore were too stunned to reply.

This was the lesson that R' Shimon ben Eliezer learned from the story of Yosef and his brothers. So devasting is the moment of truth that he compares the יוֹם הַתּוֹכָחָה, the day of rebuke, to the יוֹם הַדִּין, the day of judgment. The suffering that lies in the knowledge that one has lived his entire life in error is comparable to the judgment that one suffers as punishment for that error.

We find another profound example of the reaction of one who came to the realization that he had lived all along with a wrong preconception.

וַיֶּחֱרַד יִצְחָק חֲרָדָה גְּדֹלָה עַד מְאֹד (בראשית כז:לג).

אָמַר ר' חָמָא: – עַד מְאֹד – מֵחֲרָדָה שֶׁהֶחֱרִיד מֵעַל גַּבֵּי הַמִּזְבֵּחַ (ילקוט שמעוני קטו).

And Yitzchak trembled an exceedingly great trembling (Bereishis 27:33).

R' Chama said: 'an exceedingly' implies that it was even greater than the trembling that took place on the Altar [when Avraham was about to sacrifice him] (Yalkut Shimoni 115).

Why indeed did Yitzchak tremble so fearfully when he realized that he had given the blessings to Yaakov? It could not be that he was unhappy with having blessed Yaakov, for he reconfirmed his blessing by saying, גַּם בָּרוּךְ יִהְיֶה, *and indeed he shall be blessed (Bereishis 27:33).*

The answer is that in that instant, Yitzchak realized that his lifetime perspective of Esav was wrong. He had wanted to bless Esav for he thought that Israel would descend from him. He now realized that it was Yaakov who carried 'a scent of Paradise' with him, who would be the source of blessing in the world, and whose progeny would become the chosen people of God. There is no greater shock than the discovery that one has erred all his days; hence, אוֹי לָנוּ מִיּוֹם הַדִּין, אוֹי לָנוּ מִיּוֹם הַתּוֹכָחָה, Woe to us from the day of judgment; woe to us from the day of the rebuke.

בַּעַל פְּעוֹר

Baal Peor

לֹא תֹסְפוּ עַל הַדָּבָר אֲשֶׁר אָנֹכִי מְצַוֶּה אֶתְכֶם וְלֹא תִגְרְעוּ מִמֶּנּוּ
... עֵינֵיכֶם הָרֹאוֹת אֵת אֲשֶׁר עָשָׂה ה' בְּבַעַל פְּעוֹר (דברים ד:ב,ג).
*You shall not add to the thing which I command you
nor shall you detract from it ... You have seen with
your own eyes what God did to Baal Peor (Devarim
4:2,3).*

וַיָּחֶל הָעָם לִזְנוֹת אֶל בְּנוֹת מוֹאָב ... וַיִּצָּמֶד יִשְׂרָאֵל לְבַעַל פְּעוֹר
(במדבר כה:א,ג).
*And Israel began lusting after the daughters of Moav
... and they became attached to [their idol] of Baal Peor
(Bamidbar 25:1,3).*

Baal Peor is one of the most revolting and disgusting forms of
idol worship. The *Gemara* relates that those who worshiped
Baal Peor would consume various laxatives and then proceed to
relieve themselves before the idol. What attraction could such a
disgusting form of idolatry contain for Israel?

By way of illustrating its abominable nature, the *Gemara* relates
the story of a non-Jewish woman who became extremely ill and
pledged to worship every existing idol if she would recover. She
regained her health and proceeded to fulfill her pledge until she came

to worship Baal Peor. She inquired as to its proper form of worship. When she was told of its nature she exclaimed, "Far better that I become ill again than engage in such a manner of idol worship!" Yet despite this most degrading nature of Peor, Israel became attracted and attached to it. Wherein lay the secret of its attraction? Furthermore, there seems to be a causative relationship between the fact that Israel sinned with the daughters of Moav and the subsequent worship of Baal Peor. *Chazal* explain that the licentiousness of the daughters of Moav was intended as a lure to induce them to worship Baal Peor. What is the connection between the two?

The *Gemara* says,

מַעֲשֶׂה בְּסַבְטָא בֶּן אֶלֶס וכו'. פָּעַר בְּפָנֶיהָ וְקִנַּח בְּחוֹטְמָה. הָיוּ מְשָׁרְתֵי עֲבוֹדָה זָרָה מְקַלְּסִין אוֹתוֹ וְאוֹמְרִים מֵעוֹלָם לֹא הָיָה אָדָם שֶׁעֲבָדָה לְזוּ בְּכָךְ (סנהדרין סד:ע"א).

It happened that Savta ben Ales ... performed a disgusting act in front of Baal Peor. The idol's attendants praised him, saying, "No one has ever worshiped [so consummately]' (Sanhedrin 64a).

Savta's praiseworthy innovation was rooted in his deep understanding of what Baal Peor's essence really was. The worship of Baal Peor was an expression of degrading and humiliating one's gods. He therefore proceeded to desecrate it still further, thereby earning praise for his profound understanding of the credo of Peor.

Seen in a deeper sense, Baal Peor represents the tearing down of all moral and religious restrictions and prohibitions. Idolaters, too, had their morals manifested by their deity, and by the mode of its worship. The worshipers of Baal Peor rebelled against these very strictures, proclaiming their complete lack of recognition of any system of values whatsoever. This iconoclasm and espousal of anarchy became their very god! The more Savta showed his contempt and disrespect for Peor, the more esteemed and praiseworthy he became.

Only too well do we now understand the attraction of this idol. The allure of the ideology of permissiveness and lack of any restraints can be witnessed in contemporary society which faces an onslaught by anarchy, immorality and permissiveness.

It was precisely for this reason that Bilaam chose licentiousness as the means for bringing on Israel's plunge into the decadence of Baal Peor. The first moral restriction that humanity had set for itself was to limit promiscuous relationships. By sending the daughters of

Midian to mingle with Israel and to entice them, he succeeded in breaching the wall of the restrictions and prohibitions of the Torah. This, Bilaam knew with certainty, would culminate in the worship of Baal Peor.

This will explain the fact that even when the Torah permits something usually prohibited, such an exemption is bounded into a specific framework.

Thus the Torah, recognizing human frailty, permits a יְפַת תּוֹאַר, a gentile woman captured in war. Although the Torah sanctioned this relationship due to human weakness, it still laid down many restrictions and conditions. The purpose of these conditions is so that even the exemption granted be enclosed in a framework of restraint and should not lead to a complete dissolution of moral bonds. So, too, the גֹּאֵל הַדָּם, the closest relative to a victim of murder, was permitted to avenge the blood of the victim because כִּי יֵחַם לְבָבוֹ, *because of the heated rage of the relative*. Still, the Torah did not totally permit the taking of revenge, for then it would constitute a complete breakdown of the restraints to murder. Hence, certain areas were designated as עָרֵי מִקְלָט, *cities of refuge*, where even in moments of rage the avenger was not permitted to harm the murderer. All this, to ensure that the restraint on murder would remain. With this in mind, we may understand the verse לֹא תוֹסִפוּ . . . וְלֹא תִגְרְעוּ מִמֶּנּוּ . . . עֵינֵיכֶם הָרֹאוֹת אֵת אֲשֶׁר עָשָׂה ה׳ בְּבַעַל פְּעוֹר (דברים ד:ב,ג), *Do not add . . . and do not detract . . . You have seen with your own eyes what God did to Baal Peor* (*Devarim* 4:2,3).

The juxtaposition of these two verses is puzzling. What is the connection between these injunctions and what happened to Peor? How does the incident of Peor serve as a warning not to add to or detract from *mitzvos*?

The answer is that the essence of not adding to *mitzvos* or detracting from them is the breach of the guidelines laid down by the Torah and their replacement with one's own *mitzvos*.

The Torah serves as a fence to protect a person from the blandishments of this world, much in the manner of a fence surrounding a field. If one dislodges even one small section of the fence he has demolished not only that particular segment but has destroyed the entire effectiveness of the fence. One who dispenses with even one *mitzvah* of the Torah has in effect rid himself of *all* restraint and it is but a matter of time until the all-encompassing fence of Torah will be in shambles.

לֹא תוֹסִיף, the unauthorized addition of *mitzvos*, is characterized by *Chazal* as tantamount to the detraction of a *mitzvah* — כָּל הַמוֹסִיף גּוֹרֵעַ, *he who adds, detracts*. He who devises his own *mitzvos* demonstrates that the Torah has for him no Divinely mandated restraints. Then it is but a matter of time until everything is torn down.

This, then, is the connection between בַּעַל פְּעוֹר and בַּל תוֹסִיף and בַּל תִּגְרַע. Each begin with the breach of the restraints binding a person, and culminate in a complete destruction of Torah.

מְסִירַת נֶפֶשׁ

Martyrdom

וְעַתָּה יִשְׂרָאֵל מָה ה׳ אֱלֹקֶיךָ שֹׁאֵל מֵעִמָּךְ כִּי אם . . . וְלַעֲבֹד אֶת
ה׳ אֱלֹקֶיךָ בְּכָל לְבָבְךָ וּבְכָל נַפְשֶׁךָ (דברים י:יב).
And now, Israel, what does Hashem your God ask of
you, only . . . and to serve Hashem your God with all
your heart and all your soul (Devarim 10:12)

כְּשֶׁעָמְדוּ יִשְׂרָאֵל עַל הַיָּם הָיוּ הַשְּׁבָטִים מְנַצְּחִים זֶה עִם זֶה וכו׳. זֶה
אוֹמֵר אֵין אֲנִי יוֹרֵד תְּחִלָּה לַיָּם וְזֶה אוֹמֵר אֵין אֲנִי יוֹרֵד תְּחִלָּה לַיָּם.
קָפַץ נַחְשׁוֹן בֶּן עַמִּינָדָב וְיָרַד לַיָּם תְּחִלָּה (סוטה לז:עא).
אָמַר הַקָּדוֹשׁ בָּרוּךְ הוּא לְמֹשֶׁה מִי שֶׁקִּדֵּשׁ שְׁמִי בַּיָּם, הוּא יַקְרִיב
תְּחִלָּה (במדבר רבה יג:ז).
When Israel stood by the Red Sea, the Tribes were
arguing with each other. This [tribe] said, "I will not be
the first to descend into the sea," and the other tribe
said, "I will not go into the sea first." Nachshon the son
of Aminadav was the first to jump into the sea (Sotah
37a).
Said the Holy One to Moshe, "He who has sanctified
My Name at the sea (i.e., Nachshon) shall be the first to
bring his sacrifice [at the inauguration of the Taberna-
cle] (Bamidbar Rabbah 13:7).

This Midrash is puzzling. Why did the tribes refuse to sanctify God's Name by jumping into the sea? Generations of simple Jews sanctified God's Name by allowing themselves to be killed in order not to transgress His commandments. Can a generation which was redeemed from Egypt and was to receive the Torah be of lesser stature than many simple Jews through the ages?

This difficulty is also apparent in the preeminent importance given to the sacrifice of Yitzchak at the *akeidah*. Why is this act of heroism and sacrifice so unique when compared to similar acts of martyrdom by Jews throughout history? Were there not millions of *akeidos* in the history of the Jewish people?

The answers to the above questions lie in the realization that martyrdom is *not* a natural act. It runs counter to the very essence of human nature which is self-preservation. It was both Avraham by leaping into the furnace at Ur, and Yitzchak by allowing himself to be sacrificed, who instilled this readiness for self-sacrifice into the national psyche of Israel. The acts of martyrdom for generations to come even by the simplest of Jews are but a manifestation of this willingness to sanctify God's Name by dying which became part of the national psyche as a result of the מְסִירַת נֶפֶשׁ, *martyrdom*, of Avraham and Yitzchak.

The question regarding the tribes, however, remains unanswered. Why did they not have the courage and steadfastness to sanctify God's Name?

The answer is that the tribes had not been commanded to sacrifice themselves at the sea. Had they been so commanded, they would undoubtedly have done so without delay or procrastination as Avraham and Yitzchak did before them, and as generations of Jews did after them. Rather, they were instructed to *cross* the sea, and emerge from the other side. This was a level of faith they could not grasp. To cross a tumultuous and raging sea as if it were dry land, confident that they would emerge unscathed on the other side, was a degree of faith they had not attained. It was only Nachshon ben Aminadav who had the enormous faith that the word of God is reality itself and that no ocean exists when the word of God has paved a road to the other side.

This was characteristic of Israel's travels in the desert as a whole. The prophet describes their faith as זָכַרְתִּי לָךְ חֶסֶד נְעוּרַיִךְ אַהֲבַת כְּלוּלוֹתָיִךְ לֶכְתֵּךְ אַחֲרַי בַּמִּדְבָּר בְּאֶרֶץ לֹא זְרוּעָה, *I have remembered the devotion of your youth, the love of your betrothal, when you did go after Me in a wilderness in a land that was not sown* (*Yirmiyahu* 2:2).

The prophet is not retelling the readiness of Israel to sacrifice themselves. He is declaring rather that their love and devotion to God was so great that they were *oblivious* to the dangers and wilderness surrounding them. Israel was as a child in his mother's arms who is oblivious to his surroundings; when his mother moves, his place does not change for he is still in his mother's arms. Israel in the wilderness was in God's arms, so to speak, and wherever they moved they were still in the same place, in God's arms. The disregard of danger was not the hallmark of Israel but rather its awareness of God's immanence and omnipresence.

This understanding of Israel's relationship to God in the wilderness will help us understand a halachic difficulty. The *Gemara* (*Shabbos* 31b) raises the issue of סוֹתֵר, *demolition*, on Sabbath. The *Gemara* asks: If demolition is considered work only עַל מְנָת לִבְנוֹת בִּמְקוֹמוֹ, for the purpose of subsequent construction on the same site, how could the dismantling of the *Mishkan* be considered demolition? The re-erection of the *Mishkan* would be at a different spot and accordingly it is not סוֹתֵר עַל מְנָת לִבְנוֹת בִּמְקוֹמוֹ. The *Gemara* replies, that since the Jews traveled and stopped at God's command, 'it was to be considered as rebuilding at the same site.'

How do we understand the *Gemara's* reply? In light of what we explained before, we can understand that the physical location of Israel was irrelevant. They were totally bound up with God and his instructions. Just as a child in his mother's arms is always in the same spot, regardless of his mother's movements, so too Israel was always in one place, enveloped so to speak by the Divine.

Similarly, the *Gemara* (*Eruvin* 55b) makes the point that hut dwellers do not create a תְּחוּם, an area considered by *halachah* as one zone, for their dwellings are temporary. Israel in the wilderness was singled out as an exception, again, because "by God's [command] they camped, and by God's [command] they journeyed." The permanence attributed to their 'huts' (see *Vayikra* 23:43) is likewise due to the fact that their location was actually by "God's command," and that is permanent.

This new insight into the sanctification of God's Name, not by dying, but rather by living oblivious to one's external circumstances, will help us understand the story of Chananyah, Mishael and Azaryah.

Tosafos (*Pesachim* 53b) explains that there was no real idolatry involved when Chananyah, Mishael and Azaryah entered the furnace. They were therefore not obligated to sacrifice their lives by entering the furnace. The question arises: If they were not enjoined to give up their lives, then they were *prohibited* to do so (*Maimonides Yesodei HaTorah* 5). How then were they allowed to enter the furnace and endanger their lives?

This can be understood by a Midrash which explains that they entered the flames expecting to be saved. If so, the question reverses itself: Wherein lies their greatness if they knew that they would not perish in the flames?

The answer is that the significance of their act lay not in their willingness to die as martyrs, which was prohibited, but rather in the fact that they understood that natural causes have no effect when the Divine decrees otherwise. This is the lesson that they learned from the plague of frogs. The frogs that had jumped into Pharaoh's ovens remained alive even after the other frogs had died. It was this incident that taught them that flames cannot consume those engaged in a Divine mission. It was because of this that they were confident of being saved, and were allowed to go into the furnace. This then was the unparalleled קִדּוּשׁ הַשֵּׁם, *sanctification of God's Name*, performed by Chananyah, Mishael and Azaryah — to enter the blazing furnace, fully trusting and believing that no harm can befall those engaged in fulfilling the Divine command.

רְדִיפַת הַכָּבוֹד

Pursuit of Honor

I.

כִּי פָתֹחַ תִּפְתַּח אֶת יָדְךָ לוֹ . . . דֵּי מַחְסֹרוֹ אֲשֶׁר יֶחְסַר לוֹ (דברים
טו:ח).

For you shall surely open your hand for him ...
sufficient for his need which he lacks (Devarim 15:8).

תְּפָשׂוֹ הַקָּדוֹשׁ בָּרוּךְ הוּא לְיָרָבְעָם בִּבְגָדוֹ. וְאָמַר לֵיהּ, חֲזוֹר בָּךְ
וַאֲנִי וְאַתָּה וּבֶן יִשַׁי נְטַיֵּל בְּגַן עֵדֶן. אָמַר לֵיהּ מִי בָרֹאשׁ. בֶּן יִשַׁי
בָּרֹאשׁ.
אִי הָכִי לֹא בָּעִינָא (סנהדרין ק"ב ע"א).

The Holy One seized Yeravam by his cloak and told
him, "Repent, and then I and you and the son of Yishai
will stroll in the Garden of Eden." He asked, "Who will
be first?" [Hashem] replied, "The son of Yishai."
"If so, I do not want it" (Sanhedrin 102a).

Yeravam was meritorious enough to enter *Gan Eden* and was urged by God to repent and to reclaim the share of the World-to-Come which was rightfully his. Not only was he to enter *Gan Eden* but Hashem's declaration implied that indeed he, Yeravam, was to be the more prominent of the two: "I and *you* and the son of Yishai."

What then prompted Yeravam to ask, "Who will come first?"

The answer is that Yeravam was so obsessed with his craving for glory that he had to have his preeminence spelled out to him clearly and was not satisfied with the mere knowledge thereof. Because he so blatantly expressed his insatiable drive for honor and fame, he indeed became of lesser stature than David. His lust for honor was so overpowering that he chose to forfeit his share in *Gan Eden* over an imagined slight to his honor. Indeed *kavod*, honor, has the ability to warp a man's thinking, rendering him completely irrational.

The *Gemara* (*Kesubos* 67b) relates that Hillel ran before the carriage of a formerly wealthy person in order to satisfy the rich man's need for the trappings of affluence to which he was accustomed. The *Gemara* defines this act as compliance to the dictates of דֵּי מַחְסֹרוֹ אֲשֶׁר יֶחְסַר לוֹ, the necessity to provide the indigent with all his lacks and needs. Did this pauper not realize that he was putting Hillel, the prince of Israel, to severe effort and degradation? Surely his need was not proof of mental imbalance for if that were the case, Hillel would not have been obligated to act as he did. The answer is that although he was mentally stable, his obsession for *kavod* caused him to act in an irrational manner. He thought nothing of trampling on the honor of the great Hillel, not even stopping at turning him into a lowly servant.

Moreover, Hillel was a scholar of such stature that he would not have been allowed to forgive such an affront to *kavod haTorah* (see *Rosh, Bava Metzia* 30b, who states that a *talmid chacham* is prohibited from degrading himself on someone's behalf). This is true unless it was, as it must have been, a case of פִּקּוּחַ נֶפֶשׁ, *a matter of life and death*. It must have been, then, that this man was so desperate for his former glory that it would have constituted a situation of פִּקּוּחַ נֶפֶשׁ had he been denied this honor. So demented can one become in his drive for *kavod*.

Even in yeshivah, one sometimes allows reason to be overpowered by the senseless dictates of *kavod*, the result being the forfeiture of many opportunities to progress. One might hesitate to ask someone to learn with him for fear of being turned down, an affront to one's pride. Similarly, one refrains from asking someone to clarify a difficult point for him because of nonsensical notions of prestige.

Another factor, in the sway that *kavod* holds over man, is the insatiableness of one's appetite for it. While other passions reach a point of saturation, *kavod*, being abstract and without substance, never fills or satiates. Attesting to this is Haman before whom everyone in the world prostrated himself except Mordechai. This prompted him to exclaim:

וְכָל זֶה אֵינֶנּוּ שׁוֶה לִי בְּכָל עֵת אֲשֶׁר אֲנִי רֹאֶה אֶת מָרְדְּכַי הַיְּהוּדִי
יוֹשֵׁב בְּשַׁעַר הַמֶּלֶךְ (אסתר ה:יג).

All this is worthless to me so long as I see Mordechai the Jew sitting by the king's gate (Esther 5:13).

Not only was he not satisfied with the widespread and almost universal homage paid to him, but the honors that were accorded to him were rendered worthless so long as Mordechai, too, did not bow before him.

The fact that real *kavod* is abstract and ephemeral makes a person susceptible to the lure of false and undeserved honor. If all honor is nebulous and miragelike what difference, then, is there between real and imaginary *kavod?*

There is, however, no easy remedy to the craving for honor. Even someone who was brought up in an environment of modesty and humility has no guarantee of being free from the temptations of *kavod.*

This reality was demonstrated most clearly by Michal the daughter of Shaul HaMelech, who himself was the paradigm of humility and self-effacement, as the prophet Shmuel told him, אִם קָטֹן אַתָּה בְּעֵינֶיךָ, *Even if you are humble in your own eyes (I Samuel 15:17).* When Shaul was selected as the first king of Israel he went into hiding due to his great modesty and humility. Yet his daughter Michal could not bear what seemed to her the undignified and unbecoming demeanor of David HaMelech when he danced with all his strength before the newly returned Ark of Hashem. Smarting from what she felt to be a slight to David's prestige, she rebuked him sarcastically, "How glorious was the king of Israel today when he uncovered himself before his handmaidens, as does one of the rabble" (*I Shmuel* 6:20).

Advanced age, too, does not offer respite from the hankering after *kavod.*

R' Leib Chasman (*Mashgiach* of Chevron Yeshivah) once participated in a rabbinical conference. One of the speakers, wishing to emphasize his objectivity with regard to the issue at hand, declared, "I am an old man already and I am free of the damages of *kavod.*" Reb Leib Chasman stood up in protest. "Age does not diminish one's appetite for *kavod*; if anything, it increases it."

A most vivid example of this is Zimri ben Salu who was the prince of the tribe of Shimon and one of Israel's elders. He sinned with Kazbi, daughter of Tzur, king of Midian. The question arises as to how a man of his old age and stature (he was a son of Shimon) could succumb to that kind of temptation. The *Gemara* reveals that it was not licentiousness that lured him but rather *kavod.* Thus,

הָלַךְ שִׁבְטוֹ שֶׁל שִׁמְעוֹן אֵצֶל זִמְרִי בֶּן סָלוּא. אָמְרוּ לוֹ הֵן דָּנִין דִּינֵי נְפָשׁוֹת וְאַתָּה יוֹשֵׁב וְשׁוֹתֵק. מֶה עָשָׂה? עָמַד וְקִבֵּץ כ״ד אֶלֶף מִיִּשְׂרָאֵל וְהָלַךְ אֵצֶל כָּזְבִּי. אָמַר לָהּ הַשְׁמִיעִי לִי. אָמְרָה לוֹ בַּת מֶלֶךְ אֲנִי, וְכֵן צִנָּה לִי אָבִי, לֹא תִּשְׁמְעִי אֶלָּא לְנָדוֹל שֶׁבָּהֶם. אָמַר לָהּ אַף הוּא נָשִׂיא שֵׁבֶט הוּא, וְלֹא עוֹד אֶלָּא שֶׁהוּא נָדוֹל מִמֶּנּוּ שֶׁנִּי לְבֶטֶן וְהוּא שְׁלִישִׁי לְבֶטֶן וכו׳ (סנהדרין פ״ב ע״א).

The tribe of Shimon came to Zimri ben Salu. They complained to him, "They [i.e., Moshe and Aharon] are judging capital punishment cases and you are inactive!"

What did he do? He gathered twenty-four thousand Israelites and went to Kazbi. He told her, "Accede to my request." She replied, "I am a princess, and my father instructed me to yield only to the greatest of them." He replied, "I too am a prince, and besides [my tribe is older] being of second birth [i.e., the tribe of Shimon], while the other [Moshe] is merely from the third [i.e., the Tribe of Levi]' (Sanhedrin 82a).

The people of Zimri's tribe aroused his ire by pointing out the honor bestowed upon others, ostensibly less worthy than himself. When Kazbi told him that she is meant to sin 'with the greatest of them,' he lunged at the 'honor'! As old and as venerable as he was, he could not resist the compulsions of *kavod* even at the price of divesting himself of all that was holy and noble in its pursuit, proving in a most incontrovertible fashion that neither age nor stature weakens one's appetite for honor and prestige.

It appears that Hashem created man with such a powerful lust for *kavod* in order that he may gain a deeper understanding of how to give *kavod* to his fellow man, honor without any limitation. As much as one must distance oneself from the pursuit of honor, one must conversely work relentlessly to provide it for someone else. All the scheming and planning that is so degrading when used for one's own advancement becomes obligatory when undertaken for the sake of another, even to the extent of proffering imaginary honor if the circumstances warrant. This explains Hillel's endeavor to satisfy the senseless cravings of a formerly wealthy man and serve as his page.

Let every man look at himself. One knows how much *kavod* he wants and how much he needs for his happiness. To use it for oneself is perverse. Let him instead learn from this how much *kavod* he ought to give his friend.

II.

כֻּלָּם אֲנָשִׁים רָאשֵׁי בְנֵי יִשְׂרָאֵל הֵמָּה (במדבר יג:ג).

All of them were men of stature; the leaders of the Children of Israel (Bamidbar 13:3).

The spies sent to the land of Israel are described by the Torah as great men. *Rashi* explains אֲנָשִׁים as referring to people of stature, which indeed they were, until they sinned. *Ramban* explains that they are listed in descending order, the more prominent ones being mentioned first. Thus, four of the spies are determined as being greater than Yehoshua. Forty days later these people became the great sinners of Israel. They caused the nation to reject the land of Israel and to rebel against Moshe. They even doubted God's Omnipotence as seen from their assessment of the feasibility of conquering the land of Canaan. *We cannot go up against them for they are stronger than us.* This statement of theirs refers to the Almighty (*Bamidbar* 13:31 see *Rashi* there). How did these great leaders of Israel fall so quickly? What was their motive for denying and rebelling against everything holy and dear to Israel?

Mesilas Yesharim points out the reason for their actions:

> It was [their craving for honor] which [according to Chazal] caused the spies to slander the land of Israel, and thereby to bring the death penalty upon themselves and upon their entire generation. For they were afraid that they would be deprived of their rank upon entering the land of Israel, in that others would be appointed in their stead (*Mesilas Yesharim* 11).

Chazal have shown us how the desire for *kavod* took some of the greatest men in Israel and drove them into an abyss of no return. And what honor did they crave? The honor of being שַׂר חֲמִשִּׁים, *leader in charge of fifty people* (see *Baal HaTurim*). Can the fear of losing the status of a low-ranking official cause a sin of such magnitude?

The explanation is that when a person is caught up in the headlong rush for honor, he does not and cannot assess the goal to which he is heading nor the good that he is trampling upon. For the sake of the 'big' position of שַׂר חֲמִשִּׁים, they were willing to kill all of Israel.

The above applies to honor whose purpose is egotistic gratification. There are, however, times when the Torah sanctions the quest for honor and even requires one to insist upon it. Such honor is proper. Someone who is the recipient of such honor is to feel no personal pleasure and should feel as if the honor had been bestowed upon a third party.

An example of this type of honor is that which Yiftach HaGiladi demanded. When Ammon made war on Israel, the people came to Yiftach and asked him to lead the fight against Ammon. Yiftach replied, "אִם מְשִׁיבִים אַתֶּם אוֹתִי לְהִלָּחֵם בִּבְנֵי עַמּוֹן ... אָנֹכִי אֶהְיֶה לָכֶם לְרֹאשׁ, *If you are sending me to fight on your behalf — then I will become your leader*" (*Shoftim* 11:6-11). He repeated the terms of the agreement 'before God.'

At first glance, Yiftach's terms seem like a self-centered grab for power and prestige. In return for leading them in battle, Yiftach demanded to be made leader of Israel. However, the openness and boldness with which he expressed his demand and the fact that he repeated it again before God rule out this possibility.

It must be that Yiftach understood that his success in battle could only be assured if Israel accepted him unequivocally as their leader. It is the commitment of the people to their leader which gives him the strength to be victorious in battle. Yiftach therefore demanded leadership not as self-gratification but rather as a necessity. It was as totally impersonal as could be and therefore he could stand 'before God' and openly declare his demand to be appointed the leader of the people of Israel.

Similarly, when Shimshon beseeched Hashem:

ה' אֱלֹקִים זָכְרֵנִי נָא וְחַזְּקֵנִי נָא אַךְ הַפַּעַם הַזֶּה הָאֱלֹקִים וְאִנָּקְמָה נְקַם אַחַת מִשְּׁתֵי עֵינַי מִפְּלִשְׁתִּים (שופטים טז:כח).

O God, remember me, and strengthen me just this one

time, so that I may avenge the vengeance of one of my two eyes from the Philistines (Shoftim 16:28).

Rashi explains that "remember me" refers to "the twenty years that I judged Israel [without accruing any benefit] and I never asked anyone to pass me my stick."

Let us consider a moment. True, Shimshon never accepted benefit in a material sense, but being that Shimshon was judge of Israel he was surely shown great honor. Did he not enjoy it? Is this not to be considered having "taken from Israel" and accrued benefit from them?

It must be then that Shimshon too had reached the level where he simply did not feel the honors bestowed upon him but regarded them as being bestowed upon a third party. The prestige of being a judge and the homage paid to him did not gratify him in any way and he could truthfully declare that in twenty years of judging Israel he never derived any benefit from them.

Moshe and Shmuel too declared that they never took anything from Israel in the course of their years of leadership (see *Bamidbar* 16:16 and *I Shmuel* 12:3). The tremendous adulation and honors bestowed upon them left them totally unaffected. It was *kavod* accepted only by necessity of position and for the sake of Heaven. This ability to be totally unaffected by *kavod* is a level of consciousness that one must strive to attain, a degree of purity of character which makes one react to honor as if it were bestowed upon someone else.

אִישׁ אֲשֶׁר רוּחַ בּוֹ

Leaders of Israel

שׂוֹם תָּשִׂים עָלֶיךָ מֶלֶךְ (דברים יז:טו).
You may set a king over yourselves (Devarim 17:15).

וַיֹּאמֶר ה' אֶל מֹשֶׁה, קַח לְךָ אֶת יְהוֹשֻׁעַ בֶּן נוּן, אִישׁ אֲשֶׁר רוּחַ בּוֹ
(במדבר כז:יח).
Hashem told Moshe. Take Yehoshua the son of Nun, a man of spirit (Bamidbar 27:18).

The Torah is pinpointing the particular quality which determined the selection of Yehoshua as the leader of the Jewish people who would bring them into the land of Israel. Why was he chosen over others? His personal greatness was not the determining factor, because there were men greater than him. This is pointed out by *Ramban* who explains that the spies were listed in order of greatness, and Yehoshua is the fifth on the list. Calev, for example, was third.

Moreover, *Baal HaTurim* (*Bamidbar* 13:3) classifies the spies as being but שָׂרֵי חֲמִישִׁים, *commanders of fifty*, meaning in effect that there were thousands of people in Israel greater than Yehoshua, i.e., שָׂרֵי אֲלָפִים and שָׂרֵי מֵאָה, those in charge of groups of one thousand and one hundred. The Torah defines Yehoshua's attitude for leadership as אִישׁ אֲשֶׁר רוּחַ בּוֹ, *a man of spirit*. What is the quality of

רוּחַ, *spirit*, that makes it the key qualification for assuming the mantle of leadership of Israel?

Rashi (ibid.) defines it as שֶׁיּוּכַל לַהֲלֹךְ כְּנֶגֶד רוּחוֹ שֶׁל כָּל אֶחָד וְאֶחָד, *He is capable of adapting himself to each person in accordance with that individual's personality.* This was the intent of Moshe's request.

> רִבּוֹנוֹ שֶׁל עוֹלָם גָּלוּי וְיָדוּעַ לְפָנֶיךָ דַּעְתּוֹ שֶׁל כָּל אֶחָד וְאֶחָד, וְאֵינָן
> דּוֹמִין זֶה לָזֶה. מַנֵּה עֲלֵיהֶם מַנְהִיג שֶׁיְּהֵא סוֹבֵל כָּל אֶחָד וְאֶחָד לְפִי
> דַעְתּוֹ (רש"י במדבר כז:טז).

Master of the universe, each person's disposition is manifest to You and they are not similar. Appoint a leader who will be able to tolerate each one according to his disposition (Rashi, Bamidbar 27:16).

But how does one find it within himself to be אִישׁ אֲשֶׁר רוּחַ בּוֹ? How does one cope with the uniqueness of the individual, while leading the nation as a whole?

Let us consider the case of the prophet Hoshea.

> אָמַר לוֹ הַקָּדוֹשׁ בָּרוּךְ הוּא לְהוֹשֵׁעַ, בָּנֶיךָ חָטְאוּ. וְהָיָה לוֹ לוֹמַר,
> בָּנֶיךָ הֵם בְּנֵי חֲנוּנֶיךָ, בְּנֵי אַבְרָהָם, יִצְחָק וְיַעֲקֹב, גַּלְגֵּל רַחֲמֶיךָ
> עֲלֵיהֶן. לֹא דַיּוֹ שֶׁלֹּא אָמַר כָּךְ, אֶלָּא אָמַר לְפָנָיו, רִבּוֹנוֹ שֶׁל עוֹלָם
> כָּל הָעוֹלָם שֶׁלְּךָ הוּא הַעֲבִירֵם בְּאֻמָּה אַחֶרֶת. אָמַר הַקָּדוֹשׁ בָּרוּךְ
> הוּא, מָה אֶעֱשֶׂה לְזָקֵן זֶה? אֹמַר לוֹ לֵךְ וְקַח אִשָּׁה זוֹנָה וְהוֹלֵד לְךָ
> בְּנֵי זְנוּנִים, וְאַחַר כָּךְ אֹמַר לוֹ שַׁלְּחָהּ מֵעַל פָּנֶיךָ, אִם הוּא יָכוֹל
> לְשַׁלּוֹחַ אַף אֲנִי אֲשַׁלֵּחַ אֶת יִשְׂרָאֵל . . . בְּדוֹל עַצְמְךָ מִמֶּנָּה. אָמַר
> לוֹ רִבּוֹנוֹ שֶׁל עוֹלָם יֵשׁ לִי בָּנִים מִמֶּנָּה וְאֵין אֲנִי יָכוֹל לְהוֹצִיאָה
> וְלֹא לְגָרְשָׁהּ. אָמַר לוֹ הַקָּדוֹשׁ בָּרוּךְ הוּא וּמָה אַתָּה שֶׁאִשְׁתְּךָ זוֹנָה
> וּבָנֶיךָ [בְּנֵי] זְנוּנִים וְאֵין אַתָּה יוֹדֵעַ אִם שֶׁלְּךָ הֵן אִם שֶׁל אֲחֵרִים הֵן
> כָּךְ, יִשְׂרָאֵל שֶׁהֵן בָּנַי . . . (פסחים פ"ז ע"א וע"ב).

Hashem told Hoshea, "Your children have sinned." [To which Hoshea] should have replied, "They are Your children, the children of Your favorite ones, sons of Avraham, Yitzchak and Yaakov; have mercy upon them." Not only did he not give this reply but he said, "Master of the world, the whole world is Yours, exchange them for another people." Said the Holy One, "What shall I do with this old man? I will tell him to marry a harlot and bear children of harlotry. Then I will tell him to send her away. If he will be able to send her away, then I will be able to do so to Israel . . ." [Hoshea proceeded to do so and God told him,] "Separate yourself from her." Said he, "Master of the world, I have children by her and I cannot expel or divorce her." Said the Holy One, "If this is the way you feel about your wife who is a harlot and your children who are possibly yours, possibly someone else's, certainly I feel that way about Israel who are My children ..." (Pesachim 87a).

Here *Chazal* teach us the degree of tolerance that a leader must have for his people. It is only by considering them as his children that he can cope with their individual needs, characteristics and idiosyncracies in the way that a father relates to all his children as disparate as they may be.

This is what Moshe was referring to when he complained:

הֶאָנֹכִי הָרִיתִי אֵת כָּל הָעָם הַזֶּה אִם אָנֹכִי יְלִדְתִּיהוּ כִּי תֹאמַר אֵלַי שָׂאֵהוּ בְחֵיקֶךָ כַּאֲשֶׁר יִשָּׂא הָאֹמֵן אֶת הַיֹּנֵק (במדבר יא:יב). וְהֵיכָן אָמַר לוֹ כֵן? "לֵךְ נְחֵה אֶת הָעָם הַזֶּה," וְאוֹמֵר "וַיְצַוֵּם אֶל בְּנֵי יִשְׂרָאֵל" עַל מְנָת שֶׁיִּהְיוּ סוֹקְלִין אֶתְכֶם וּמְחָרְפִין אֶתְכֶם (רש"י שם).

Have I carried this nation? Have I given birth to it that You tell me, "Carry it in your lap as a nurse carries the suckling babe" (Bamidbar 11:12)?

Where did [God] speak to him thus? [As it says,] "Go lead this nation," and it says concerning Israel, "[Take charge of them]' — even though they stone you and humiliate you (Rashi ibid.).

If leadership of Israel requires tolerating stones and insults, then it is only possible if one considers his mission as parental. A stranger will decline responsibility if the difficulties become intolerable, unlike a parent who will remain a parent forever, even if the child rebels against him. It is in this aspect of leadership that we perceive Moshe's task, as that of a mother carrying her suckling child.

Why indeed could Moshe not relate to Israel as a parent? The answer is that the relationship must be reciprocal. If Moshe is to relate to Israel as a parent, then Israel must relate to him as children. A child, notwithstanding his differences with his father, still feels that his father is acting in his (the child's) best interest. If Israel did not reciprocate the child-parent relationship with Moshe, he could not feel that way about them. This is implied in the comment of *Sforno*:

A father can lead his children despite differences of opinion, because they feel that he loves them and acts on their behalf and for their benefit. But these people [i.e., Israel] do not trust me at all and are suspicious of me, testing me as to what I can do for them (ibid.).

But, to return to Hoshea, why could he not consider Israel as his children? After all, a prophet is like a father to his people, as Elisha exclaimed when he mourned Eliyahu the prophet, "Father, father . . ." (*II Melachim* 2:12). Moreover, since God created the world by the word of His mouth, creating reality by His mere utterance, then using the Divine word "your children" should have been reason enough for Hoshea to relate to them as his children.

The answer is that a father's love is begotten by the work and sacrifice on behalf of his children. One comes to love another person as a result of giving to him and not, as is mistakenly thought, as a result of receiving from him.

Chazal say, *If you wish to love your friend and to cleave to him, exert yourself on his behalf* (*Derech Eretz Zuta*, 2). Similarly the love of Heaven (God) is acquired specifically by מְסִירַת נֶפֶשׁ, by sacrificing oneself for the sake of Heaven. Thus, *Ramban* cites a Midrash on the verse לְאֹהֲבַי וּלְשֹׁמְרֵי מִצְוֹתָי, *to those who love Me and to those who keep My commandments* (*Shemos* 20:6).

ר' נָתָן אוֹמֵר: לְאֹהֲבַי וּלְשֹׁמְרֵי מִצְוֹתַי, אֵלּוּ שֶׁהֵם יוֹשְׁבִים בְּאֶרֶץ יִשְׂרָאֵל וְנוֹתְנִים נַפְשָׁם עַל הַמִּצְוֹת. מַה לְּךָ יוֹצֵא לַהֲרֵג? עַל שֶׁמַּלְתִּי אֶת בְּנִי. מַה לְּךָ יוֹצֵא לִשָּׂרֵף? עַל שֶׁקָּרֵאתִי בַּתּוֹרָה וכו' הַמַּכּוֹת הָאֵלּוּ גָּרְמוּ לִי לֵאֱהוֹב לְאָבִי שֶׁבַּשָּׁמַיִם (רמב"ן שם).

R' Nosson said: "To those who love Me and to those who keep My mitzvos" refers to people who dwell in Eretz Yisrael and give their lives for the sake of mitzvos. "Why are you being executed?" "Because I circumcised my son." "Why are you being burned?" "Because I learned Torah." "These blows have caused me to love my father in Heaven" (*Ramban* ibid.).

Hoshea lacked this prerequisite of a father's love. He had never toiled or endangered himself for Israel, and so he *could not* possess a father's tolerance. Only one who gives and gives becomes a father, and only a father has the patience and forbearance to tolerate all his children's shortcomings and wrongdoings.

רַב וְתַלְמִיד

The Teacher-Disciple Relationship

Torah, unlike other areas of knowledge, cannot be acquired by study alone; it must be transmitted from teacher to pupil. This characteristic of Torah study is called שִׁמּוּשׁ תַּלְמִידֵי חֲכָמִים, *apprenticeship to a Torah scholar*, and it is considered of greater importance than the act of study itself. *Chazal* declare גְּדוֹלָה שִׁמּוּשָׁהּ יוֹתֵר מִלִּימוּדָהּ, *The service [of Torah] is greater than its study* (based on *Derech Eretz Zuta*).

Ri Mikorvil ruled that while one must interrupt his study of Torah for the sake of burying the dead, one should not do so if it means interrupting one's studies with his teacher. And if he does he is considered as if 'he had shed blood.' The explanation for this is that while one may attain knowledge on his own, there is no way for one to grow and develop if not in communion with a *rebbe*. The time that one disrupts from study under a teacher prevents him from attaining his true stature and magnitude, and is therefore comparable to the shedding of blood.

Chazal have compared the teacher-disciple relationship to life itself.

The *Gemara* (*Makos* 10a) rules: תַּלְמִיד שֶׁגָּלָה מַגְלִין רַבּוֹ עִמּוֹ, שֶׁנֶּאֱמַר, וְחַי, עָבִיד לֵיהּ מִידִי דְּתֶהֱוֵי לֵיהּ חִיּוּתָא, *A disciple who has been exiled [to* the cities of refuge,] his teacher is exiled with him, as it says, "so that he might live," which means provide him with whatever he needs to live.

There is no shortage of books and texts in the עָרֵי מִקְלָט, the cities of refuge. Yet without a personal teacher it is not considered a place fit to live in.

Rabbi Eliezer's disciples, surrounding his deathbed, vividly portrayed this profound relationship.

תָּנוּ רַבָּנָן. כְּשֶׁחָלָה רַבִּי אֱלִיעֶזֶר נִכְנְסוּ אַרְבָּעָה זְקֵנִים לְבַקְּרוֹ. רַבִּי טַרְפוֹן וְרַבִּי יְהוֹשֻׁעַ וְרַבִּי אֶלְעָזָר בֶּן עֲזַרְיָה וְר׳ עֲקִיבָא. נֶעֱנָה רַבִּי טַרְפוֹן וְאָמַר, טוֹב אַתָּה לְיִשְׂרָאֵל מִטִּפָּה שֶׁל גְּשָׁמִים שֶׁטִּפָּה שֶׁל גְּשָׁמִים בָּעוֹלָם הַזֶּה וְרַבִּי בָּעוֹלָם הַזֶּה וּבָעוֹלָם הַבָּא. נֶעֱנָה רַבִּי יְהוֹשֻׁעַ וְאָמַר טוֹב אַתָּה לְיִשְׂרָאֵל יוֹתֵר מִגַּלְגַּל חַמָּה, שֶׁגַּלְגַּל חַמָּה בָּעוֹלָם הַזֶּה וְרַבִּי בָּעוֹלָם הַזֶּה וּבָעוֹלָם הַבָּא. נֶעֱנָה רַבִּי אֶלְעָזָר וְאָמַר טוֹב אַתָּה לְיִשְׂרָאֵל יוֹתֵר מֵאָב וָאֵם שֶׁאָב וְאֵם בָּעוֹלָם הַזֶּה וְרַבִּי בָּעוֹלָם הַזֶּה וּבָעוֹלָם הַבָּא (סנהדרין קא:ע״א).

The Rabbis have taught. When R' Eliezer fell sick, four elders came to visit him, R' Tarfon, R' Yehoshua, R' Elazar ben Azaryah and R' Akiva. R' Tarfon said, "You are more valuable to Israel than the drop of rain. For rain [is precious] in this world while a teacher [is] both in this world and in the World-to-Come." R' Yehoshua said, "You are more valuable to Israel than the sun. The sun [gives benefit] in this world, while a teacher [is] both in this world and in the World-to-Come." Said R' Elazar ben Azaryah, "You are more precious to Israel than a father and a mother. For a father and mother are in this world while a teacher is in this world and in the World-to-Come (Sanhedrin 101a).

Each one of the disciples defined another aspect of the *talmid-rebbe* relationship. R' Tarfon pointed out the impetus for growth which the teacher imparts to the student as does the rain to the seedling. The soul of a person buried in his earthly body is very much a dormant seedling waiting for the 'rain' to cause it to sprout. Without an external force to awaken it, it remains inanimate, blossoming forth only due to the inspiration of the teacher.

R' Yehoshua expressed the comparison to the sun which acts not only as a stimulant for growth, but is the source of light which protects man from *thorns and briars, wild animals and robbers* (see

Sotah 21a). So is one's teacher; he develops and causes his students to grow and mature. He also illuminates their path in life; helping them avert stumbling blocks, clearing up doubt, and enlightening them with regard to *halachic* questions. A true teacher will arm his disciple with the required protection to ward off potential threats to his spiritual well-being.

R' Elazar ben Azaryah compared one's *rebbe* to one's parents. The indispensability of parents lies not merely in their tangible assistance to their offspring, but more importantly in the atmosphere conducive to spiritual and physical growth engendered by their very presence. An orphan is by his very nature a helpless and pitiful person. So, too, is a person without a *rebbe*.

Indeed, the verse כַּאֲשֶׁר יִשָּׂא הָאֹמֵן אֶת הַיֹּנֵק, *as the nurse carries the suckling infant (Bamidbar* 11:12), refers to the relationship between Moshe and his people, his disciples. A teacher must bear his charges as would a mother her suckling infant (*Sanhedrin* 8a).

The extent to which disciples can become attached to their master and the power of this bond is most vividly portrayed in the description of Moshe Rabbeinu's death:

וַיְדַבֵּר ה' אֶל מֹשֶׁה בְּעֶצֶם הַיּוֹם הַזֶּה לֵאמֹר: עֲלֵה אֶל הַר הָעֲבָרִים (דברים לב:מח, מט).

בִּשְׁלֹשָׁה מְקוֹמוֹת נֶאֱמַר בְּעֶצֶם הַיּוֹם הַזֶּה נֶאֱמַר בְּנֹחַ . . . לְפִי שֶׁהָיוּ בְּנֵי דוֹרוֹ אוֹמְרִים . . . אֵין אָנוּ מַנִּיחִים אוֹתוֹ לְהִכָּנֵס בַּתֵּבָה . . . אָמַר הַקָּדוֹשׁ בָּרוּךְ הוּא הֲרֵינִי מַכְנִיסוֹ בַּחֲצִי הַיּוֹם וְכָל מִי שֶׁיֵּשׁ בְּיָדוֹ כֹּחַ לִמְחוֹת יָבֹא וְיִמְחֶה. בְּמִצְרַיִם נֶאֱמַר בְּעֶצֶם הַיּוֹם הַזֶּה . . . לְפִי שֶׁהָיוּ הַמִּצְרִיִּם אוֹמְרִים . . . אֵין אָנוּ מַנִּיחִין אוֹתָם לָצֵאת וכו'. אַף כָּאן בְּמִיתָתוֹ שֶׁל מֹשֶׁה נֶאֱמַר בְּעֶצֶם הַיּוֹם הַזֶּה לְפִי שֶׁהָיוּ יִשְׂרָאֵל אוֹמְרִים . . . אֵין אָנוּ מַנִּיחִין אוֹתוֹ אָדָם שֶׁהוֹצִיאָנוּ מִמִּצְרַיִם וְקָרַע לָנוּ אֶת הַיָּם וְהִגִּיז לָנוּ אֶת הַשְּׂלָיו וְהֶעֱלָה לָנוּ אֶת הַבְּאֵר וְנָתַן לָנוּ אֶת הַתּוֹרָה אֵין אָנוּ מַנִּיחִין אוֹתוֹ אָמַר הַקָּדוֹשׁ בָּרוּךְ הוּא הֲרֵינִי מַכְנִיסוֹ בַּחֲצִי הַיּוֹם וְכָל מִי שֶׁיֵּשׁ בְּיָדוֹ לִמְחוֹת יָבֹא וְיִמְחֶה (רש"י שם).

Hashem spoke to Moshe on that same day, saying: Ascend the mountain of Avarim (Devarim 32:48, 49).

The term "on that same day" appears in three places. Noach's contemporaries said, "We will not let him enter the ark." Said the Holy One, "I will let him enter in the middle of the day and whoever has the power to prevent it, let him do so." It appears in Egypt when the Egyptians said, "We will not allow them to leave" — and again, regarding the death of Moshe the term "on that same day" is employed — for the Jewish people said, "We will not allow the one who delivered us from Egypt, split the sea, brought down the manna, provided us with quails, furnished us with a well and gave us the Torah — [to go]." Said the Holy One, "I will take him in the middle of the day and he who has it in his power to prevent it, let him come and prevent it" (Rashi ibid.).

The comparison between Moshe's death, Noach's ark and the redemption from Egypt is astonishing. We can well understand how a mob of people could think they would be able to prevent Noach from entering the ark or how a multitude of Egyptians could have prevented Israel from leaving Egypt. But how could Israel ever think they would be able to prevent Moshe from dying?

What becomes apparent is that the people of Israel — having come to the profound recognition of Moshe's role as their teacher and liberator, as the man who guided them in this world and afforded them the opportunity to merit the World-to-Come — thought they would be able to cling to him and to prevent his death. They were so tightly bound to him that nothing but a special miracle of Hashem would be able to tear Moshe away from them.

This, on a smaller scale, was the thrust of the remarks by R' Eliezer's disciples. By emphasizing and acknowledging his role as their mentor and teacher, they were attempting to prevent his death.

We too are obligated to apprentice ourselves to a *rebbe*. Let no one say that there is nobody living worthy of serving, for each generation is endowed with men fit to be its leaders.

Chazal emphasize this point.

וּבָאתָ אֶל . . . הַשֹּׁפֵט אֲשֶׁר יִהְיֶה בַּיָּמִים הָהֵם (דברים יז:ט).
אֲפִילוּ אֵינוּ כִּשְׁאָר שׁוֹפְטִים שֶׁהָיוּ לְפָנָיו אַתָּה צָרִיךְ לִשְׁמוֹעַ לוֹ.
אֵין לְךָ אֶלָּא שׁוֹפֵט שֶׁבְּיָמֶיךָ (רש״י שם).

And you shall go ... to the judge who will be during those days (Devarim 17:9).

Even if he is not like other judges who preceded him, you must listen to him. You have no one but the judge of your time (Rashi ibid.).

This is not meant to imply that although the earlier leaders were greater, we must regardless obey the judges of our generation. Rather it means that the leaders of each generation are those most suited to its needs. This is evident from the Midrash which states that if Aharon would have been alive during Yehoyada or Tzadok's generation (both of whom were High Priests), the latter two would have been greater than Aharon (*Koheles Rabbah* 1:8). In the absolute sense, Aharon was certainly greater. However, they were more suited to the needs of their specific generation.

This is most vividly demonstrated by Choni HaMagel, who slept for seventy years. The *Gemara* relates that when he awoke ...

אֲזַל לְבֵית הַמֶּדְרָשׁ שַׁמְעִינְהוּ לְרַבָּנָן דְּקָאָמְרֵי נְהִירָן שְׁמַעַתְּתִין כִּבְשְׁנֵי חוֹנִי הַמְעַגַּל, דְּכִי הֲוֵי עַיְל לְבֵית מִדְרָשָׁא, כָּל קוּשְׁיָא דַּהֲוּוּ לְהוּ לְרַבָּנָן הֲוָה מְפָרֵק לְהוּ אָמַר לְהוּ אֲנָא נִיהוּ. לֹא הֵימְנוּהוּ וכו׳. חֲלַשׁ דַּעְתֵּיהּ בָּעֵי רַחֲמֵי וּמִית (תענית כג:ע״א).

... *he went to the Beis Midrash and overheard the scholars saying the law is as clear as in the years of Choni HaMagel, for whenever he came to the Beis Midrash he would settle any question that the scholars posed. He [Choni] said to them, "I am he [Choni]." They refused to believe him [and as a result] he became distressed [and] prayed for [death] and died (Taanis 23a).*

Why did Choni not prove his identity by once again answering all questions that were asked in the *Beis Midrash?*

The answer is that Choni's interpretations did not carry the same meaning for the succeeding generation as it had for his. The studies they were engaged in when he entered had indeed originated with Choni, but the one capable of transmitting it to succeeding generations would now have to be a different *rebbe*, the teacher suited to that generation.

The bond between teacher and student is mutual. Just as a pupil cannot survive spiritually without his master, so too a *rebbe* cannot exist without his *talmid*. Therefore, not only is a teacher exiled along with his student, but so also are the students of an exiled teacher exiled with him.

The *Gemara* (*Bava Metzia* 84a) relates that when Reish Lakish the colleague-disciple of Rabbi Yochanan died, R' Yochanan lost his mind from anguish. The Rabbis prayed for his death to relieve his misery and so he died broken hearted.

Another point: Why did the Rabbis pray for him to die? Why could they not pray for him to regain his sanity, as we find elsewhere in the *Gemara*? The answer must be that the Rabbis comprehended the depth of R' Yochanan's anguish at having lost his disciple. They realized that even were they to pray for him to recover his sanity, it would be of no avail because he would immediately lose it again as a result of the unremitting anguish of Reish Lakish's death.

It is amazing that it was this same R' Yochanan who was so strong, as *Chazal* tell us, that even after the death of his ten sons he was able to carry in his pocket a small bone of his tenth son and comfort people with the fact that he, too, had undergone great tragedy. Yet R' Yochanan was unable to bear the loss of his disciple.

Indeed, so indispensable is a teacher to his disciple and vice versa, that *Rambam* (*Hilchos Rotzeach* 7:1) describes a disruption of this very relationship as "the life of wise people and searchers of wisdom is as good as terminated if there is no study of Torah!"